Key Concepts

The Falmer Press Library on Aesthetic Education

Series Editor: Dr Peter Abbs, University of Sussex, Brighton

The aim of the series is to define and defend a comprehensive aesthetic, both theoretical and practical, for the teaching of the arts.

The first three volumes provide a broad historical and philosophical framework for the understanding of the arts in education. The subsequent volumes elaborate the implications of this comprehensive aesthetic for each of the six major art disciplines and for the teaching of the arts in the primary school.

Setting the Frame

LIVING POWERS:
The Arts in Education
Edited by Peter Abbs (1987)

THE RATIONALITY OF FEELING:
Understanding the Arts in Education
David Best

A IS FOR AESTHETIC:
Essays on Creative and Aesthetic Education
Peter Abbs (1988)

THE SYMBOLIC ORDER:
A Contemporary Reader on the Arts
Debate Edited by Peter Abbs (1989)

The Individual Studies

FILM AND TELEVISION IN
EDUCATION:
An Aesthetic Approach to the Moving
Image Robert Watson

DANCE AS EDUCATION:
Towards a National Dance Culture
Peter Brinson

MUSIC EDUCATION IN THEORY
AND PRACTICE
Charles Plummeridge

LITERATURE AND EDUCATION:
Encounter and Experience
Edwin Webb

THE VISUAL ARTS IN EDUCATION
Rod Taylor

THE ARTS IN THE PRIMARY
SCHOOL
Glennis Andrews and Rod Taylor

EDUCATION IN DRAMA:
Casting the Dramatic Curriculum
David Hornbrook

Work of Reference

KEY CONCEPTS:
A Guide to Aesthetics, Criticism and the Arts in Education
Trevor Pateman

THE FALMER PRESS LIBRARY ON AESTHETIC EDUCATION

Key Concepts:
A Guide to Aesthetics, Criticism and the Arts in Education

Trevor Pateman

 The Falmer Press

(A Member of the Taylor & Francis Group)
London • New York • Philadelphia

UK   The Falmer Press, 4 John St, London WC1N 2ET
USA   The Falmer Press, Taylor & Francis Inc., 1990 Frost Road, Suite 101, Bristol, PA 19007

First published in 1991

A Catalogue record for this book is available from the British Library

Library of Congress Cataloging-in-Publication Data are available on request

Typeset in 10/11.5 Bembo
by Graphicraft Typesetters Ltd., Hong Kong
Printed and bound in Great Britain by
Burgess Science Press
Basingstoke

Contents

Contents

Preface

The arts can only thrive in a culture where there is conversation about them, animated conversation, informed conversation, articulate conversation. This is particularly true of the arts in an educational context: in schools, colleges, polytechnics and universities. Yet, often, the discussion is poor because we do not have the necessary concepts for the elaboration of our aesthetic responses or sufficient familiarity with the contending schools of interpretation. In brief, as Matthew Arnold argued in relationship to his own time, there is not a sufficiently animating *current of ideas*. There is a poverty of collective interpretation; yet it is simply not the case that there are no ideas. For example, for decades continental thinkers — Roland Barthes, Michel Foucault, Jacques Derrida, Julia Kristeva — have been challenging our traditional reading of art; while in the last two decades, employing a very different idiom, some major English writers — Roger Scruton, Peter Fuller, George Steiner — have been questioning that influence and offering radically different formulations. The problem, then, is that there would seem to be an invisible wall between the philosophers and the critics, on the one side, and busy teachers of the arts and the general public, on the other. The aim of Trevor Pateman's *Key Concepts* is to penetrate this invisible barrier and to engender a broad and broadly informed conversation about the arts and the complex and various issues they raise.

The word 'conversation' has been chosen carefully because the various entries — ranging, as the reader will see from a quick perusal of the contents, from 'Structuralism' to 'Sublime' from 'Deconstruction' to 'Tears and Laughter' — have their origin in his own teaching. For the best part of ten years the author has been teaching arts teachers on the MA Language, Arts and Education course at the University of Sussex, and the tone and approach of the book derive from his own style of teaching which is deeply Socratic. The aim of a typical entry is thus *not* to decide definitively an issue from the author/teacher vantage point but, rather, to start a conversation around it, to indicate various ways of looking at it, to point to some of the confusions, and then to suggest further lines of enquiry and, of course, in the manner of all good seminars, to offer productive suggestions for further reading. In this indirect and accumulative manner the volume, taken as a whole, offers a map of aesthetics, critical theory and the arts in education; it takes it readers down some of the major thoroughfares and also unexpectedly some of the minor roads and alleys just to see what happens. The aim is, partly, to point out the main features and monuments, but it is also, and more importantly, to provoke readers into becoming travellers themselves.

Key Concepts, in brief, is not offered as a concise work of reference or infallible dictionary (if such is possible); such works exist in abundance. This book is better termed a Socratic guide to aesthetics, criticism and the teaching of the arts. Yet there are exceptions to this general approach. A small number of major entries covering some of the key movements in critical reflection and artistic expression are more descriptive in nature. It was thought that some of these movements (such as feminist criticism, Marxist criticism, modernism and post-modernism, structuralism and post-structuralism) required such a treatment. At these points the conversation gives way to a burst of direct teaching; as a consequence, the tone and the format of the entry alter. The writing is more impersonal in nature and more synoptic in aim. This is also true for another small but substantial series of entries. These relate most specifically to the Library on Aesthetic Education, of which this volume is an essential part. They involve the history and teaching of the arts. In this respect there is an entry on each arts discipline: dance in education, drama, literature, music, film and the visual arts. In relationship to teaching there is a short history of the idea of the arts as a generic community, a concept often invoked but rarely examined in the light of its educational history. These accounts have been written by authors who have contributed to earlier volumes in the series.

Spanning the arts in education, the major schools of modern criticism and the philosophical and ethical issues they raise, Trevor Pateman has produced an informed and distinctive guide. It should be of immediate interest to all teachers of the arts (at whatever level), to all those embarking on the study of aesthetics, and to those reflective friends of the arts who wish to keep abreast of current thinking. If the volume further refines and extends our conversations about the arts, both in education and in society at large, it will have served an invaluable purpose — for we are in need of a broad current of potentially liberating and expanding ideas in our civilization, as never before.

Peter Abbs
Centre for Language, Literature and the Arts in Education
University of Sussex
February 1991

Note

All the entries are by Trevor Pateman except where they are followed by initials. The initials represent the following authors: PA Peter Abbs, PD Pauline Dodgson, AC-H Anna Carlisle-Haynes, DH David Hornbrook, CP Charles Plummeridge, MS Maggie Semple, RW Rob Watson, EW Edwin Webb, RT Rod Taylor.

Acknowledgments

I have been privileged to teach on the University of Sussex's MA in Language, Arts and Education since its inception in 1982. My contributions to this book come from that teaching experience, and my first acknowledgment is to the students who have listened to me and prompted me in new directions. Some of them will, I hope, find the trace of their influence in what follows. I am conscious of specific debts to a number of students, friends and colleagues: Angela Barry, Stephanie Cant, Lisa Dart, Terry Diffey, Carol Dyhouse, Lucy Green, Terry Hodgson, Stuart Hood, Robin Morris, Michael Stephan and Alan Wright. Peter Abbs, my editor, has striven very hard to make me make this a better book than it is, assisted by Jeanette Gabbitas. As the reader will recognize, my daugthers, Izzy and Mitzi, have provided delight and inspiration. Above all, Shirley Wright helped me keep the project alive through a difficult time in my own life.

I should be interested to receive suggestions for additional sections which might be incorporated in a second edition of this book, should one be possible. Clearly, a book such as this has no obvious point of closure.

Trevor Pateman

Aesthetic/Aesthetics

The concept of the aesthetic is central to the Falmer Press Library on Aesthetic Education, nor is this centrality innocent. It is intended to encourage thinking about the arts in terms of aesthetic categories — beauty, judgment, taste, imagination (q.v. entries under these headings) — in contrast to thinking about the arts in terms of the categories of history, sociology or psychology. This is made clear in the entries for 'Aesthetic Field', 'Aesthetic Intelligence' and 'Arts in Education'. Thinking about the arts in terms of the aesthetic is a way of bringing out what distinctive contribution to a child's education is made by the arts, and also facilitates thinking about the arts together and comparatively.

The philosophical discipline of aesthetics has existed in recognizable form since the eighteenth century, but this is not in itself a guarantee that there exists a subject matter which corresponds to the subject. For aesthetics to be a legitimate subject, the aesthetic must, in some sense, exist. So what is the aesthetic? Why do some doubt that it exists? How does the aesthetic relate to art?

Suppose, as a first shot, one characterized the aesthetic as whatever it is in things which makes them pleasing or displeasing to the senses. This makes the scope of aesthetics potentially very wide, since a good wine, a subtle perfume, a fine silk are all pleasing to the senses. More worryingly, it seems to exclude from the scope of aesthetics consideration of at least the bulk, if not all, of literature. It is simply untrue that a great novel is pleasing to the senses. The pleasure we get in reading the novel is a mental or intellectual pleasure. The novel touches our imagination and our emotions. The same might, of course, be said of music, and it might easily be denied that the pleasure we take in music is principally a pleasure in hearing: fine music is not fine because it pleases the ear like a fine wine pleases the palate. It is fine because it involves us intellectually or mentally, exciting the imagination and/or the emotions. Pursuing this line of thought, even the scenery or the painting which 'pleases the eye' might be said to please the eye because it pleases the mind at work in the eye: the mind which is pleased by (for example) harmonious configurations, patterns and forms.

In short, it is useless to define the aesthetic as whatever it is in things which is pleasing to the senses. But suppose we took out 'the senses' from the initial characterization and replaced it with 'the mind'. We now have another set of problems. Undoubtedly, there are pleasing ideas. I may be pleased by the thought that my grandchildren may pick apples from this very tree which I am planting. I experience an inner glow and satisfaction. But it sounds odd — indeed wrong — to characterize my experience as an aesthetic one. To this the obvious response is: quite right, because the pleasurable idea has no connection to any specific or particular experience of the senses. This response suggests that the aesthetic has to do with an experience both of the senses and of the mind, and connected in a particular way. Could we say: the aesthetic is whatever it is in things which is pleasing through the senses to the mind ... or: pleasing to the mind as made active by a connected sense experience ... or some variant formula?

This is more promising, except that it still leaves the novel as a problem. After all, I may read a novel, using my eyes; have it read to me, using my ears; or read it in Braille, using my fingers. That being so, there is no connection of the mind to a *particular* sense experience (as there is, say, with music: reading the score is *not* a substitute for hearing the music). Since the novel can be experienced using any one of three senses, one should clearly conclude that the experience of the novel — whatever it is — is *not* a sense experience, and that whatever pleasure we take in a novel is not connected to a defining sense experience.

One could cut the knot at this point and say that the novel does not have aesthetic properties, and so is not an object of aesthetic experience, but of some other kind of experience. The trouble then is that many people think that the pleasures afforded them by novels, paintings and musical perform-ances are in some sense related, and that one ought to define 'aesthetic' in a way which would capture this relatedness.

A possible way of doing this is to locate the aesthetic not in properties of the object, or directly in qualities of the experience of the object, but rather in an *attitude* taken up towards objects, an attitude often characterized as con-templative or disinterested though directed towards pleasure or enjoyment. So it is said that taking an aesthetic attitude towards an object precludes having (at that moment) the desire to possess that object, or thinking about its material value, or considering to what useful purposes it might be put. I walk through a garden in the cool of the evening, enjoying the scent of flowers. I don't think of picking the flowers; I don't think, 'How much money must have been spent on this!'; I don't think, 'I must bring my mother here. It would cheer her up.' I simply take pleasure in the scent of the flowers, which I consciously locate (this is the contemplative moment), free of any desire to alter or otherwise use their location (this is the disinterested moment). In the same way, it is said, I listen to a concert or (ideally) look at a painting.

Put like this, the aesthetic attitude sounds rather like a recipe for en-joying (more of) what there is to be enjoyed in life than is possible if one (always) looks upon the world with a view to appropriating it for oneself or putting it to some other use than it presently has. If the aesthetic attitude is a recipe for enjoying oneself, it looks as if aesthetics will consist in the injunction: Relax! But what we hoped for from aesthetics was surely some sense of what it is that makes something (aesthetically) pleasing, and how it is that we can experience things as (aesthetically) pleasing. In contrast, the aesthetic attitude sounds like a *preliminary* to aesthetic enjoyment — as putting on one's spectacles is a preliminary to reading a novel.

But the two questions — what is it that makes something (aesthetically) pleasing? and how is it that we can experience things as (aesthetically) pleasing? — sound like requests, respectively, for accounts of 'Beauty' (q.v.) and 'Taste' (q.v.). If we can say what beauty and taste are, then perhaps we have said what the aesthetic is, and also what is the subject-matter of aesthetics.

So far nothing has been said which suggests that *art* has any particular connection to the aesthetic. For all I have said, one could think that we have the aesthetic and aesthetics, and art and the philosophy of art, and that it is an interesting but coincidental fact that there is an overlap: some art objects have aesthetic properties, some do not; some but not all objects of aesthetic experience are art objects. Is this the right way to think about the relation of the aesthetic to art?

There is certainly a long tradition of treating certain kinds of natural objects as exemplary for understanding aesthetic properties and aesthetic experience. Scenery, natural forms of flowers, shells and animals, cloud formations, etc. have all been used in this way. Likewise, I have suggested that some art objects — specifically the novel — might not have aesthetic properties, hence might not be objects of aesthetic experience. If this is so, it would require that we be able to answer the question, 'What is art?' without mentioning the aesthetic (q.v. 'Art World').

At this point some thinkers would protest against the hopelessly simplified, dichotomized way of thinking which expects a quick and easy account of the aesthetic and of art. They might say that art and the aesthetic are merely more and less helpful shorthand ways of getting at aspects of the fabric of human activity and experience, a fabric woven of many strands, not one of which need be supposed to run the whole length of the fabric, such that it can be removed for analysis. Life is more complex than the categories 'aesthetic' and 'art' allow. Not only this, but it may beg a very real question to suppose that the aesthetic and art must have a definable *essence*. Perhaps there is no essence of the aesthetic or of art; perhaps these terms function rather to direct our attention now this way, now that — and perhaps not innocently either. Perhaps 'aesthetic' and 'art' are primarily categories of ideology, of an illusory way in which a culture makes sense of itself to itself. They are categories which should be treated with suspicion, not treated with a reverence which suggests that with enough patience they will surely yield up their essence to the honest enquirer after truth. For such alternative approaches to art and the aesthetic, q.v. 'Art World; Institutional Theories of Art', 'Marxist Critical Theory'.

Aesthetic Field

The term 'aesthetic field' is first employed in an educational context in *Living Powers: The Arts in Education,* edited by Peter Abbs (1987). It is intended above all to denote the dynamic interactive element both in art-making and in and between works of art. As the term has developed, it has come to have two related but conceptually distinct meanings. The first concerns the actual process of art-making; the second the nature of the symbolic system in which all art is made.

In the first sense aesthetic field denotes the four successive stages through which a work of art passes, namely, making, presenting, responding and evaluating. These stages are seen to be equally applicable across all the arts and to be one mark of their unity.

In the first phase of making, an individual creates an expressive symbolic form by engaging with the specific medium of the art in question (with clay, with musical notes, with gestures, with words, etc.) When the work is complete, it is then presented to an active audience. In the different arts this presentation takes different forms. In drama, dance, mime and music (the 'performing arts') the work is performed; in the visual arts it is exhibited or displayed; in the case of written works it is published (although it can also be performed); and with film and video it is shown. This presentation releases the third stage of response. The audience responds largely through its feelings, its senses and its imagination, namely through pre-discursive aesthetic response. Finally, as the audience reflects on the nature of its aesthetic response in relationship to the art, it attempts to make a judgment, an evaluation of the experienced work. Acts of evaluation, to be worthwhile, require the intellectual formulation of aesthetic response, and this, in turn, requires for its development an awareness of artistic convention, of inherited traditions and contemporary practices as well as a knowledge of various critical commentaries. This dynamic concept of the art-making process has come to provide one possible model for the teaching of the arts.

The second related use of the term 'aesthetic field' refers to the whole symbolic system in which the individual work is made. In this sense the concept is very close to that of 'the simultaneous order' first put forward by T.S. Eliot in 'Tradition and the Individual Talent' (1917). Eliot claimed that:

the historical sense compels a man to write not merely with his own
generation in his bones, but with a feeling that the whole of the
literature of Europe from Homer and within it the whole of the
literature of his own country has a simultaneous existence and com-
poses a simultaneous order. This historical sense, which is a sense of
the timeless as well as of the temporal and of the timeless and of the
temporal together, is what makes a writer traditional. And it is at the
same time what makes a writer most acutely conscious of his place in
time, of his own contemporaneity. (p. 14)

Eliot's insight, if not his formulation, is here strikingly close to that of the
structuralist movement (q.v. 'Structuralism'). The aesthetic field, then, refers
to that complex interactive system of allusion, reference and structure in
which individual expressions of art are necessarily constituted, from Sappho
to Anne Stevenson, from the cave paintings of horses to Elizabeth Frink,
from Balinese music to Britten and John Adams (q.v. 'Tradition').

There is nothing inherently fixed or in any way metaphysical about the
concept of the aesthetic field. Just as in quantum physics the field creates a
variety of forms which it sustains, then takes back, then creates again in new
patterns, so in the aesthetic field the complex relationships between the parts
are changing all the time, recast in different ways at different times, by the
driving power of different ideological movements, critical theories and artistic schools. Thus, to take a small example, Donald Davie reviewing the work
of the until recently obscure English poet, Ivor Gurney (1890–1937), writes,
'in Gurney we have to reckon no longer with a wistful and appealing figure
in the margin but with a poet whose achievement, now that we can measure
the full scope of it, demands a rewriting of the accepted accounts of English
poetry in this century' (*The Independent*, 25 August 1990). It is a critical claim
which, if accepted, has the power to change the prevailing pattern of literary
mapping. Any major and widely accepted re-evaluation alters the relationships between all the other works in the field. This is now happening on a
grand scale across all the arts with the challenging of modernism by the
contending forces of post-modernism and anti-modernism (q.v. 'Modernism
and Post-Modernism'). In our own century feminism (q.v. 'Feminist Critical
Theory') has profoundly altered the simultaneous order of the arts. It is a
vital process activated by the contending claims of critical and artistic movements and the counter-claims to which they in turn give birth. The model is
not a static one of fixed canons, although certain figures in any of the
symbolic systems are likely to remain constant (Homer, George Eliot, Picasso, Kurosawa, Mozart, Martha Graham), although the ways in which we
interpret them will change constantly and at times quite radically.

The implications of such a conception for the teaching of the arts are
enormous and deeply challenging to many entrenched practices in our
schools. Above all, it suggests that the primary task of arts teachers is to
initiate their pupils into the vast, interactive symbolic system of their disciplines, and to do so in the manner of engaging aesthetic experience, not inert
knowledge. Thus it is neither a traditional prescriptive view of teaching the

arts, nor is it a progressive view. It provides a new model based on a dual recognition of the dynamic phases of art-making (first meaning of aesthetic field) and of the interactive nature of symbolic systems (second meaning of aesthetic field).

PA

Aesthetic Intelligence

According to the *Oxford English Dictionary*, '"aesthetic" derives from the Greek word meaning "through the senses".' The definition runs as follows: 'of or pertaining to aestheta: things perceptible by the senses, things material (as opposed to thinkable or immaterial) also perceptive, sharp in the senses.' Thus, consistent with its original denotations, the first use of the word 'anaesthetic' in English in 1721 meant 'a defect of sensations as in Paralytic and blasted persons.' The three definitions are given as (1) insensible, (2) unfeeling, (3) producing insensibility. Similarly, other related words — 'synaesthetic' (feeling with), and 'kinaesthetic' (movement feeling) — record and depend upon the same matrix: of sense, of feeling, and of sensibility.

The etymology reveals the contiguity between sensation and feeling, of sensory experience and sensibility. Again and again the practices of our language, the inherited conjunctions and the daily alliances of our speech suggest the intimacy of this relationship. 'To keep in touch' is both to keep in contact and to remain close in feeling. To touch an object is to have a perceptual experience; to be touched by an event is to be emotionally moved by it. To have a tactile experience is to have a sensation in the fingertips; to show tact is to exhibit an awareness of the feelings of others. The very word 'feel' embodies the conjunction; one can feel both feelings *and* objects, and one can do both simultaneously. The analysis discloses that the aesthetic involves both the perceptual and the affective. The education of aesthetic intelligence is therefore concerned with the development of sensation and feeling into what is commonly called sensibility.

The aesthetic denotes a mode of response inherent in human life which operates through the senses and the feelings and constitutes a form of intelligence comparable to, though different from, other forms of intelligence, such as the mode of logical deduction. If these propositions stand, it becomes clear that the aesthetic is a much broader category than that of the artistic; it includes all manner of simple sensuous experiences from, say, the pleasure of tasting food to enjoying the breeze on one's face. In *The Ideology of the Aesthetic* Terry Eagleton claims that his own definition of the word merges into the idea of bodily experience as such. But, at the same time, the arts depend on the aesthetic modality because they operate through it. The

7

various arts comprise the differentiated symbolic forms of the aesthetic modality. Through aesthetic intelligence we are able to apprehend a realm of meaning and value essential to any full concept of human existence. In the development of understanding the aesthetic mode is as important as the discursive mode, and it is the arts which develop sensuous intelligence for by their very nature they work through it and on it in both their creation and their reception.

For further views on the nature of aesthetic experience see Susanne Langer's *Feeling and Form*, Herbert Marcuse's *The Aesthetic Dimension*, Terry Eagleton's *The Ideology of the Aesthetic* and the contributions by Roger Scruton, Peter Abbs and George Whally in *The Symbolic Order*. The view outlined here, central to the Falmer Press Library, can be described as essentially Kantian and has its main historical source in *The Critique of Judgement*. For some if its problems, particularly in relationship to the novel, q.v. 'Aesthetic'.

PA

Alienation Effect
(q.v. 'Mimesis and Katharsis')

It is generally thought that one of Brecht's major contributions to the theory and practice of theatre was to propose as a dramatic object the creation of emotional distance as an alternative to the solicitation of emotional identification. Emotional distance would allow and encourage the theatre audience to be thoughtful and reflective in response to the unfolding dramatic representation. Equally, the actor would present or represent a character rather than seek to identify with a role.

This is not inaccurate as an account of Brecht's thinking, but is incomplete insofar as Brecht was not looking to create theatre which offered no emotional experience. In *The Messingkauf Dialogues* he describes the alienation effect as

> an artistic effect [which] leads to a theatrical experience. It consists in the reproduction of real-life incidents on the stage in such a way as to underline their causality and bring it to the spectator's attention. This type of art also generates emotions; such performances facilitate the mastering of reality; and this it is that moves the spectator. The A-effect is an ancient artistic technique; it is known from classical comedy, certain branches of popular art and the practices of the Asiatic theatre. (p. 102)

Elsewhere in the *Dialogues* Brecht describes the A-effect in terms which indicate his indebtedness to Russian formalist thinking. Thus he writes, 'If empathy makes something ordinary of a special event, alienation makes something special of an ordinary one. The most hackneyed everyday incidents are stripped of their monotony when represented as quite special' (p. 76). The idea here is identical to that of 'making the familiar strange' found in Russian formalism (q.v. 'Form, Formalism'), and this is another source of Brecht's thinking. Though 'alienation' is a key concept in Marxist theory, the roots of Brecht's idea of the alienation effect are elsewhere.

In general, one might say that the A-effect is pedagogic in intent, privileging instruction in contrast to entertainment, and Brecht authored a number of didactic plays and dramatic sketches, explicitly designed for subsequent discussion by an audience (see *The Measures Taken and Other Lehrstücke*).

Archetype

'What marks the serious artist for a lifetime is the authorization which comes from the knowledge that an illimitable repertory of images is within each one of us, only asking to be brought upwards to consciousness.' So wrote the art critic John Russell in relationship to the work of the sculptor Henry Moore. Such an inner repertory of images Carl Jung (1875–1961) named the 'archetypes', locating them in what he called the collective unconscious. Philosophically, the archetypes could be defined as a priori images analogous to the a priori categories of Immanuel Kant. Jung envisaged the archetypes as powerful mobilizing images which expressed, in visual and concrete form, the nature of the various human instincts. They are part of the inherited structure of the psyche; they manifest themselves spontaneously and are seen to account for some of the striking symbolic similarities across cultures, e.g. in the widespread appearance of the Divine Child, the Eternal Mother, the Trickster, The Goddess of Love.

Jung claimed that if the energy attendant upon the life of instinct were not to be lost, it was essential for individuals to adapt these powerful archaic images to the more complex and differentiated requirements of civilization. The implications of such a view for the arts are as rich as they are manifold. The work of such artists as William Blake, Henry Moore and Cecil Collins can be illuminated by the notion of archetype, as can, for example, the operas of Mozart, Wagner and Tippett or the poetry of Coleridge, Yeats and T.S. Eliot. However, by no means all artistic work gains from the application of the category. Applied to the wrong kind of art, or applied in too blunt a manner, it can easily give birth to a diffuse, question-begging, pseudo-mystical kind of exegesis.

For a moving description of Jung's own encounter with the primordial images of the collective unconscious see Chapter 6 of his *Memories, Dreams, Reflections*. For more systematic accounts of the archetypes see Carl Jung's *The Archetypes and the Collective Unconscious*; *The Spirit in Man, Art and Literature* and Anthony Stevens' *Archetype: A Natural History of the Self*. For its development and use in visual arts education see *Rosegarden and Labyrinth* by Seonaid Robertson. And q.v. 'Symbol, Symbolism'; 'Unconscious/The Unconscious'.

PA

Arts in Education: The Idea of a Generic Arts Community

While the place of *some* art in education has long been recognized, it is only recently that the arts have been conceived as forming a family of related disciplines, a generic community, which should form an essential part of any curriculum claiming width and balance.

An historical study of the arts in British education discloses their isolation from each other and their general state of fragmentation. Literature, for example, was first envisaged as one of the humanities (often linked to history) and has largely remained so. Dance was seen as part of physical education and has been forcibly returned there by the 1988 Education Reform Act; drama for the best part of fifty years has presented itself either as a form of enactive psychotherapy or as a learning medium; while film existed only on the very margins of the curriculum. Music and the visual arts, in contrast, established themselves early on as autonomous arts disciplines but were seldom envisaged as part of any larger aesthetic enterprise. In brief, the history of the arts in the British curriculum (see Peter Abbs (Ed.), *Living Powers*) reveals a sad story of insularity and conceptual confusion.

One of the first books to propose something resembling a concept of a common arts community in an educational context was the volume *The Arts in Education*, edited by James Britton (first published in 1963 under the title *Studies in Education*). I write in an *educational* context because one must not forget that ten years before this volume, in 1953, the philosopher Susanne Langer first published her philosophical study of the arts, *Feeling and Form*, which defined a common philosophy for the arts and gave individual studies of art, drama, dance, music, literature and even, as an epilogue, film. It was to take over thirty years for her great conception to impinge fully on educational thinking. However, in the spring of 1963 James Britton gathered together a number of arts teachers and lecturers to give a programme of lectures across the arts (in the Institute of Education, London), which were then published in the following year. With the exception of film, all the main art forms were fully represented. In an exceptionally brief editorial note to the slim volume James Britton wrote:

The question poses itself: who will read this book? No doubt there will be those who turn straight to the section of their specialist concern, but it may be hoped there will be many more whose curiosity ranges wider and who will be concerned to find out what claims in common are made for the various arts and what differences are indicated between them. (p. vii)

Britton himself, in his own chapter on 'Literature', revealed briefly the kind of educational advance that can come from an active comparison across the arts. But for the most part the various lectures, shot through with some of the deadly and dated assumptions of modernism and progressivism, revealed little collective coherence and offered no sustained comparative analysis. The editor may have had some vague idea of unity, but most of his contributors disclosed a stubborn enclosure within their own subjects. If there was any common theme, it lay in the concepts of 'self-expression' and 'self-discovery'. Had James Britton written a long afterword analyzing the various unities and differences, with an eye to creating philosophical coherence, he might have created a book of historic significance. As it was, the book failed to delineate the terms necessary for any synoptic understanding of the arts.

The first project which made a serious attempt at formulating the nature of the common ground was called Arts and the Adolescent. It was set up in 1968 for four years, was directed by Malcolm Ross and Robert Witkin, and resulted in two publications, *The Intelligence of Feeling* (1974) and the Schools Council monograph, *Arts and the Adolescent* (1975). Here, too, the notions of 'self-expression' and 'self-discovery' were given further formulation and made, alas, all but axiomatic in the teaching of the arts. Indeed, around this time, between 1963 and 1974, the idea of any reference to a cultural tradition that stretched back through the ages became badly disrupted. From this period into the 1980s the child was to express himself in a growing vacuum, often without the means of adequate articulation, without exemplars, without predecessors and without the challenge of great art. On the other hand, for the first time the arts *were* brought together with the informing notion of a common epistemology.

The project based at the University of Exeter had set itself three main aims:

What materials and methods in the field of the arts are most likely to elicit a lively response among young people? The arts for this purpose are taken to include visual art, music, dance, drama, literature, film and photography.

How do young people view their own involvement in the arts in school and out of school; how much connection is there between these two forms of often disparate activity?

How much connection can be made, and how much transfer of interest is possible, between one art and another, and between the arts and other subjects in the curriculum?

Out of these holistic questions came the first major attempt *in education* to formulate a common philosophy and common practice of arts education for state secondary schools.

In their various discussions with teachers of the arts Malcolm Ross and Robert Witkin found what they saw as a lamentable lack of intellectual clarity. There was, they claimed, a fund of enthusiasm but a paucity of reasoning. What was needed, and what Robert Witkin felt he could provide, was a conceptual framework which could be used for the empirical study of the arts and which could act as an ideal model for their systematic reconstruction. Early in 1969 Ross took the reformulated programme to the Schools Council:

> When I met the Schools Council to discuss the proposal I was able to offer them the prospect of a language which would enable arts teachers better to understand and control their work: a language that would have to be equally applicable to all the arts. This language would emerge as part of a more far-reaching study of the educational function of the arts based upon original work in the psychology of affect, on which Robert Witkin was already engaged.
>
> (Ross 1975, p. 12)

The diagnosis was surely as right as the prescription was, in the last analysis, partial and, at critical moments, fundamentally misguided. At the same time the attempt to bring unity where there had only been isolation and confusion was well worth making.

The major work deriving from the project, *The Intelligence of Feeling* by Robert Witkin, was turned down by the Schools Council on the grounds that it was too obscure for teachers to understand; it was subsequently published by Heinemann Educational Books to become an important and controversial book in a growing national arts debate.

In *The Intelligence of Feeling* Witkin struggled to forge a common language for the arts in the context of the secondary curriculum. His basic argument was that the arts were primarily concerned with subjectivity and its conversion into symbolic form through a continuous and developing interaction between the expressive impulse of the art-maker and the expressive medium of the art form. All the arts were concerned with the reflexive understanding of feeling within itself. Moving outwards from his own psychological commitment to the study of affects, Witkin proposed five common categories for the collective examination of the arts; they were as follows: 'self-expression and individuality'; 'control of the medium'; 'the use of the realised form'; 'personal development' and 'examinations and assessment'. Then in Chapter 8 he offered an account of the creative act common to all the arts, moving from the release of impulse or what he termed 'setting of the sensate problem' to 'the making of a holding form' to 'a movement through successive approximations to a resolution'. According to Witkin, an understanding of the creative process in the arts allows the teacher to enter structurally, as a kind of guiding co-artist, the pupil's expressive act.

Here was a study which brought all the arts together. In the select bibliography each art form is listed (English, art, drama, music, dance, film), though in the study only four arts are examined according to the established categories, namely, English, drama, art and music. Yet a terrible contradiction has to be recorded, for, at the same time as the explicit argument moves towards the conception of a generic arts community, another argument weaving its way through the text seems to resist and all but disown art in its inherited and symbolic nature. Again and again in his writing Malcolm Ross has attacked the formal arts and insisted only on the value of *expressivity* in education. In *The Claims of Feeling* (1989) he wrote: 'We were not after all advocating education in the arts — still less an apprenticeship for school children in the high Western artistic tradition. Real art and real artists were all but incidental to the thesis of human expressivity that the project was advancing.' (p. 8)

In brief, the idea of the arts community was almost discovered and exploded at the same moment. Perhaps it could not have been otherwise, starting from 'the psychology of affects' and an 'approach rooted in social science'. The art was bound to remain secondary as it lay outside the primary and defining terms of interest. Thus the contribution of *The Intelligence of Feeling* was ambiguous and slippery; it did much to establish the arts as a family, but, ironically, deprived them of their intrinsic content. It is not for nothing that Malcolm Ross called his work 'iconoclastic', for it served to discredit the living icons of the aesthetic field.

The next major step towards a unified conception of the arts came in 1982 with the publication of the Gulbenkian Foundations's report, *The Arts in Schools*. This project was chaired by Peter Brinson, while the report was written partly by David Aspin (who wrote the opening philosophical chapters) and partly by Ken Robinson (who wrote the remaining pragmatic chapters). The report located the need for a comprehensive view of the arts in the curriculum: 'Our arguments in this report refer to all of the arts — music, dance, drama, poetry, literature, visual and plastic arts. We do not deal with them separately because we want to emphasise what they have in common — both in what they jointly offer education and in the problems they jointly face' (p. 10). The philosophical argument derived from a central European tradition in aesthetics going back through the writing of Louis Arnaud Reid to the work of Susanne Langer and Ernst Cassirer, back to the philosophical writings of Kant.

In *The Arts in Schools* the arts are seen to provide a unique kind of knowledge of the world, in particular, a knowledge of *feeling* and *value*, and hence to form an indispensable part of any complete curriculum. The emphasis is on knowledge and aesthetic intelligence; but this knowledge is understood as materializing both through the actual practice of art-making as well as through aesthetic engagement with works of art, both contemporary and traditional. What the report advocates is not history or sociology but sustained practice with all kinds of artistic media. The hope and energy generated by the report were taken forward by the Arts in Schools Project directed by Ken Robinson.

This project, which included eighteen Local Education Authorities, drawing on more than 500 teachers, art-makers and advisers and working in over 200 schools, was launched in September 1985 and completed under the auspices of the National Curriculum Council in August 1989. The project culminated in the publication of a set of related books. It is too early to judge properly the influence and importance of this national initiative. Some have been deeply critical of it. Malcolm Ross in *The Claims of Feeling* called it a bureaucratic exercise serving the interests of political totalitarianism and claimed that the project would probably be best remembered for its data bank; while David Best accused the project of being conceptually muddled on the crucial concepts of 'aesthetic' and 'artistic' and philosophically vacuous. Others have been more positive, seeing it as the collective and pragmatic development of ideas set out in the Gulbenkian Report.

A further initiative followed in the wake of the Gulbenkian Report, *The Arts in Schools*. It was that of the Falmer Press Library on Aesthetic Education, a series of twelve related volumes on arts education. In 1987 the first volume in the series, *Living Powers*, put forward the notion of the arts as a generic community based on philosophical propositions deriving largely from the work of Susanne Langer. However, in the library the notion is *not* seen logically to entail integrated or combined arts programmes. The logic is to move from the genus to the distinctive species to a consideration of possible connections and areas of overlap. There is no way in which one art form can be simply dissolved into another or seen as simply equivalent. For this reason in the library each great art form has its own volume.

Yet at the same time as the Arts in Schools project and the Library on Aesthetic Education were taking shape, the Conservative Government, taking unilateral action over the heads of the teachers and educationists, instituted the National Curriculum. It passed into law as the Education Reform Act in the summer of 1988. The effects on the arts were dramatic and contrary to the direction of the dominant argument inside education itself. In the various National Curriculum documents literature was seen as an integral part of English teaching; drama was also seen as a subsidiary part of English; dance was similarly returned to physical education; while film as an arts discipline more or less disappeared off the map. Music and visual arts, in contrast, were first given the status of foundation subjects and then made optional after 14. The full implications of the National Curriculum for the arts are still being worked out and will take a decade to become completely clear. At the moment the government shows very little understanding of the arts and has constructed a curriculum which either fragments them, once again, into isolated, unequal and competing parts, or treats them as 'servicing subjects' working across the curriculum. For the time being the National Curriculum has made structurally difficult, if not impossible, the realization of a unified arts curriculum based on the idea of the generic community.

For further reference see Robert Witkin, *The Intelligence of Feeling*; the Gulbenkian Report, *The Arts in Schools*; P. Abbs (Ed.), *Living Powers: The Arts in Education*; Peter Abbs, 'A Formal Aesthetic for the Teaching of the Arts', in *A Is for Aesthetic*; Malcolm Ross, *The Claims of Feeling*; and DES *The Arts 5–16: A Curriculum Framework*.

PA

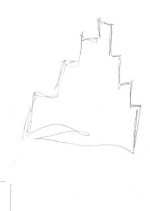

Arts in the Primary School

> ... the arts are not only for communicating ideas. They are ways of having ideas, of creating ideas, of exploring experience and fashioning our understanding of it into new forms ... the arts are among the ways in which we move from merely experiencing to understanding and controlling it. (Gulbenkian Report)

The arts represent a fundamental way of knowing to do with the aesthetic and creating fields. They are experienced through the direct use of the senses and engage both feelings and mind. They share a special capability of penetrating to the very core of human existence, having the potential to deal with every facet of life, from the most light-hearted and humorous to the most disturbing and profound. They should therefore constitute as important a part of the youngest pupil's education as of any pupil in any other phase of learning. Also, because of the nature of how learning generally takes place in the primary schools, the arts can assume a particular relevance there because that learning can be both *in* and *through* the arts in ways which the traditional secondary school timetable frustrates. When properly handled in the primary sector, they can be enjoyed in their own right and for their own sake, but can also imbue other areas of the curriculum with greater relevance and meaning. They also make the most potent contribution to the personal and social education and development of the children, and have an unrivalled potential to enrich the whole school environment, able to make it into a learning resource with a special ethos.

Unfortunately, though, as the final pieces of the National Curriculum jigsaw fall into place, all the indications suggest the risk of further marginalization of the arts in primary education, rather than the advances which were promised in some quarters. That it was necessary to introduce something as complex, drastic and wide-ranging as the National Curriculum in a phased way over a considerable period of time can be readily appreciated. In practice, along with the accompanying rhetoric, undue weighting has been given to the core subjects, widely perceived as having been introduced in an order of priority according to their assumed importance. The sheer number of programmes of study and attainment targets associated with the core, allied to the fact that national testing in these subjects will be the main means whereby schools are to be made accountable, risks distorting the primary curriculum throughout, much as the 11+ patently did at the later stages. In this total scenario the arts appear to have been dealt with superficially in passing — the verbal arts and drama — or last on the basis of least — music, the visual arts and dance. Is it surprising that some already overburdened teachers, insecure in the arts because of their own inadequate initial training, are inevitably choosing to treat the arts as peripheral? Is it surprising that some primary schools are turning to the secondary-type timetable patterns which have traditionally served the arts so badly?

'From Policy to Practice' states that, through the Education Reform Act, the entitlement of all pupils within the maintained sector will be met through a curriculum which is balanced and broadly based and which, as the Act says, 'promotes the spiritual, moral, cultural, mental and physical development of pupils at the school and of society; and prepares such pupils for the opportunities, responsibilities and experiences of adult life.' Nobody would argue with these laudable aims, but they are in danger of being distorted through the adoption of a woolly compromise. Instead of pruning back the overabundant fleshy growth of the core subjects, all the signs are that restrictions of time and scope are being placed on the arts subjects in particular. In place of the promised 'balanced and broadly based' curriculum, the most likely outcome in many schools will be yet another return to the so-called 'basics', even though there is abundant evidence that when these are taught in isolation at the expense of the rest of the curriculum, the resulting work is invariably arid and lacking in content. A 'top' stratum of children are usually able successfully to put capital letters and full stops in the right places, making only a minimum of spelling mistakes in their use of a restricted vocabulary.

As the National Association for Education through the Arts (NAEA) aptly observes:

> We believe that the present situation is one in which the Arts should play a central role. Arts education offers the young unique opportunities for exploring and sharing their experiences and adapting to the human implications of societal change. Any attempt to inculcate academic disciplines or social and life skills without reference to feelings, to the moral values which feelings imply and reveal, or to peer-group attitudes, cultural norms and individual aspirations, dooms the young to an education which continues to ignore their real world and must inevitably fail to bring about the results called for by government.

The case for the arts occupying a more central place in the primary curriculum is overwhelming, and there is much that any staff can collectively do, notwithstanding the adverse pressures upon them. They are preparing their pupils for life in a world which is now changing so rapidly that we can only but vaguely begin to envisage what it might be like for them as adults. They are going to have to be adaptable, and the arts, with their rare capacity for allying thoughts with feelings and vigorously to pursue individual concepts to their conclusion, are essential to the cultivation and development of the types of divergent thought and action which will prepare children to operate adequately in this changing world.

Whole school policies are essential to this process. Without them, the chances are that arts experiences will be spasmodic and fragmentary at best, with some children missing out altogether. To this end there should be an arts post commensurate in status with any other, and its holder should have sufficient confidence and expertise to support other teachers whose main skills are elsewhere, so that all children benefit from an arts education which has coherence, relevance and continuity. Each teacher might then begin to relate more effectively what is done throughout a specific year to what the children have previously experienced and are to undertake next.

From the earliest age and throughout their education all pupils should have ongoing access to the arts as practised by established makers and performers. The aesthetic field of making, presenting, responding and evaluating in all its implications is as relevant at the primary phase as at any other, with even the youngest pupils capable of utilizing the experiences gained from contact with other practitioners to the benefit of their own practice — a process which, in turn, invariably extends and deepens their awareness of the arts as practised by others. Frequently expressed fears that contact with adult practitioners impairs pupils' own creativity and originality are being dispelled as a relevant body of evidence builds up to show that, with sensitive teaching, primary pupils are more than capable of transposing and drawing from what others have done, making it relevant to their personal needs and stage of development, frequently confounding normal expectations in the process.

A particularly acute and complex problem in the primary sector is that of which art forms should be practised when, but all children should have the opportunity to be involved in at least some of the arts all of the time. How knowledgeable and informed might they become if it became an accepted norm that they gradually and relentlessly increase their awareness and understanding of the arts and their place in society through ongoing and systematic opportunities from the beginning of school days onwards? Just imagine how articulate they could become if these experiences were allied to constant discourse about the arts, with each developing a vocabulary commensurate with their age and ability! Imagine what might be achieved through the continuity of secondary education building upon primary achievements, as opposed to always starting afresh at age 11! What sophisticated, complex and powerful concepts might young people begin to give expression to through their practice, and how positively might they begin to determine the form and nature of their environment! Education might then, at last, be appropriately shaped to prepare young people for the world of tomorrow. It is of

A thoroughgoing sociological approach has found favour especially in relation to the visual arts — and no doubt especially because paintings and sculptures are sought-after, portable and saleable commodities, the most impressive feature of which may be their price tag. But related theories have also been advanced for literature, especially for the construction of literary meaning. Thus, rather than see the meaning (q.v. 'Meaning') of a literary work as given by the author's intentions (q.v. 'Intention and Convention') or by the words on the page (q.v. 'Text and Context') — admittedly always subject to interpretation (q.v. 'Interpretation') — there are those who have seen literary meaning itself as constructed or manufactured by the institution of criticism, by the community of critics and academics who write the articles and the books which tell us what a work *means*. This view has been championed and popularized in recent years by Stanley Fish, notably in his book, *Is There a Text in This Class?*, discussed more fully in the other sections of this book referred to in this paragraph.

There is a sense, but not a trivial one, in which Fish and fellow social constructionists are clearly right. Without human beings to animate and reanimate them, a painting is merely paint on canvas, a literary work merely ink marks on paper: works of art are not like atoms and gases. They need human beings to keep them in existence *as* works of art — as intentional objects of thought, feeling and imagination. The spectator, the audience cannot be left out of the account of art. Too often they have been left out, or left implicit, and the consequences (it is said) have been seriously misleading theories of art.

But what has just been said does not license any claim to the effect that works of art are mere Rorschach ink-blots on which we are free to project any meaning we choose, or that Carl André's bricks mean what the Tate Gallery pays them to mean, or that the only relevant questions concern who is to be master of the game of calling this art, that beautiful, this tasteless and so on. For art works are produced within traditions (q.v. 'Tradition'), using conventions (q.v. 'Intention and Convention') and within art worlds to which the artist as well as the spectator and critic are party. Art is a social as well as an individual practice (Marxists would agree to that), a public and accountable activity within what Wittgensteinians would call a form of life. All this sets constraints on the meanings which can plausibly be attributed to a work of art (q.v. 'Aesthetic Field').

Yes, indeed, says Stanley Fish: I agree entirely with the previous paragraph. But nothing in it undermines my position; rather it is précis of what I say myself. Art works are kept alive, meanings assigned to them, in the context of a communal, not individual, activity. And this is what we mean by social construction. We may indeed be able to talk and argue about What is art? and What is beauty? and What does the poem mean? But we must never forget that we have created the categories and the meanings we talk and argue about. That also means that we are capable of changing the categories, rethinking the meanings — just the sort of thing the Tate Gallery was a party to and initiator of when it bought Carl André's bricks!

The idea of art as an institution was discovered practically by the early twentieth century visual arts avant-garde, notably Dadaism. 'Works' such as Duchamp's 1917 urinal are reactions to notions of autonomous art, aestheticism and *L'art pour L'art*. See Peter Bürger's *Theory of the Avant-Garde*.

Beauty (q.v. 'Judgment', 'Taste')

'A thing of beauty is a joy forever.' Thus we represent the belief that beauty in an object is timelessly recognizable and can be responded to despite all manner of changes in economy and society, all manner of changes in political, moral, religious and even artistic beliefs. Indeed, we take it as evidence for the (surpassing) beauty of an object that it withstands the test of time: on the nature of this test we even have a philosopher's book, Anthony Savile's *The Test of Time*. But we also say, 'Beauty is in the eye of the beholder', suggesting that what is picked out as beautiful will vary from person to person, period to period, culture to culture. To cancel this implication we would instead have to say, 'Beauty is in the eye the beholder, and the eye is the same at all times, in all places.'

Indeed, there has been no shortage of attempts to specify what it is in something which will unchangeably please through the senses (the ear as well as the eye), and lead anyone to judge it beautiful. At their most concrete and practical these attempts are exemplified in 'classical' rules for composition, whether in music, painting or prose. We know now that such rules are too restrictive and that we judge to be beautiful objects which are made in wilful or ignorant violation of such rules. So it is false that *only* works made in accordance with such rules are beautiful. But it may still be true that *all* works made in accordance with such rules will be judged beautiful or, at least, not displeasing. We may judge a musical composition or painting done according to the rules to be uninspiring or insipid or feeble, but not actively displeasing hence positively ugly. There is clearly a fine line here: if a work done according to the rules is tedious, surely it is displeasing; in which case following the rules cannot *guarantee* beauty, But the fault may be in the fallible humanly-created Rule Book, not in the idea that there are, in fact, definable features of things which always — everywhere — tend to please and tend to elicit a judgment of beauty. For example, it may be said that in itself harmony in a work (whether music, painting or poetry) will always tend to please, though we may be hard put to spell out rules of harmony in advance of actual instances of things found harmonious.

This point leads to a central claim made in Kant's *Critique of Judgement* (1790) and influential through all subsequent discussions of aesthetics. This is the claim that whereas the ordinary and scientific understanding fits instances of things, events, perceptions to pre-existing rules, concepts, schemata or categories, in aesthetic judgment we (in some sense) frame a rule, concept or category to fit the (unique) instance presented by the work of art before us. We do this in an act of imagination, or of what Kant calls 'reflective judgment'. The work of art thus constitutes a challenge, and in meeting the challenge, we experience a characteristic pleasure which is the touchstone for the subsequent judgment of beauty.

Can one illustrate this idea? Let me try, but with one preliminary condition spelt out. This is that everyone has to engage imaginatively with a work of art *for himself or herself*; there can be no 'secondhand' experience. So, positioned before a particular canvas by Cézanne, the idea is that the possibility of taking pleasure in it, and thence judging it beautiful, is dependent on my ability to conceptualize (in some sense) an account of what it is Cézanne is doing, or what it is that the painting is about, or what it would be an achievement to have done such that this painting would be an instance of such an achievement. Of course, I may be helped by having already heard about or read about Cézanne. But to take *pleasure* in Cezanne's painting, I need to make the categories or concepts I have already encountered my own. Otherwise, there is merely recognition of an instance (scientific or ordinary understanding) of something, not a discovery of a (pleasurable and fresh) way of seeing — hence no reproduction or reliving of whatever it was that Cézanne was about. (This last point indicates that the imagination is not operating arbitrarily in its encounter with the art object, but is in some sense responsible to the (artist's) imagination which created the work.)

In sum, the Kantian idea is that though authentic encounter with a work of art is not mediated through pre-existing rules, categories, etc. — so that the encounter is fresh and ground-breaking — it can result in the *creation* of a rule, category, etc. which is the basis on which the work can subsequently be talked about. Where the imaginative creation is pleasurably experienced, we end up seeing the work as beautiful, and convinced that this is an objective fact of which we can assert a true judgment (q.v. 'Judgment'). There is an extended account of such a Kantian idea of beauty in Mary Mothersill's *Beauty Restored*, and a companion Kantian account of imagination in Mary Warnock's *Imagination* (q.v. also 'Imagination'). For the present, I pause to consider one or two difficulties.

First, the Kantian approach tends to downgrade the importance of the (merely) sensuous in art, the (merely) pleasing. Things which can be enjoyed — like wine or fruit — without imaginative engagement (reflective judgment) do not count as highly as art proper which does require those things. Yet some art has a strongly sensuous character. Is it the worse for that? And when we are talking about imagination and reflective judgment, are we talking about these as exercised consciously or as acting below the level of consciousness? (Compare hearing or grasping a melody with conceptualizing the point of Molly Bloom's soliloquy in Joyce's *Ulysses*.)

In fact, Kant has to draw a sharp distinction between the beautiful and the merely pleasing in order to ground the idea that judgments of beauty make an objective claim to validity which merely subjective expressions of pleasure or displeasure do not: beauty is 'out there', intersubjectively accessible, whereas pleasure is 'in here', a fact about me, not about the world (q.v. 'Judgment').

Second, imagination or reflective judgment, as Kant describes it, is not uniquely exercised in relation to art, whatever Kant may have thought. For though so-called 'normal' science may be about fitting new phenomena into established categories or laws, creative ('revolutionary') science involves finding new categories or laws, often for 'old' phenomena: it involves what Karl Popper calls 'conjecture' and C.S. Peirce called 'abduction' (as distinct from deduction and induction). When Copernicus 'saved the phenomena' (accounted for the phenomena) of planetary motion by imagining that the earth moved and the sun did not, he exercised precisely what Kant calls reflective judgment. If, as in Kant, reflective judgment is linked to pleasure and thence to the judgment of beauty, why should Copernicus not have experienced pleasure in framing his theory and from thence derived a judgment of the beauty of the movement of the spheres?

Why not, indeed? We do speak of the beauty of the universe and the beauty (or elegance) of the theories which describe its laws. We do see a close connection between artistic and scientific creativity (q.v. 'Creativity'). All we now have to say à propos of Kant is that it is *not only* works of art which engage the imagination or reflective judgment, which produce pleasure in the act of grasping their concept (rule, law, category), and which lead us to ascribe beauty to them. Art differs from nature in that its works are instances of freely created beauty, but pleasure taken in the beauty of a work of art may not be so very different, subjectively, from pleasure taken in grasping the laws of nature.

Classicism and Romanticism

In a famous book, *The Mirror and the Lamp* (1953), M.H. Abrams distinguishes theories of art and criticism in terms of whether and how they privilege one or more terms or relationships in a set diagrammed like this (p. 6):

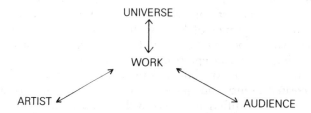

So, some of our oldest theories of art define and value (or, in Plato's case, condemn) art in terms of the relationship of *mimesis* (q.v.) which obtain between works of art and the universe, the world to which it relates. This is a major element of classicism. Likewise, there are long traditions which characterize and value art in terms of its ability to 'please and instruct', and consequently focus on the rhetorical or pragmatic relationship between work and audience. There is a line from Greek theories of *catharsis* (q.v. 'Mimesis and Katharsis'), through the history of rhetoric (q.v. 'Figurative and Literal') to contemporary reader-response criticism, as surveyed, for example, in Robert Holub's *Reception Theory* or Elizabeth Freund's *The Return of the Reader*.

One might say that before the Romantic movement (say, 1770–1830) most theories of art simply took for granted the unimportance of the relationship between artist and work; where it obtruded itself (as in lyric poetry or the self-portrait), they responded by regarding those genres as minor and not worth theorizing. In the eighteenth century, says Abrams, Shakespeare's sonnets — unlike his plays — were simply ignored or condemned (p. 246).

Romanticism is, then, a critical watershed as well as a permanent possibility of artistic orientation, an orientation which emphasizes and values the work of art as *expressive* of the artist's mind. Historically, the romantic movement — for example, in English poetry and the theorizing of it by Wordsworth and Coleridge — wants the work to be expressive of the artist's emotions and feelings: poetry, says Wordsworth in the 'Preface' to the *Lyrical Ballads* (1800), 'is the spontaneous overflow of powerful feelings', not oriented in origin to any external audience, and illuminating the objective world with the lamp of a subjective experience.

In romanticism as a movement, poetry as the expression of emotion is categorically contrasted with science as representation of reality. It is not opposed to prose (which may be poetic or scientific, according to its informing subjective or objective drive). But one might say that there is no reason not to regard as 'romantic' any theory or practice of art which values the self-realization of artist in his or her work, even when what is realized is more like a vision, or ideas and beliefs, than like a realization of 'simple' emotion. In this way one would be led to distinguish the question of whether self-expression or self-realization is important in or defining of art from the question of whether certain traditionally romantic oppositions — between feeling and reason, subjective and objective, emotion and fact — are tenable. There are, of course, many good arguments to suggest that the stock romantic oppositions are untenable; for a survey see David Best's *The Rationality of Feeling* and q.v. 'Expression'; 'Self-Expression'.

Romanticism as a movement implied and articulated significantly fresh evaluative criteria for art, notably sincerity and spontaneity. What we now think of as later aestheticism and decadentism is, in part, a reaction against such criteria as inadequate to judge a work of art. Thus Oscar Wilde in 'The Decay of Lying' (against, inter alia, Mrs Humphry Ward's *Robert Elsmere*) and, in another context, Baudelaire's address to the 'hypocrite lecteur, mon semblable, mon frère', Modern neo-classicism is, one might say, a cleaned-up version of aestheticism and decadence, which insists against the romantic orientation and the romantic criteria on the autonomy of the work of art, on judging the work itself, 'the words on the page', all considerations of biography (and hence of sincerity and spontaneity) excluded. Though associated with theorists of notably conservative and illiberal persuasions — the American 'New Critics' and T.S. Eliot, notably — neo-classicism has also had its radical spokesmen, notably Brecht, whose epic theatre is consciously anti-romantic (see, for example, his *Messingkauf Dialogues*).

Of course, for educationists the romantic orientation and criteria were and remain of immense importance. This extends beyond the romantic emphasis on self-expression, sincerity and spontaneity to the connected romantic claim that poetry (art) does not 'please and instruct' but is directly effective as an emotionally and, more generally, morally educative force. For Wordsworth, says Abrams, 'poetry, by sensitizing, purifying and strengthening the feelings, directly *makes* us better' (p. 330). John Stuart Mill, in an 1835 essay on Tennyson's poems, states the claim in its grandest terms, speaking of 'the noblest end of poetry as an intellectual pursuit, that of acting upon the desires and characters of mankind through their emotions, to raise them towards the perfection of their nature' (cited in Abrams, p. 334).

This is still a characteristic way of justifying the arts in education, the background matrix of which is an equation of imagination, sympathy and moral development (see, for example, in this series the contributions of Rex Gibson and L.C. Knights to *The Symbolic Order*). But after Auschwitz, says the German critic Theodor Adorno, such claims are unsustainable — worse, 'to write lyric poetry after Auschwitz is barbaric' (in Bloch *et al.*, *Aesthetics and Politics*, pp. 188–9). It is worse than insensitive to go on as if the redemptive claims of the romantic movement had not been hopelessly discredited by history, says Adorno (q.v. 'Holocaust').

Of course, there is an enormous shift in arts education away from the orientations and values of romanticism, or, more specifically, self-expression, as is evidenced in Peter Abbs' contribution to this series in *Living Powers* and *A Is for Aesthetic*. Romanticism yields to a neo-classical emphasis on the work itself, on its forms and genres, its traditions and techniques, and arts education becomes less the search for sincerity, spontaneity and self-expression than the patient initiation of pupils into the forms of artistic knowing. But, on the other hand, if there is nothing to be known — felt, imagined, concretized — through the forms of artistic knowing, then they have no more claim to our interest than a parlour game. Deprived of a link to deep human concerns (q.v. 'Morality and Art'), poetry would be no better than bar billiards.

The key texts of the Romantic movement include Wordsworth's 'Preface' to the *Lyrical Ballads* (1800).

Communication

Is the artist a communicator? Is an artistic medium a medium of communication? These questions are deceptively simple, and to answer 'yes' to them may commit one to a view of art which, upon reflection, one would want to reject.

Suppose I have a message I want to communicate to you, and that what matters is that you get the message, not how you get it. Then, obviously, I am indifferent whether you get the message by letter or by 'phone, in English or in French. My choice of medium for the message will be determined simply by considerations of efficiency. The medium has no effect on the message, which is supposed to pre-exist it — what we naturally think is that the message already has a verbal formulation in the sender's mind.

Now it is (in general) not true that an artist uses a medium as an efficient way of communicating a message; nor is it true that the artist uses his or her medium to represent, translate, notate or express a message which already exists fully formed in the artist's mind. If you do have a fully formed message in your mind, the best thing to do is just spit it out. Why go to the bother of writing a symphony or a novel? The history of the novel with a thesis (*roman à thèse*) suggests that the bother is *not* worthwhile. The artist's medium is better thought of not as a medium of communication but as a medium of expression or representation (q.v. 'Medium', 'Expression', 'Representation'). It follows that artistic works should not in general be thought of as 'making statements' or 'bearing messages' which need decoding, though some artists may indeed conceive their work in these terms and require this kind of response. Of course, the interpretation and placing of individual works in a historical, cultural context involve treating individual works as bearers of collective messages; but this is no longer to be responding to the individual work as a work of art with aesthetic properties.

A useful distinction has been drawn by philosophers and linguists between communication (or communicative action) and information (or informative behaviour). Your blush or your stutter may tell me a lot about you — it provides me with information about you. But insofar as you do not intend to blush or stutter, or intend to provide me with information by means of blushing or stuttering, you are not engaged in communicative action. In a slogan: no communication without an intention to communicate. Despite the slogan, the topic is a complex one, and the nature of the intention to communicate and the dependence or independence of *what* is communicated (the *meaning* of what is communicated) on the intention to communicate it has been extensively debated (q.v. 'Intention and Convention', 'Meaning'). Nonetheless, there is a world of differenc_ between the accidental fall and the pratfall; between the actor who corpses and the actor who pretends to corpse; between the halting speech of an actor forgetting his lines and the halting speech which signifies a character. In each of these cases it is the difference between informative behaviour and communicative action which makes the difference.

The slogan, 'No communication without an intention to communicate', can be paralleled by another possible slogan, 'No art without an intention to make art'. What we find in nature may be aesthetically pleasing, but it is not art. The unintended beauty of a porcelain urinal does not constitute the urinal as a work of art; something more is needed. Whether Duchamp's gesture is enough to make the urinal into a work of art remains hotly debated (q.v. 'Art World; Institutional Theories of Art').

Creativity (q.v. 'Genius')

What is creativity? There is no answer to this question currently available, any more than there is to the question, what makes an individual (highly) creative? Part of the problem is that since creativity is generally thought to be a good thing, the word is used to describe many things which are not creative.

One might begin by trying to distinguish between *creativity* and *novelty*, or alternatively between *extraordinary* and *ordinary* creativity. For example, in *Music of the Common Tongue* Christopher Small writes that 'an improvised performance is not unlike a conversation ... both depend on the existence of a commonly agreed language' (p. 290). Now, on one account of language, the sentences produced in the course of an ordinary conversation are ordinarily merely *novel*: they are sentences which may not have been uttered before, though the possibility of their utterance already existed and was defined by the pre-existing 'commonly agreed language', that is, a vocabulary and a grammar. Knowing a language is knowing how to produce such novel sentences to serve one's purposes. If language is as just described, and if a musical language is just like language, then in the course of an improvised performance, musicians will normally do no more than produce novel combinations of notes, the possibility of which was pre-defined in the musical language known to the musicians and without which they would not be able to play together. There is nothing especially *creative*, on this view, in either a conversation or an improvised performance — there is merely novelty. In his *Autobiography* John Stuart Mill in a state of depression was 'seriously tormented by the thought of the exhaustibility of musical combinations'.

In contrast, on this approach, 'true' creativity arrives when individuals break old rules or invent new ones. The writer's use of language is creative to the extent that it violates an existing rule of grammar, or invents and then shows the use of a new rule. To take an example used elsewhere (q.v. 'Death of the Author'), creative writers invented and developed the linguistic device known as free indirect speech or free indirect discourse in which, when John says, 'I'll come tomorrow', they write not the 'John said he would come on the following day' of indirect speech but the 'John said he would come tomorrow' of free indirect speech. The free indirect form is both a rule violation of the standard indirect form, but also embodies and historically develops as a new rule.

Similarly, inventing twelve tone music involved the creative development of a new set of rules, framework or matrix for composition. On the other hand, the idea that creativity can be evidenced *simply* in breaking or violating rules seems to make creativity too easy: *A* scarcely deserves to be called a more creative poet than *B* because *A* writes doggerel verse which wilfully breaks rules of meter while *B* writes rule-conforming and beautiful poems.

Nor is everyone who has thought about this topic willing to accept a sharp contrast between novelty and creativity linked to a contrast between rule-following, on the one hand, and rule-breaking or rule-making, on the other. For it is not by any means agreed that there is always a well defined set of rules of the language or rules of the art which pre-exist individual (non-creative) contributions which simply draw on those rules. The rules may be ill defined and at least partly made up as one goes along. Creativity is then much more a matter of sniffing out and exploiting an area of ill definition and taking the initiative in making up the rules as one goes along.

A good illustration of what is involved in such a way of thinking is provided by the formation of words by analogy. No doubt everyone reading this passage is happy to accept that 'Redness' is a well defined word of English: 'There was a redness and swelling on the face.' The same goes for 'Greyness': 'I was appalled by the greyness of the lives they lead.' But how about blueness, purpleness, Hooker's greeness, magentaness, ochreness, . . .? One can immediately see what these words might mean, but doubt whether they actually *exist*. In such a situation a writer can be creative in finding a context such that a possible word can be deployed in a way which makes it acceptable as an actual word. In this way the writer contributes to changing what is perceived to be part of the language. Such an approach, rejecting the sharp contrast between novelty and creativity, is central to the aesthetics of Benedetto Croce and his followers, who included linguists and stylisticians like Karl Vossler and Leo Spitzer. See, for the full argument, B. Croce, *Aesthetic: As Science of Expression and General Linguistic*; for the approach first considered there is a good chapter in F.D'Agostino, *Chomsky's System of Ideas*, (Ch. 4). In Kantian terms the contrast of the approaches is between considering rules of language as involved in *determinant* judgments of grammaticality, which merely involve the application of rules, and considering them as involved in *reflective* judgments, which create new rules.

There are, of course, quite other ways of thinking about creativity. For example, one may think of creativity as centrally manifested in *problem-solving* activities, and argue that artists are involved in problem-solving: either problems presented by a tradition or problems invented by the artist (q.v. 'Tradition'). Alternatively, one can define creativity in terms of the exercise of *imagination*, so that to give an account of imagination is at the same time to give an account of creativity. Thus the distinction between creativity and novelty corresponds to Coleridge's distinction between imagination and fancy: the imagination involves the artist's whole being in a creative act; fancy simply recombines already available materials (q.v. 'Imagination').

Creativity could be linked to creating, and seen as involved in all *making*: so that there is an exercise of creativity in all making. This is, in effect, the position of the early Marx in the *Economic and Philosophic Manuscripts of 1844*. It is because making is so central to the growth and exercise of human powers, including human creativity, that alienation from making is so devastating for the human spirit, and thus the basis for a moral critique of alienating economic and social relations. The concept of making is central to the idea of aesthetic education developed by Peter Abbs (see, for example, his *A Is for Aesthetic*, Ch. 1). The idea of making as centrally involving creativity can be underpinned in terms of psychological and psychoanalytic theory, notably from the work of D.W. Winnicott where emphasis is placed on the child's making something new (something *else*) out of something old (something *other*): a piece of old blanket becomes a cuddly — a transitional object in D.W. Winnicott's terms — a stick becomes a hobby horse (see Ernst Gombrich's essay, 'Meditations on a Hobby Horse'). On such approaches work and play are closely connected, since the child's purposive making is inseparable from play. Hence the old slogan that a child's play is its work (for relevant discussion see D.W. Winnicott, *Playing and Reality*).

Dance in Education

It was not until the post-war era and the rise of progressive education that a major initiative to establish dance as a significant aspect of physical education occurred. As early as 1909, the traditional, if unaesthetic, location of dance in the physical education department appears to have been settled when Cecil Sharp's national drive to revive and popularize folk dancing prompted the Board of Education to include it as an appropriate physical training activity in public elementary schools. A considerably broader aesthetic perspective was introduced over the next three decades by a small number of pioneers inspired by Isadora Duncan's revolutionary concepts of expressive dance. Nationally their impact was marginal, but forms of 'natural movement' the 'revived Greek dance', 'eurythmics' and 'music and movement' became a feature in the syllabi of some schools and physical training colleges. Their rationale cohered to place a common stress on the 'holistic' nature of rhythmic movement, and their emphasis on the psychological and therapeutic value of dance foreshadowed the tenets upon which dance education was to stand and progress for the next forty years.

In 1938 Rudolf von Laban, the most distinguished pioneer of Central European modern dance, arrived in England as a refugee from Germany. Not only did Laban's work attune to the holistic philosophy of earlier dance educators; it also connected closely with the progressive approach. In addition, its relevance to the development of physical education (under pressure to formulate a more creative curriculum) was quickly noted. In 1941, after a conference to investigate the educational potential of Central European dance, the Physical Education Association issued a formal request to the Board of Education to promote 'modern' dance in schools.

Although Laban is today considered a major theoretician and originator of what is currently termed 'community dance', he was also a dancer, choreographer and opera director. In the early 1940s his formulation of what came to be known as 'modern educational dance' was to be aesthetically restricted by the cultural climate here in which it was shaped. The creation and growth of modern dance as an art form in Central Europe and America was virtually unknown in England until the 1970s. Lacking reference to any British models of modern dance, there was thus no opportunity to align dance education to the formal techniques and skills of dance as a performance art. Modern educational dance was cast in close correspondence to the characteristic features of progressivism, and 'movement', as the common link between physical education and dance, became the primary source of subject material. Reference to formal aesthetics became absorbed in the general concept of the 'art of movement'.

For the next three decades dance education concerned itself with the practical and theoretical study of Laban's analysis of the principles of movement. There was an emphasis on self-expression, creativity, spontaneous improvisation and absorption in process. The focus was experiential; the aims towards personal growth and development. For the majority of physical educators, teaching dance as one aspect of the syllabus, reference to the aesthetics of theatre dance was a peripheral consideration. By the late 1960s, however, a number of influential dance educators were voicing concern at the ways in which a refusal to expand the parameters of dance education had effectively led Laban's work into a cul de sac. The boundaries between dance and physical education had become blurred and philosophy and practice confused.

Such critiques were sharply highlighted in the early 1970s when dance became an examinable subject and validating bodies pressed for a clarification of aims and objectives. In addition, Ballet Rambert and London Contemporary Dance Theatre began to tour England with a repertoire of contemporary dance works. Out of the ensuing and fiercely divisive debates which were waged throughout the next decade a new perspective emerged to connect dance education to a world outside the gymnasium. This pressed for an alignment of dance in the area of expressive arts; for a formal concern with the development of three major strands: choreography, performance and appreciation; and for the inclusion of such theoretical aspects as dance analysis, criticism, history, aesthetics and notation.

Although 'modern educational dance' was skilfully updated to encompass the directive to teach dance as art form, the influence of Laban's work diminished and dance educators turned heavily and somewhat uncritically to the pool of expertise presented by the London Contemporary Dance Theatre and the contemporary American technique of Martha Graham. A look at current practice illustrates a number of ways in which this has contributed towards a clarification of the conceptual framework for dance education; towards the gradual rise in standards of technical expertise, performance skills and choreography; towards lifting and popularizing the profile of dance education. What was questionable is the preoccupation with a form of dance whose tradition is limited to a period of no more than forty years.

An attempt to undo the restrictions of this situation was presented in the early 1980s by Janet Adshead in *The Study of Dance*. Herein she set down 'a coherent account of the totality of dance study'. While reiterating the concepts of dance-making, performance and appreciation as central organizing principles, she insisted that a sole focus on the contemporary dance as art orientation ignored the eclectic nature of dance and the rich variety of dance forms which exist outside this specialism. She further insisted that dance

education should be free of ethnocentricity and what can be seen retro-
spectively as a tendency to become overly influenced by current practice,
stylistics and fashions. (Ironically, the dramatic formalism of Graham and the
abstractions of minimalism have now moved out of fashion, and the naturalism of 'new dance' and the demands of 'dance theatre' point directly back
towards Duncan and Laban.)

Adshead's conception of dance education places it in alignment with
other arts disciplines. The implications for its implementation are daunting,
since the lack of a recording system until this century rendered dance historically inaccessible and textually impoverished. It is clear, however, that the
influence of such recommendations is beginning to be reflected in current
PGCE and degree courses and incorporated into GCSE and A-level syllabi.

At a point in the history of dance education when the elements for a
broad and coherent philosophy are available, when a pathway towards a
logical articulation with the expressive arts has opened up, the dictates of the
National Curriculum have bracketed dance back into the physical education
department. While the recommendations of the working party concerned
with physical education insist that dance be compulsory for key stages 1–4,
dance educators wait with some anxiety the publication in July 1991 of the
government's final decision to determine the future of dance education in the
curriculum.

For further reading see J. Adshead, *The Study of Dance*; V. Preston
Dunlop, *Dance Education*; A. Haynes, 'The Dynamic Image: Changing Perspectives in Dance Education', in P. Abbs (Ed.), *Living Powers*.

AC-H

Death of the Author

On Monday, I talk to John. He says, 'I'm going to Paris tomorrow.' On Friday, I talk to Jill and say to her, 'I met John on Monday. He said he was going to Paris the next day.' Or I may say, 'I met John on Monday. He said he was going to Paris on Tuesday.' What I cannot say is this: 'I met John on Monday. He said he was going to Paris tomorrow' — since 'tomorrow' would here be taken to refer to Saturday. Nor can a third party say, 'Trevor met John on Monday. John said he was going to Paris tomorrow', since 'tomorrow' would refer to the day following that on which these words were uttered. But a *writer* can write these words which cannot be spoken; for example, the words, 'John said he was going to Paris tomorrow', and the 'tomorrow' will be understood as referring to the relevant Tuesday, that is, *John's* tomorrow. When a writer does this, he or she is producing an instance of free indirect discourse. This contrasts with direct discourse (which here would involve writing, 'John said, "I'm going to Paris tomorrow"') and with indirect discourse ('John said that he was going to Paris the next day').

In free indirect discourse a word uttered by an original speaker which has a reference determined by its origin with that speaker speaking at a particular time is nonetheless retained in the discourse of a third person, the writer, yet is understood to have its reference determined by its original circumstances of utterance. This is a remarkable phenomenon. A sentence in free indirect discourse is, strictly, unspeakable just because it does not consist in the words of just one speaker, but of more than one. The fact that it can be written suggests that writing is not to be thought of as the 'utterance' of a single 'speaker', the writer. This can be the springboard for an understanding of literary texts as things which do not acquire their meaning from (the intentions of) a writer, an author. Going further, the so-called writer or author can come to be thought of as a (mere) *scriptor* of words which do not issue from a single source, which are not the expression of a single voice, and are not to be understood by reference back to their authorial origin. The upshot is that we get articles like the famous one by Roland Barthes entitled 'The Death of the Author' (1968).

To understand what is being suggested here, and what is at stake, we need to understand more about free indirect discourse and related phenomena, and how it can serve as a springboard to a more general conception of literary texts as speakerless and internally heteroglot (as opposed to monoglot). Sources for this often abstruse discussion include V. Volosinov, *Marxism and the Philosophy of Language*; M. Bakhtin, 'Discourse in the Novel', in *The Dialogic Imagination*; R. Pascal, *The Dual Voice*; A. Banfield, *Unspeakable Sentences*; K. Hamburger, *The Logic of Literature*.

Free indirect discourse (FID) was remarked as a phenomenon present in literary texts as long ago as 1887. In every case it involves carrying over into the representing language of the author/narrator features of the represented language (or consciousness) of characters which under the rules for indirect discourse would only be permitted within quotation marks. In the absence of quotation marks, the reader is nonetheless expected to be able to refer the language back to its origin with a character and thereby establish its meaning or reference.

In stream of consciousness novels, for example in Virginia Woolf, FID is omnipresent. It can also be found in novels where the representing language is supposedly distinct from that represented. For example, Zora Neale Hurston's novels are written in Standard American English (SAE) though her characters speak Black English Vernacular (BEV). The gap between the two is bridged by taking up into the representing language features of the language represented. Thus in the following passage from *Their Eyes Were Watching God* BEV 'nohow' and 'good and proper' are taken up without quotation marks into the SAE representation of a character's (Tea Cake's) consciousness:

> Tea Cake didn't say anything against it and Janie herself hurried off. This sickness to her was worse than the storm. As soon as she was well out of sight, Tea Cake got up and dumped the water bucket and washed it clean. Then he struggled to the irrigation pump and filled it again. He was not accusing Janie of malice and design. He was accusing her of carelessness. She ought to realise that waterbuckets needed washing like everything else. He'd tell her about it good and proper when she got back. What was she thinking about nohow? He found himself very angry about it. (pp. 259–60)

In the work of Mikhail Bakhtin the idea of FID is the springboard to a more generalized concept of *heteroglossia*, which is taken up via the work of Julia Kristeva by Roland Barthes and rendered as the idea that 'the text is a tissue of quotations drawn from the innumerable centres of culture' or, alternatively, 'a text is not a line of words releasing a single "theological" meaning (the "message" of the Author-God) but a multi-dimensional space in which a variety of writings, none of them original, blend and clash' ('The

Death of the Author', p. 146). Bakhtin originally developed such ideas in a reading of Dostoyevsky's novels in which he suggests that we should not read them in terms of seeking a character who expresses Dostoyevsky's point of view, or read them asking, what did Dostoyevsky believe? — but rather read them as representations made up of what are, in effect, quotations from expressions of rival world views, all of which are *shown* and none of which is *asserted* by the author (as true). (See M. Bakhtin, *Problems of Dostoyevsky's Poetics*; and for an introduction M. Holquist, *Dialogism*).

This notion that the novel, paradigmatically, *shows* rather than *asserts* is just another way of saying that the sentences of a literary work are not the *utterances* of an author to whom they must be related back. For other art forms it is equally possible to think of the work as showing rather than asserting something — art works are not statements (q.v. 'Communication') and many paintings, for example, as much as the novel are citational, using motifs and techniques drawn from other paintings. (Numerous examples are given in Richard Wollheim's *Painting as an Art*).

None of these very interesting and reasonable claims, however, supports any kind of notion that the audience for an art work can reasonably respond in any way they please. All that they support is an idea that the reader must be attuned to hearing or seeing the 'play' of voices in a literary text, or other art work, continuously clashing and merging and re-accented with each and every use. Nor does this preclude the possibility or necessity of referring back the play of voices to the intentions of an artist who has deliberately constructed such a multi-voiced work, though some would simply say th. artists must construct multi-voiced texts, willy-nilly, whether they intend to or not. (q.v. 'I', 'Tradition').

Deconstruction
(q.v. 'Post–Structuralism')

The lights are on, but is there anyone in the house? We have the big and difficult books by Jacques Derrida (1930–), we have the glamour and the razzamatazz. But do we actually have any ideas or methods which help advance our understanding of anything?

Deconstruction can be, and often is, thought of as a set of methods for approaching written texts and other materials (paintings, for example). As such, it consists in a number of injunctions: look out for binary oppositions in a text; look out for key words through which one can unlock a text's secrets; pay attention to marginal features of a text, such as footnotes, which (as Freud long ago remarked) may, for example, be places where the unconscious escapes from censorship. As a set of methods, deconstruction may offer worthy advice, but nothing really new to anyone; and it is certainly not the intention of deconstructionists to be worthies.

Derrida's writings are much more concerned to develop a philosophy, and specifically a philosophy of language and culture, than to propose a set of methods for approaching texts. At the heart of this philosophy is a scepticism about the possibility of truth, arising from the sense that we are always caught in a web of words ('there is nothing outside the text', says Derrida), words which are not sustained in their meaning by some referential link to reality ('presence') but only by their differential relation to each other ('absence'). This idea is a radicalization of Saussure's insight into the differential character of a language's phonemic structure (q.v. 'Structuralism') and produces one of Derrida's key concepts, that of *différance*, by means of which the idea that meaning can never be fixed or pinned down, but is always subject to endless circulation or deferral, is articulated.

Scepticism about the possibility of truth can produce either depression or frivolity. In Derrida's case it produces frivolity. His followers are often enough depressingly serious people, incapable of gaiety, and given to imitations of the master which make ordinary academic prose seem, in comparison, positively irresponsible. For introductions to Derrida see Christopher Norris *Derrida* or Christopher Norris's *Deconstruction: Theory and Practice*. Of Derrida's own books, *Margins of Philosophy* contains some of his more accessible writing.

Drama Education

Drama has been a significant presence in English schools since the end of the Second World War. In the years that followed the founding of the Educational Drama Association in 1943 and the appointment of Peter Slade as Drama Adviser for Staffordshire, drama quickly became accepted as 'an established and worthwhile part of school life'.[1]

The acknowledgment of drama as an educational force in the 1940s echoed the spirit of the times. The 1944 Education Act, together with parallel health and welfare legislation, reflected a new confidence in the possibility of a fair and humane society. Educational drama, its post-war exponents argued, had a key part to play in the social, moral and imaginative development of the children of the new age.

In many schools drama had long been accepted as an 'extracurricular' activity, most commonly in the form of the school play. For the advocates of curriculum drama, however, the emphasis was not to be on learning lines and performing but on creative self-expression. Drawing their inspiration from the progressive movement in education and heavily influenced by psychological theories of child development, post-war drama educationalists eschewed the 'counterfeiting' of the actor in favour of what they saw as the 'sincerity and absorption' of children's play.[2]

For the next four decades the distinction insistently drawn between drama-in-education and drama-in-theatres effectively manacled educational drama to forms of spontaneous improvisation. These made little reference to a wider theatrical culture or to the skills and knowledge normally associated with drama in the world beyond the classroom. As a result, quite fundamental aspects of drama, such as the performing and watching of plays, received little attention.

Denying themselves the subject content of comparable arts disciplines, educational drama practitioners turned their attention instead to the processes of the drama lesson itself. Highly sophisticated teaching methodologies were developed and drama became widely advertised as a tool for learning across the curriculum. Self-expression (q.v.) was displaced by role-play in a range of strategies for engaging young people in practical empathy. By the mid–1980s devices such as 'hot-seating', 'mantle-of-the-expert' and 'forum theatre' had become the drama teacher's stock-in-trade.

When the government published its proposals for a national curriculum cobbled together from pre-war models, the educational drama community was much shaken by the omission of drama from the list of foundation subjects.[3] Yet a consistent failure to address the question of specific subject content made the highlighting of drama's servicing role at the expense of its place as an arts discipline less than surprising. In the event the English Working Group and National Curriculum Council both gave drama some prominence in their recommendations. The NCC's non-statutory guidance for English covers most of the techniques developed in the name of dramatic pedagogy.[4] As part of a core subject, these aspects of drama have now a relatively secure position within the curriculum.

However, few drama teachers are likely to be satisfied by such limited recognition, particularly as visual art and music have the privileged status of independent foundation subjects. While it remains to be seen how this arbitrary hierarchical distinction will affect the overall arts provision in schools, it is clear that drama must put its curricular house in order with some urgency. Only by arguing the case for parity on the basis of a sound disciplinary structure will drama ever stand a chance of securing its legitimate place within the arts. Certainly, it is difficult to see how drama could retreat to its earlier position as an expressive and developmental process within progressive education; for all the idealism and real strengths of progressivism, its tenets are unlikely to sustain the confidence of schools and parents in the 1990s. Instead, drama must find a new way of defining its place among the arts which acknowledges developments across the aesthetic field. (q.v. 'Aesthetic Field').

We could do worse than to start with what is now surely most people's experience of drama. The hard fact is that today dramatic fiction is presented to us not so much in theatres as on the flickering screens in the corner of our living rooms. We should remember that as a result of television children will see more drama in a week than their great-grandparents would have witnessed in a lifetime. For drama-in-education, the watchers of dramas have never been a priority. Self-expression, after all, requires no witnesses; role-play is strictly a non-spectator sport. Yet while few of us are likely ever to perform in plays, the ubiquitous presence of film and television means that we all watch dramas in unprecedented quantities. The new dramatic curriculum must have at its core the key relationship between a performance and its audience.

By borrowing from media education the idea of the play as 'text' we are also able to put to rest the long and wearisome debate within drama-in-education between process and product. Text used in this sense — what we witness when we watch a drama — is simply the outcome of a *production process*. As the text is played out before us, we receive its messages and respond to them — we read and interpret what we see and hear.

Most importantly, the formulation of production, text and reception allows us to relocate school drama in a wider aesthetic culture. It is possible to speak of the dramas of everyday life, the great dramas of religion or of the state, the dramas that are infinitely reproducible on film or videotape. Above all, we can reinstate the theatre as the legitimate concern of drama in schools, and begin to look with greater clarity at progression in drama and at questions of quality and achievement.

Education in drama covers all these matters and should seek to replace the narrow concerns of drama-in-education with an altogether more eclectic curriculum of dramatic art. Above all, students of drama at all ages should regard what they do and what they learn as part of a varied and deeply rooted aesthetic vocabulary, spilling over into dance music and visual art and incorporating forms from all historical periods and all the world's cultures. By thinking of it in this way, we can recognize drama as an art form rich in signification and powerful in its ability to articulate the structures of feeling within which we live and by which we are made. To engage in drama is to participate in one of the oldest and most sustaining forms of social interpretation. The dramatic curriculum must provide for students the experience, knowledge and skills which will enable them to become more than bit-part players on this diverse and powerfully resonant stage.

For further reference see B. Brecht, *Brecht on Theatre: The Development of an Aesthetic* (edited and translated by John Willett); J. Allen, *Drama in Schools*; M. Esslin, *The Field of Drama*; D. Hornbrook, *Education and Dramatic Art* and *Education in Drama: Casting the Dramatic Curriculum*.

Notes

1 From an unpublished 1951 Ministry of Education committee report.
2 Rousseau believed that the actor diminished his own authenticity by 'counterfeiting himself'. Similarly, writers on educational drama in the 1950s and 1960s saw 'sincerity and absorption' as key signifiers of success.
3 Those who think the exclusion of drama was a conspiracy should look to their history. The 1988 national curriculum is little different from the 1904 version and identical to that introduced in 1935, except that then the arts were represented by singing and drawing.
4 See the section on drama in National Curriculum Council (1990) *English: Non-Statutory Guidance*.

DH

Expression

An artist, working in any medium, may set out to *represent* an object, person, event or situation (q.v. 'Representation') or to *express* a belief, a feeling, an emotion, a mood or both.

In order to express something, it is not necessary that the artist be possessed by or in possession of that something (belief, mood, feeling) at the time of executing the work. Beliefs can be imagined, emotions recollected in tranquillity. A work can express something without being a symptom, an effect, an index, of the artist's having such-and-such a belief or being affected by such-and-such an emotion. So much is now commonly agreed: see Susanne Langer, *Philosophy in a New Key* (1942) or Alan Tormey, *The Concept of Expression* (1971).

But how can an inanimate object — a painting or a piece of instrumental music, say — express something as living and distinctly human as an emotion or a feeling of sadness, joy, terror, melancholy, anguish, ...? How does the artist do it, and how do we recognize what has been done?

According to Richard Wollheim (*Painting as an Art*, Ch. II), the answer involves recognizing that the possibility of artistic expression is built on the natural ability to perceive things *as* expressive, even when they express nothing. This parallels the situation in which the possibility of representation is built on the natural ability to see something in something else: to see a face in the fire, a man in the moon (q.v. 'Representation'). So we look at a drooping flower and see it as sad, knowing full-well that the flower is not and cannot be (literally) sad. Seeing the flower as sad is expressive perception on the spectator's part; the possibility of artistic expression is built on our capacity to experience things expressively.

The artist is guided by his or her own sense, as a spectator, of what it is their work will be perceived as expressing. This is not to say that they are always successful in getting audiences to perceive in their work whatever they expressed in it, and the expressive qualities of a work may be (deliberately or not) ambiguous. It is not only because is provides the music for 'I vow to thee my country' that Holst's *Jupiter* (from *The Planets* suite) is expressively ambiguous. Jupiter is supposed to be 'the Bringer of Jollity'. I confess I have never been able to hear a clear expression of jollity, but rather the stately, nostalgic, recessional or simply melancholy qualities of the music.

However, this is not to say that we are free to see or hear whatever expressive qualities we like in a work. As with representation, the standard of correctness for expression is set by the artist's intention (q.v. 'Representation', 'Intention and convention'). It is, however, an interesting and rather complex question whether a work which expresses or manifests qualities which we would describe by using emotional predicates ('sad', 'joyful', melancholy') must or can be said to *symbolize* those qualities. The same query arises if we ask whether a work which expresses or manifests certain metaphysical beliefs or qualities (beliefs or qualities which have to do with our sense of our place in the cosmos) must or can be said to symbolize them.

For example, there is a much reproduced painting by Sir Henry Raeburn (1756–1823) of *The Reverend Robert Walker Skating on Duddingston Loch* (the original hangs in the National Gallery of Scotland). The painting expresses or manifests a sense of the possibility of a harmonious relationship between mind and body (a vicar skating) and between man and nature (the elegantly dressed reverend is not ill at ease on the frozen loch). But does the painting symbolize the harmony of mind and body, man and nature? Is the painting a symbol of harmony? It does not seem right to answer 'Yes' to either of these questions (q.v. 'Symbol, Symbolism'). One might look at the way in which Wollheim in *Painting as an Art* discusses the landscape paintings of Caspar David Friedrich (pp. 131–140), which express a particular religious world-view. Wollheim nowhere says that the paintings *symbolize* it. For a discussion of metaphysical qualities in relation to literature see Roman Ingarden, *The Literary Work of Art*, pp. 290–300.

The concept of expression is clearly related to that of 'Self-Expression' (q.v.) and to expressionism as an artistic movement, but these are, as indicated, separately discussed, the latter under the title 'Mapping Some -isms'.

Feminist Critical Theory

Women students are well represented in the language and literature, art and drama departments of universities, polytechnics and colleges, and English has long been a favourite subject for girls to study at A-level. Girls are encouraged to take arts subjects because they are said to be sensitive and better able than boys to respond to the feelings expressed in art and literature and because they are 'good at' understanding traditional categories such as characterization. Yet the majority of works studied or plays performed are by male artists and writers and reflect the patriarchal societies in which women have lived throughout the ages.

In art, literature and music women have been allocated subsidiary roles as wives, mothers, sisters and daughters within the institution of the family or as lovers outside it. We can see this tendency in the English romantics (Mary Shelley, Dorothy Wordsworth, Mary Lamb) and in the Pre-Raphaelite movement, aptly named the 'Brotherhood' (Jane Morris, Christina Rossetti); other examples are Camille Claudel (the sister of Paul Claudel and lover of Rodin, but also a sculptor herself), Clara Schumann, Cosima Wagner and Gwen John. During Robert Schumann's lifetime his wife Clara suppressed her own composing talent in order to nurture his, and Dorothy Wordsworth, a capable and sensitive writer as her journal shows, turned herself into a household drudge to look after her brother William.

Wealthy women could be patrons of the arts; some women became the much maligned hostesses of artistic and literary salons. Talented women are commonly identified with the muse which suggests that their role is to provide inspiration for male artistic creativity and to sublimate their own talent. However, whether patron, hostess or muse, the role of these women in relation to male artists has not been unproblematic. John Fowles portrays the relationship of male writer to female muse in a worryingly uncritical, even sado-masochistic, fashion in his novella, *Mantissa*, and the usually gentle Ivan Turgenev presents an uncharacteristically cruel portrait of a blue-stocking hostess in *Fathers and Sons*.

In music and drama there are few women composers or dramatists before the twentieth century. An exception is the seventeenth century dramatist Aphra Behn, who also wrote an important early novel, *Oroonoko*.

This absence can partly be explained by the exclusion of women from the public spheres of music and the theatre. As is well known, Shakespeare created wonderful female roles which had to be played by boys, and even when women were allowed to perform on the public stage, women who entered the acting profession had to put up with taunts about their 'loose' morality. Even in private there were restrictions on the type of play which it was thought appropriate for men and women to act in together, as can be seen if we consider the moral indignation Fanny Price feels when her cousins and the Crawfords decide to perform the risqué 'Lovers' Vows' in Jane Austen's *Mansfield Park*.

Private music recitals showed how accomplished a woman was, but it is now difficult to know whether women in musical families actually composed much which is attributed to the male members of the family. It is interesting to ponder over the choice made by the eighteenth century painter Angelica Kauffmann. Her painting, *Angelica Hesitating between the Arts of Painting and Music*, depicts the artist herself between two female allegorical figures, one holding a sheet of music and the other a palette and brushes. One wonders whether these symbols have equal weight. The palette and brushes are for her to use, but Music offers her a composition already written (see Illustration 50 and discussion of the painting in Rozsika Parker and Griselda Pollock, *Old Mistresses: Women, Art and Ideology*).

It can be argued that music and drama are fields which require collaborative work. Musicians, singers, designers, actors, directors, composers, writers all play a part in production and performance. But how much freedom do women have as interpreters and performers of work by others? In Greek and Renaissance tragedy, women are often depicted as rebels who put their own desires before society's need for order and stability: Clytaemestra, Medea, Electra, Lady Macbeth, the Duchess of Malfi, Beatrice-Joanna in *The Changeling* — the list is endless. Similarly, the heroines of nineteenth century opera often played a symbolic role: the Wagnerian daughter who challenges her father; Verdi's courtesan who sacrifices the man she loves at his father's insistence and is reunited with him only on her deathbed; Puccini's Turandot who executes her would-be husbands and can only be 'cured' by love. All inhabit a world where women's desires and power must be suppressed to assuage male fears and fantasies. This can also be seen in classical ballet, an art form associated with women although most choreographers are men. *Swan Lake* and *Giselle* both associate sexual love with death. Given that it is hard for women to offer alternatives to these roles when working with major companies, it is not surprising that those women who want their feminism to inform their artistic work sometimes choose to work in all-women companies, for example, Red Shift or Women in Music.

However, literature is the one area of the arts where it is acknowledged that there are 'great' women, even if their number is few. They are predominantly English and most of them lived in the historical period which extends from the late eighteenth century to the twentieth (some exceptions are the women writers of the Middle Ages, e.g. Hildegard, Christine de Pisan and Marie de France, and in the seventeenth century, Aphra Behn and Madame de Sevigny, the author of *La Princesse de Cleves*). It is also significant that they were mainly writers of novels, a relatively new form which Jane Austen felt had to be defended from masculine accusations of frivolity (see her defence of the novel in *Northanger Abbey*).

Much Anglo-American feminist literary criticism centres on women writers and not only studies the great women writers but also endeavours to recover writing by women, who were often popular in their time, but whose work has not been included in the literary canon. Elaine Showalter discusses the work of a number of little known British women writers in *A Literature of Their Own: British Women Novelists from Brontë to Lessing*. One significant writer who has been rediscovered is Kate Chopin whose late nineteenth century novel, *The Awakening*, was criticized at the time of its first publication because it depicts a woman who wishes to go beyond the mild flirtation allowed by polite Louisiana society and find a more worthwhile self-fulfilment. The recovery of work such as this, which has created a new literary category, writing by women, has been assisted by the new publishing houses such as Virago and The Women's Press which publish only work by women.

The study of women's writing in the Anglo-American tradition tends to emphasize biography, and to a lesser extent this is also the case in other fields of enquiry. Kate Millett's work, *Sexual Politics*, studies the representation of women in work by male authors but moves outside the texts to consider the male writer's views on women. There is also a biographical element to some studies which consider women as readers, for example, on women and romance, but the emphasis shifts from the lives of the authors to the effect of the works on the lives of the readers. Helen Taylor has written a fascinating study analyzing readers' and viewers' responses to the novel and film, *Gone with the Wind*.

Whereas Anglo-American feminist literary theory has been author-centred, French feminist criticism is centred on the text and has been greatly influenced by psychoanalysis and deconstruction (q.v.). French feminists argue that Western culture is phallocentric; it places man at the centre as a unified being and defines those who are not male as other. Man's dominance is maintained through language which is integral to what, in Lacanian terms, can be described as the symbolic order or the law of the father (given that it is established at the point when the child separates from the mother). According to Julia Kristeva, it is possible for writers to return to a pre-Oedipal stage when the identification with the mother is complete and the father excluded and the child has not learnt through language that he or she has a separate identity. For Kristeva (unlike Helen Cixous and Luce Irigaray who advocated an affirmation of difference through *écriture feminine*), what is important is not to find an alternative discourse for women but to challenge the category of 'the subject' and the notion of difference.

Black feminist writers have preferred to draw on the oral tradition in order to recover the female experience of slavery. Alice Walker, Toni Morrison and Sherley Williams attempt to recover a suppressed language and experience through the writing of the new narrative 'herstory' which examines critically the patriarchal and racist attitudes of past and present. To teach Walker's novel, *The Color Purple*, one has to consider the importance of literacy to Celie (why is it written in the epistolary form?) and how Celie's dialect relates to the oral tradition and Alice Walker's aim of recovering the language of her grandmother. It is also important to encourage students to think about how Celie achieves a sense of her own worth through her relationship with another woman and growing awareness of her sexuality as something which can give her pleasure when previously she had only known pain. On reaching the end of the book, students can discuss why Walker refers to herself as 'author and medium'. *The Color Purple* is a useful text for feminist criticism because its form makes it impossible to talk convincingly about it in terms of characters and plot.

Virginia Woolf pointed to the relationship of economics and aesthetics when she wrote in *A Room of One's Own* that in order to write, women need their own physical (as well as inner) space and financial independence. Until recently, few women had this independence; even today, women are likely to be closer to the poverty line than men. Oral history is, therefore, also a rich source for the lives of working-class women.

A perennial problem for both men and women is integrating the personal and the political. Mary Wollstonecraft, the author of *Vindication of the Rights of Women*, which censures men who see women as 'objects of pity', tried to drown herself when she was deserted by the adventurer Gilbert Imlay and, finally, sadly and ironically, like many less liberated women she died in childbirth. Perhaps autobiography helps to make sense of theory. Carolyn Steedman's *Landscape for a Good Woman: A Story of Two Lives* explores her relationship with her mother and the contradictions in both their lives as Simone de Beauvoir had done earlier in her autobiographical work and in *A Very Easy Death*.

Feminist theories of art have considered how in Europe in the eighteenth and nineteenth centuries the male art establishment began the process of denying women artists their place in art history until in the twentieth century it was accepted that there were no major women artists before 1900. Studies by Rozsika Parker and Griselda Pollock (*op. cit.*) and by Germaine Greer (*The Obstacle Race: The Fortunes of Women Painters and Their Work*) have rekindled interest in the work of the Renaissance painter Artemisia Gentileschi and the Impressionist Berthe Morisot among many others and have situated their work within ideological practices. Parker and Pollock argue persuasively that it was the changing role of the family in the late eighteenth and early nineteenth centuries which led to the domestication of women and took them out of the public domain of art. Feminists have also drawn attention to the way in which a hierarchy of the arts was created in industrial Europe which privileged painting and sculpture and relegated craftwork, often work done collectively by women, such as embroidery or quilting, to a separate inferior category.

Much work has been done on feminism and film theory and practice, especially in terms of film and psychoanalysis. Laura Mulvey's article, 'Visual Pleasure and Narrative Cinema', published in *Screen*, 16, 3 (Autumn 1975) and reprinted in her collection of essays, *Visual and Other Pleasures*, remains essential.

Growing interest in feminism and in the politics of gender has in recent years been met by an equally determined attempt to maintain the social constructions of masculinity and femininity. Perhaps the attitudes behind Clause 28 of the Local Government Bill reflect this. It is difficult for teachers to encourage boys, who are already reluctant, to dance in such a climate. However, it is important for teachers to ensure that boys and girls have equal access to arts subjects. Discussion of the process of creativity and how it relates to our imaginative, intellectual and physical capabilities can help students to break down gender divisions and find new possibilities for themselves.

For further reading see: W. Chadwick, *Women, Art and Society*; C. Clement, *Opera, or, the Undoing of Women*; J. Mayne, 'Feminist Film Theory and Criticism', *Signs*, 11, 1 (Autumn 1985); T. Moi, *Sexual/Textual Politics*; and R. Parker and G. Pollock, *Old Mistresses: Women, Art and Ideology*.

PD

Figurative and Literal (q.v. 'Meaning', 'Symbol, Symbolism')

In his *Essay on the Origin of Languages* Rousseau describes a solitary man, living in a state of nature, coming upon one of his likes for the first time and exclaiming, 'A Giant!' Only later when his shock subsides does he realize that it is really only another man. Thus, for Rousseau, the figurative use of language precedes the literal: to Rousseau's natural man another man is (figuratively) seen as a giant, and only subsequently recognized as (literally) another man. Rousseau thus inverts the usual assumption that first there is a literal meaning, and only subsequently figurative meaning.

Figurative and literal are *uses* of words; the word 'sun' can be used literally or figuratively: 'The sun is in the sky' and ' Juliet is the sun' are literal and figurative uses of the word 'sun'. But what *is* a literal use of a word? The philosopher John Searle states the standard view in terms of a literal meaning hypothesis that, 'Every unambiguous sentence, such as "The cat is on the mat" has a literal meaning which is absolutely context free and which determines for every context whether or not an utterance of that sentence in that context is literally true or false' ('Literal Meaning', p. 125). Searle goes on to challenge the literal meaning hypothesis, arguing that the notion of literal meaning is only applicable relative to a set of background assumptions which are not themselves specifiable in advance. For our own purposes, however, the important idea is that of words *having* a literal meaning, such that a literal *use* of a word is a use of it *with* its literal meaning. In contrast, there are no figurative *meanings* of words, only figurative *uses*. So 'Juliet is the sun' does not draw on a figurative *meaning* of sun; it uses the word 'sun' figuratively.

How is this possible? How do we understand figurative uses? At school, emphasis on the difference between metaphor and simile is unhelpful if it is the case, as many theorists have argued, that all metaphorical uses of language are basically similes. So 'Juliet is the sun' is understood because we understand it as a (true or false) assertion that Juliet is *like* the sun in certain (unspecified) respects. Like the sun, Juliet is the source of life, of warmth, and she is herself radiant. But how do we know that these are the relevant (kinds of) respects in which Juliet *is* like the sun? Why, for example, do we not conclude that Juliet is like the sun in being round, fiery and a long way away?

This question suggests two possible answers. One is that the idea of the sun is itself associated with a set of stereotypical features of which some are more prominent than others: it is true of the sun that it is a long way away, but this feature is less prominent in our (most people's) minds than that it is a source of life and warmth. An obscure metaphor, like an obscure joke, would be a figurative use of language which drew on recessive features associated with the object of metaphorical comparison. But a second possibility is, instead, that we can understand aright the implied comparison between Juliet and the sun because of what we already know about Juliet as well as about the sun. We may know that she isn't round and a long way away, for instance.

Both possible answers do, however, tend to make out metaphor to be a rather mechanical thing in which the relevant points of comparison can, in principle, be fully spelt out: Juliet is like the sun insofar as she is *a, b, c*.... This does leave figurative language looking rather like shorthand, circumlocution or, in Freud's terms, condensation. Yet surely a good metaphor, a vivid figurative use of language, is precisely one which gives us something new, which expands a horizon of possibility, and which is not completely paraphrasable — which remains in some measure ineffable.

In contemporary literary theory two kinds of figurative language use — metaphor and metonymy — have assumed particular prominence, particularly because they have been connected, notably by Jacques Lacan, to the two key processes of what Freud in *The Interpretation of Dreams* calls the dream work, namely, condensation and displacement. In metaphor, multiple meanings are condensed into one word or visual image. In metonymy, meaning is displaced onto a part or associated element of a whole object, just as in sexual fetishism desire is displaced onto a part object. See Roman Jakobson's essay, 'Two Aspects of Language and Two Types of Aphasic Disturbance'; and more generally, A. Ortony (Ed.), *Metaphor and Thought*.

Film in Education

Film is an assemblage of recorded sounds and images, and an aesthetic approach to the subject would emphasize the processes, purposes and effects of that putting together of recorded pieces; most approaches in English education have emphasized recording instead.

An accurate recording serves that which is to be recorded, the spectacle itself constituting the true subject. Much film and video, especially on television, aspires to neutrality or transparency of form so that the viewer experiences (apparently) the unmediated reality of the event. Where the illusion that its recording and transmitting media have no significant existence is successfully achieved, film may be supposed to have little aesthetic interest; if the *film* makes no shaping contribution to the narrative or dramatic experience it conveys, then we simply look *through* the screen/window *at* the subject. We see and hear what happens inside the frame, but cannot taste, touch and smell what is 'also' there, cannot step through to disrupt the event. Given such limitations, accurate recording allows access to real enough worlds which may not be as immediately available by other means.

Even that would make film a valuable educational tool — anything from historical events to scientific experiments and school sports days might be recorded and shown repeatedly — but in its humble service capacity the medium already draws on a distinctively filmic set of conventions. Once that is recognized, the value of an education in film has a greater potential; indeed, until it is adequately recognized, film will remain an interesting but underused resource.

The dominant educational approach has been social rather than aesthetic. Film, television and, latterly, video have been perceived as components of the popular culture. Richards (1924) and Leavis and Thompson (1933) were influential in making the mass media subjects for study, but their purpose was corrective: commercial entertainment was pervasive and corrosive, inculcating 'stock attitudes and stereotyped ideas',[1] and exploiting 'the cheapest emotional responses'.[2] Elsewhere these critics were often sensitively concerned with scrupulous discrimination of meaning and value, but film, evidently, could be dismissed with generalizations based on the assumed passive helplessness of the ordinary viewer — academic stock attitudes based on stereotyped ideas. Presumably this was because they could not see film as an art. Collingwood (1938) was aware than an earlier popular form of entertainment, Renaissance theatre, *had* produced great art, but film, he reasoned, could not, because it did not allow 'collaboration between authors and actors on the one hand, and audience on the other',[3] because, that is, it was not live theatre but only recorded film. The medium itself got in the way of art, yet was at the same time disregarded as a salient, indeed crucial, factor.

Gradually attitudes to popular culture shifted, until what had been negative could be seen as positive. Film still occurred 'at the lowest level of abstraction of all the arts', though, and so could 'serve to stimulate discussion.'[4] If it was art, at least its art could be left out of account; stories, characters, plots, issues could be discussed immediately, as if they were unfolding in reality just beyond that window. Later, in addition to studying media content (largely divorced from form), the media institutions themselves became subjects of study; eventually film became passé as other media were seen to be more popular, powerful and socially relevant.

Film as itself a constructive medium of thought and feeling seems scarcely to have been considered in English schools and colleges, despite the seminal work of Pudovkin, Eisenstein, Kuleshov, Arnheim, Kracauer, Spottiswoode and others, and despite a widespread (if, one must assume, largely perplexed) admission that some of the key art works of the twentieth century have been made by film-makers such as Griffith, Chaplin, Keaton, Ford, Hawks, Hitchcock, Murnau, Eisenstein, Bunuel, Bergman, Kurosawa, Ozu, Godard, Herzog, Klimov, Tarkovsky, Antonioni, Renoir and so on. Admittedly the English contribution has been slight, but that hardly seems a sufficient reason for effectively denying generations of students access to a discipline which may have as profound an influence on their lives as any of the arts.

Discourses and ideologies less sympathetic to commercial popular culture than to high culture, tradition and the individual talent (the last gaining prominence just when the notion of the director as author was promising to make film study enough like literary study for English academics to take it up — albeit, like Richards *et al.*, with scant attention to the ways in which film differed from theatre and the novel) delayed the adopting of film as an arts discipline; but so, more prosaically, did the practical difficulties of hiring films, setting up projectors and screens in blacked-out rooms, purchasing cameras and raw film stock, arranging editing facilities. For many teachers film was more trouble than it was worth, despite its dramatic immediacy. Even then, while the film was being shown, it was difficult to teach around: interruption, exegesis, repetition, analytical discussion, none of the conventional approaches to textual study was easily translated into the darkened classroom.

The remarkable advance of video cameras, recorders and software has, however, transformed the situation so far that the aesthetic field is now fully accessible. Television and film technologies are not identical, the primary difference being that radio waves allow instantaneous and uninterrupted transmission (neutral recording); similarly, a videotape can record continuously for several hours, far longer than has ever been physically possible on film. Put in practice the convention of a relatively brief shot-length, with a new camera position or movement for each succeeding shot until the sequence is constructed, produced a kind of grammar which television adopted. Consequently, although video cameras *can* be used non-filmically, emphasizing the neutrality of recording, there is no established precedent for doing so. The creative emphasis is on assemblage from recorded pieces, on reconstructing a continuous dramatic narrative from a world of discontinuous and diverse materials.

A film cannot be made and need not be watched as if the recording media just happened to be present. The processes of composition and execution are sometimes similar to, though never the same as, those undertaken by the writer. In addition to the dramatist's concern with dialogue and relationship through the positioning and movement of actors, the film-maker continually adjusts the relationships of actors and environments to the framed composition. For example, at this point in a sequence do we want a general description of a room, a specific significant detail, or a nondescript background? Do we want a close up of the speaker, or of someone listening, or of a hand tapping, or should we show how both characters interact at this moment? From what distance and at what angle should we see this scene? How long should the shot be held, and what position will we cut to for the next one? If the camera moves *with* one of the actors, it will encourage audience identification, but if it moves independently, it may imply an authorial intrusion or the presence of another character whose viewpoint implicates the audience. Of course we may not want to show actors or room at this point, we may allow the dialogue to continue but show a bit of newsreel, a landscape, a painting — whatever serves the 'writing' of the film. The composition of the physical elements within the frame can be made more or less arresting by the disposition of light and shade, the brightness of parts of the image, the dominant colours and tones. Then again we must consider sound: do we simply want an exchange of dialogue at as naturalistic a level as possible, or should we record a voice over later, for our protagonist's thoughts or our narrator's memories? Should sound levels change during the sequence? What about other significant sound effects? Music — an on-screen source or not? And how does all this relate to the visual exposition? Is there an overall style? A tendency for inclusive long shots and long takes of several minutes' duration, for example? Is the camera predominantly at shoulder-height and static, or tracking, craning, zooming? Where does the cutting rhythm change, and why? Are camera movements smooth or bumpy? Why use that particular piece of music? What are all these effects *saying*, how do they modify our experience, and how would the tones and emphases alter if other positions, movements and sounds were used?

An education in film is an education in visual and aural story-telling which, almost as a by-product, can deepen the understanding of how verbal narratives work, how complex relationships and actions are formed and informed by the creative intervention of thought and a recording medium, with all its conventions, generic patterns and expressive potentialities. 'Everything that moves on the screen is cinema.... In my view cinema is nothing but a new form of printing — another form of the total transformation of the world through knowledge.'[5] Everyone is affected by looking through the window. The point is to step back, see that it is largely and sometimes challengingly an illusion, and then begin to experience and create the art.

Notes

1 I.A. Richards, (1924) *Principles of Literary Criticism*.
2 F.R. Leavis, and D. Thompson, (1933) *Culture and Environment*, p. 3.
3 R.G. Collingwood, (1938) *The Principles of Art*, p. 323.
4 J. Kitses (1966) *Film and General Studies*, p. 2.
5 J. Renoir (1974) *My Life and My Films*, p. 11.

RW

Form, Formalism

Formalism, simply as a preoccupation with the form of a work of art, exists in three domains. Artists can be preoccupied with form; aesthetic experience can be located in relation to the experience of form; and critics and theorists can concern themselves with the form of works.

First, it is hard to imagine an artist not preoccupied with form, though Oscar Wilde in 'The Decay of Lying' (1891) complains that neglect of form is all too common. There are poets and novelists so urgently oppressed by the need to express themselves or transmit a message that they quite neglect to consider how best to express or transmit what they have to say. Such artists will, of course, generally experience form in its coercive aspects, as when they are told by a potential publisher or producer that their novel simply has too many characters or that their play is too long (and boring). For artists not negligent of form, content and form may be experienced as antagonistic: the content refuses to fit the form, the form alters the (meaning of the) content. But then it is often said that the artist's real creative achievement occurs when he or she finds a way of relating form and content in such a way that they are no longer antagonistic but reinforce each other or even fuse, so that we no longer have a 'mechanical' union of 'form' and 'content' (which can be broken) but an 'organic' whole, which cannot be disassembled into parts.

In teaching, the idea that art involves a mechanical union of form and content is frequently reinforced by the tasks set: 'Write a poem about such-and-such using alliteration', and not even 'Find a subject for a poem which cries out for use of alliteration.' But the latter task is clearly a much more difficult one, and if it is only in significant artistic achievements that we find form and content inseparably united, perhaps we should not ask for it to be accomplished in the context of a (routine) pedagogic assignment.

But what of the 'merely formal' exercise? Is it part of a good pedagogic strategy to ask students merely to play with forms: to write limericks about anything, to write a variation on any old theme, to paint anything in classical (Renaissance) perspective? Can such exercises be justified as part of an education (or training) in gaining facility with technique? Or must all arts education work *from* the meaningful *to* form and technique, rejecting mere formalism? In Chapter 1 of *A Is for Aesthetic* Peter Abbs argues that expressive impulse and form should be kept in a reciprocal relation within the aesthetic field of a particular arts discipline. This is a recurrent theme in other volumes in the Library on Aesthetic Education.

Second, formalism also exists as the claim that aesthetic experience just is the experience of form, experienced as pleasing or beautiful when its object is good form or significant form. In a famous little book, *Art* (1913), Clive Bell develops an argument as follows: sensibility is the precondition of having aesthetic experience; aesthetic experience is experience of a peculiar emotion; works of art are what produce this peculiar emotion; works of art differ enormously in medium and content; but it is only in virtue of something that they have in common that works of art can produce a common response; what they have in common is significant form. In relation to paintings, with which alone Bell is concerned, this means that 'lines and colours combined in a particular way, certain forms and relations of forms, stir our aesthetic emotions. These relations and combinations of lines and colours, these aesthetically moving forms, I call "Significant Form"; and "Significant Form" is the one quality common to all works of visual art' (pp. 17–18).

Significant (that is, meaningful) form produces an emotion distinct from that aroused by the contemplation of natural beauty (p. 20), but this distinction should not lead us to think that it is the representative content of a work of art which makes the difference from an object of natural beauty. Bell is quite insistent on this:

> if a representative form has value, it is as form, not as representation. The representative element in a work of art may or may not be harmful; always it is irrelevant. For, to appreciate a work of art we need bring with us nothing from life, no knowledge of its ideas and affairs, no familiarity with its emotions. Art transports us from the world of man's activity to a world of aesthetic exaltation.... The pure mathematician rapt in his studies knows a state of mind which I take to be similar, if not identical. He feels an emotion for his speculations which arises from no perceived relation between them and the lives of men, but springs, inhuman or super-human, from the heart of an abstract science. (p. 27)

Now this is formalism with a vengeance. An obvious objection to make is that Bell has got off on the wrong foot from the start with his assumption that works of art produce just one peculiar emotion. After all, if it is only one emotion which is produced, why don't we get bored with works of art? Or, alternatively, why do we need to experience more than one work? One could say that the novelty of fresh works combats the possible boredom of endless-ly re-experiencing the same emotion in virtue of the *different* significant forms offered by new works. One might be tempted to compare our appetite for sex and for changing sexual positions or partners: the appetite is for the same thing in different forms. But then someone might reasonably object that this misses the idea of personal relationships and the idea of love, making sex too much a matter of appetite. Equally, one might say that Bell's aesthetic emotion is too appetitive, missing the dimension of our involvement with the world of the work of art — its content, for want of a better word, though content will cover much more than naturalistic representation of objects, and will include, for example, mood. (So the work of an 'abstract' expressionist like Mark Rothko is not devoid of content; it overflows with the content of moods and emotions.) Again, Bell's idea of an aesthetic emotion is too singular, too blithely discounting the possibility that our responses to works of art might range across an indefinite number of emotions. What might be singular and distinctive is the presence not of a peculiar emotion, but of an attitude of disinterestedness, which, since Kant, has been held to characterize the aesthetic encounter (q.v. 'Aesthetic/Aesthetics'). But this attitude is one adopted towards or defining of art (as purposefulness without purpose), not a relationship to the form of art in particular.

There is something in what Bell says, and that is whatever is valid in the reaction to romanticism which goes under the various names of aestheticism, art for art's sake, decadence and, in Bell's case, formalism.

Third, at the same time as the doctrines of Clive Bell's *Art* became influential in thinking about the visual arts, a group of Russian writers, critics and theorists was generating related ideas which have had a continuing powerful influence on critical thinking, especially about poetry and the novel. These were the Russian formalists, headed by Roman Jakobson (1896–1982) in Moscow, and Viktor Shklovsky (1893–1984) in Leningrad. There is an extended discussion in Victor Erlich's *Russian Formalism*.

Shklovsky in his 1914 essay, 'The Resurrection of the Word', wrote: '"Artistic" perception is that perception in which we experience form — perhaps not form alone, but certainly form' (cited in Boris Eichenbaum's (1926) 'The Theory of the "Formal Method"', p. 112). Poetic language in particular is distinguished from everyday language by the fact that its language is perceived as having an independent value, which means that it does not primarily (or at all) function as a means of communicating. This independent value is as an object of aesthetic perception. In the poetry of the Russian futurists, with whom the formalists were closely allied, this emphasis on the independent value of words as sound and syntax extends to the creation of a 'nonsense' language, as in the trans-sense poetry of Khlebnikov. The job of the formalist theorist is to study the structures of poetic language or, as Roman Jakobson put it in 1921, 'The object of the science of literature is not literature, but literariness.' In the case of the novel the formalists pioneered the study of narrative technique, drawing a key distinction between the story (*sjuzhet*) and its telling (*fabula*). A work like Gerard Genette's *Narrative Discourse* is the lineal descendant of Russian formalism.

Jakobson sustained the idea of a contrast between 'ordinary' and 'poetic' language throughout his extraordinary, long career: see, notably, his 1960 essay, 'Closing Statement: Linguistics and Poetics'. But it is challenged in many contemporary studies; see, for example, Chapter 1 of Mary Louise Pratt's *Toward a Speech Act Theory of Literary Discourse*.

The Russian formalists had many more ideas to contribute besides the

idea of form as focus of aesthetic interest and of a contrast between poetic
and prosaic (communicative) language. Shklovsky in his 1917 essay, 'Art as
Technique', offers an account of the function of art, and an associated sketch
of the dynamics of historical change in artistic styles and genres.

> Habitualization devours works, clothes, furniture, one's wife, and
> the fear of war.... Art exists that one may recover the sensation of
> life; it exists to make one feel things, to make the stone *stony*. The
> purpose of art is to impart the sensation of things as they are
> perceived and not as they are known. The technique of art is to make
> objects 'unfamiliar', to make forms difficult, to increase the difficulty
> and length of perception because the process of perception is an
> aesthetic end in itself and must be prolonged. (p. 12).

In other words, art opposes the tendency to 'automatism' of perception, and
Shklovsky is able to cite numerous examples from Tolstoy's writings to
support his claims — for example, Tolstoy's story 'Kholstomer', in which
events are narrated from the point of view of a horse. Shklovsky calls this use
of technique 'defamiliarization' or 'making strange' (*ostraneniye*), and it becomes an account of artistic change when it is argued that the purpose of a
new form is not to express new content, but to change an old form which
has lost its aesthetic quality — that is, its ability to impede perceptual
automatism. (Coleridge in *Biographia Literaria* had attributed just this purpose
to Wordsworth, saying that he aimed 'to give the charm of novelty to things
of everyday', 'awakening the mind's attention from the lethargy of custom,
and directing it to the loveliness and the wonders of the world before us; an
inexhaustible treasure, but for which, in consequence of the film of familiarity and selfish solicitude, we have eyes, yet see not, ears that hear not, and
hearts that neither feel nor understand'; it is only the last phrase which
Shklovsky would not have been ready to write.)
     Yet Shklovsky was a writer as well as critic and he uses techniques of
defamiliarization in his wonderful — and moving — autobiography, *A
Sentimental Journey*, a chronicle of war and revolution seen through a tem-
perament. The idea of defamiliarization was also picked up by Brecht on a
visit to the Soviet Union and is important to his development as a playwright, since it is the basis of his theory and practice of the 'alienation' or
'estrangement effect' (*Verfremdungseffekt*) (q.v. 'Alienation Effect'). The idea
of impeding perception is also important in music when it reacts against the
idea of the 'easy' melody, and it is used consistently to delay or frustrate
gratification in the work of a film-maker like Godard. One might add that
one of the most interesting features of contemporary film has proved to be its
ability to make a whole repertoire of classical music tantalizingly alive by use
of interrupted snatches of classical compositions. This is exemplified by
Godard's *Passion*. In these cases it seems right to say that one is dealing with
artistic practices which can be systematically illuminated by the work the
Russian formalists undertook between 1910 and 1930, at which latter date

they were, in effect, suppressed as a matter of Stalinist policy. Formalism in theory was seen as of a piece with aestheticism and decadentism and, more generally, modernism in artistic practice (q.v. 'Modernism and Post-Modernism').

Genius (q.v. 'Creativity')

The idea of genius is the idea of extraordinary talent, usually in one only among the major fields of human activity. It is the idea of a talent which is innately based to the extent that it may manifest itself even without early and intensive education or training. The ideas of genius and precocity go together, even though precociousness is no guarantee of adult achievement: some precociously talented children 'come to nothing', just as some major human achievements are the work of hard-working plodders who are not geniuses in the conventional sense. No one, for example, would have picked out the youthful Charles Darwin as a genius, but Darwin revolutionized a whole area of scientific enquiry, and a culture's view of the place of human beings in nature.

Mozart and Picasso both showed precocious talent in the art form in which they also made their adult contributions, but there have been many precocious child artists who have not become Mozarts and Picassos. Precociousness in one domain may be accompanied by backwardness in others; for example, we have documented the case of Nadia, a very precocious child artist who was also autistic, and whose artistic abilities waned with the loss of her autism (see Lorna Selfe, *Nadia*).

There is no genius without a ready facility in mastering the medium in which the genius manifests itself, whether the medium be chess, painting, music or mathematics. But there is also no genius without an imaginative ability to use the medium to some (creative) purpose. Thus there is a big difference between the calculating prodigy who has an extraordinary facility with numbers and the mathematical genius who can conjecture and/or prove significant mathematical theorems. Similarly, virtuosity on a musical instrument is not a guarantee of any ability to compose music, though we expect of a virtuoso performer the capacity to interpret musical compositions in significantly fresh ways. Thus Pablo Casals is not a major composer, but his renderings of 'cello compositions, notably Bach's, were the manifestations not only of instrumental virtuosity (evidenced at a very young age) but of a significant creative imagination.

It is an interesting question whether in all domains hard work, application and training can compensate for lack of extraordinary talent. If hard work, lucky breaks (the voyage of *The Beagle*) and a modicum of imaginative ability gave Darwin his pre-eminence in developing the theory of evolution, could they equally have made a Mozart out of a Salieri? Or is music different in such a way that no amount of hard work or being in the right place at the right time can make up for a deficit of talent? It would be silly to attempt a short answer to this question, but one relevant dimension of the answer will have to do with assessing whether there are natural age limits to significant contributions to a domain. It is often said and generally acknowledged that no one contributes anything new to mathematics after the age of 30. So achieving her doctorate at the age of 18, having begun her university career at age 12, leaves mathematical prodigy Ruth Lawrence with twelve years to make a difference to mathematics. That does limit the scope for hard work to compensate for indifferent ability, compared to a domain where significant achievement might come late in life on the basis of extensive knowledge of the domain. No one is surprised if a novelist or philosopher makes a major contribution at the age of 60. (Kant published his *Critique of Pure Reason* at the age of 57; his early works do not portend the genius of his later productions.)

Genius flourishes in the context of a culture where ordinary talent is substantially applied to the domain in question. Mozart and Picasso have their place in rich musical and visual art cultures. From the point of view of educational policy there is little or no sense in going genius-spotting. There are not that many geniuses, and identifying them in advance is a hazardous affair. (Even Ruth Lawrence may come to nothing as far as the history of mathematics is concerned.) Much more to the point is identifying and nurturing ordinary talent, without which the cultural milieu will not exist in which extraordinary achievement can occur. Mozart grew up in a culture of a thousand youth orchestras and choirs.

For recent work see *Genius: The History of an Idea* (1989), edited by Patricia Murray, and Anthony Storr's *The School of Genius* (1988).

Holocaust

The representation of extreme suffering is commonplace in Western art; in the visual arts, for example, the crucifixion of Christ must be one of the most frequently painted and carved subjects. But this familiarity has not prevented the questions being asked whether one can or should artistically represent historically occurring situations of great suffering. These are questions about both the aesthetics and the ethics of such representations. In the case of representations of the crucifixion, a theological justification is offered; but in other cases this justification is not available.

The aesthetic problem is roughly this. If an art work is designed to produce (aesthetic) pleasure, how can it have as its subject matter something the encounter with which can only be, or ought only to be, distressing or in other ways unpleasurable? One traditional answer — that of Aristotle — has been that there is a pleasure to be taken in purging real or imagined distressful emotions; this is the idea of catharsis (q.v. 'Mimesis and Katharsis'). Another answer has been that artistically successful representations of extreme suffering avoid representing the grosser and most distressing features of the suffering depicted. For instance, artists do not linger over the loss of control of bowel and bladder which extreme fear may produce. In his *Laocoön* (1766) Lessing discusses in some detail how the sculpture of Laocoön and his sons crushed in the serpent's coils avoids causing (aesthetic) offence. The sculptor, says Lessing,

> was striving after the highest beauty, under the given circumstances of bodily pain. This, in all its full deforming violence, it was not possible to unite with that. He was obliged, therefore, to abate, to lower it, to tone down cries to sighing; not [in the view of the Greeks] because cries betrayed an ignoble soul, but because they disfigure the face in an unpleasing manner. (Section II, p. 65)

(Lessing is, in fact, characterizing and justifying an aspect of what we still call 'poetic licence'.) But both these answers, in seeking to reconcile the representation of suffering with possibilities of gratification, invite ethical or quasi-ethical objections. At least some versions of the idea of catharsis appear to sanction 'getting off' on other people's suffering. If the suffering is the imaginative creation of an artist only, as in *King Lear*, the pleasure taken in the tragedy of Lear may be puzzling, but not offensive. But if the suffering is re-created by the artist from real suffering, as it is in Holocaust literature, the sense of offence is at the least intelligible. What possible right does an artist have to seek to give an audience pleasure out of the real suffering of others? Ought one not to be offended by a crucifixion painting rather more than by a nude painting of the King's mistress (say, Lely's of Nell Gwynn)? The former must surely be more obscene than the latter. Children often find crucifixion paintings upsetting; paintings of the nude do not trouble them. Adults may think of crucifixion paintings as having a redemptive function, and so react differently from children. As for the second answer, that artists clean up suffering before representing it to an audience, that may be all right for merely imagined suffering, but surely for real suffering it devalues it, limits our feeling for the awfulness of real suffering, and is at least half-way towards a downright romanticization of suffering (as in the old, old lie, *dulce et decorum est pro patria mori*).

It is in such a context that vindications for a genre like Holocaust literature have been and have to be produced. The idea of cosmeticizing suffering in order to produce art is rejected, as is the idea of catharsis as what is to be sought from such art. Those who have written literary works out of their own experience of the Nazi holocaust have not avoided representation of the effects on the bowel and the bladder. Nor are they seeking to provide catharsis for an audience. Rather, they have characterized their work in terms of the concepts of witnessing and redemption.

The idea of bearing witness or giving testimony is a way both of characterizing what Holocaust literature is about (but, then, how is it *literature* rather than autobiographical documentary record?) and of giving it legitimacy. Someone who has not experienced extreme suffering cannot bear witness to it, and — on one view — only witnessing is an ethically acceptable form for the representation of extreme suffering. Outsiders ought not to try to recreate, imaginatively, such *real* extreme suffering. They will inevitably end up exploiting it, however sound their intentions. On such a view it is as illegitimate for Maggie Gee to make use of the experiences of the victims of the nuclear bombing of Hiroshima in her anti-nuclear *The Burning Book* as it is for D.M. Thomas to use the Babi Yar massacre in his sensationalist *The White Hotel*.

The idea of redemption, of repairing damage done, is also used in discussion and justification of Holocaust art, sometimes as the idea that such art may contribute to ensuring that 'it never happens again'. But the brutal question is simply how any of this might relate to providing other, non-suffering, people with a good night out. If one takes a work like Penderecki's *Threnody to the Victims of Hiroshima* or Christopher Bruce's *Ghostdances*, the fact is that they only attract audiences to the extent that they give pleasure, and no one ought to feel that someone else's awful suffering is redeemed, repaired or prevented from reoccurring by the good time I have had listening to the music or watching the dance performed. It isn't, and it can't be. The

German critic, Theodor Adorno, objects to Schoenberg's *Survivor of Warsaw*: 'The so-called artistic representation of the sheer physical pain of people beaten to the ground by rifle–butts contains, however remotely, the power to elicit enjoyment out of it' (Bloch *et al., Aesthetics and Politics*, p. 189).

Teachers generally assume that they have a responsibility to introduce their pupils to the facts of extreme suffering, as produced both by nature (drought, earthquake, disease, ...) and by culture (war, persecution, ...), and to elicit or build a shared sense of their awfulness as a prerequisite to shared endeavours to reduce human suffering. Some of this responsibility they will seek to discharge through the use of artistic representations of human beings suffering individually and collectively. The greatest dangers are probably those of eliciting a voyeuristic pleasure (as when young boys avidly read accounts of torture) and of alternating bewilderment and complacency when pupils are faced with representations of suffering on a scale we often call unimaginable, as, for example, that created in the First World War. But if some kinds and magnitudes of suffering are truly unimaginable, then it may well be for the best that we should not try to imagine them. There is also an ethics to silence, and it may be that what matters is simply to *know* that the trenches of the First World War or the Nazi concentration camps were scenes of unimaginably vast and intense suffering. One might have to accept that there can be no proper imaginative grasping of that suffering through art, and that both aesthetics and ethics dictate a large measure of silence on such matters. A work like *Oh What a Lovely War!* is wholly improper if it is meant to make pupils appreciate the horrors of war; entirely proper as a way of alerting pupils to the fact that perfectly decent people, well-dressed and well-spoken politicians and generals, are capable of organizing and accepting the manufacture of suffering on a scale and of a kind which we have no proper way of expressing.

Human Nature (Natural, Innate)

It would seem at first glance to be a fairly straightforward empirical question: what is natural to human beings as a species? Yet not only are there rival answers, but these divide people as sharply as conflicting opinions on questions of politics or religion. For some people a great deal is natural to humans; for others nothing at all, or at any rate nothing that matters.

Part of the problem is that the question is not so straightforwardly empirical as it seems. The new-born infant may respond in certain ways to sights, sounds, inner sensations of hunger and so on. But these 'natural' reactions are immediately responded to and thereby, it is said, shaped by the infant's caretakers. Without those caretakers the infant would die. So-called wolf children have always been minimally cared for and hence socialized before they are abandoned to their fate. They can tell us nothing about human nature.

Rather more promising as a source of evidence for claims about human nature are those children who are unable to experience the natural or social world through one or more of the five senses. Yet despite their handicaps, blind children will draw and deaf children seek to communicate through invented signs with their hearing caretakers. In these cases we have 'output' without any corresponding 'input'. If blind children then produce similar drawings and deaf children produce similarly structured signs, it seems that we have some evidence for how the human mind works as such and independently of cultural shaping. In recent years evidence from these sources has been intensively explored, since it has been realized that these children offer us the equivalent of a deprivation experiment, in their case a naturally occurring one; see, for example, H. Feldman *et al.*, 'Beyond Herodotus: The Creation of Language by Linguistically Deprived Deaf Children', in A. Lock (Ed.), *Action, Gesture and Symbol*.

To such studies one might add the report of a rather unpleasant deliberate deprivation experiment reported in J. Hochberg and V. Brooks, 'Pictorial Recognition as an Unlearned Ability ...', *American Journal of Psychology* (1962), pp. 624–8. Here a child of nineteen months, previously deprived of sight of pictures and photographs, could immediately recognize and name objects in photographs and line drawings when (at last) shown them, suggesting an unlearnt basis to picture recognition. More recently it has been claimed that there is a specific genetic basis for the rare ability known as perfect pitch, the ability to identify a musical note from memory without the need for a reference sound.

Less scientifically secure, but still credible to most observers, are the observations of infantile responses which appear to be triggered by a stimulus, yet where there is no basis for supposing that the behaviour is imitative or that it has been shaped. New-borns are selectively attracted to the colour red and show signs of interest and excitement when red objects enter their field of vision. Infants who are just beginning to toddle will stop and move their bottoms rhythmically if music (of virtually any kind) is played in their hearing. Young children being read to will burst into tears over a sad story: I recorded this for my daughter, Mitzi, at age 2 years 1 month. In none of these cases is there any reason to suppose that the reaction is shaped by or modelled on the reactions of the caretakers. In his book, *The Rationality of Feeling* (1991), David Best regards such innate propensities to respond, common to the species, as the basis on which depends the possibility of all later learning and teaching of the arts. For some writers this is not just a point of conceptual ot background relevance; it informs their entire approach to the understanding of later learning. For example, in a book entirely indebted to Noam Chomsky's approach to the study of language development, Fred Lerdahl and Ray Jackendoff see our musical development as triggered rather than shaped by our encounters with musical stimuli, and further argue that a-tonal music is not learnable as a first music. That is, we cannot become fluent in it on the basis of limited exposure, in contrast to the way we can become fluent in a tonal musical language on the basis of encounters with a restricted sample of tonal music; see their *A Generative Theory of Tonal Music*, and more accessibly, John Sloboda, *The Musical Mind*.

Whereas it is usual to think of the child and adult's later initiation (socialization, enculturation) into the artistic traditions and conventions of its culture as an enrichment of his or her possibilities for expression and response, there have always been theorists of art who have been suspicious of established culture as in some ways cramping and blocking to self-expression and authentic response. They have looked for ways of recovering in art the innate or natural, or regressing to the infantile (as equivalent to the innate or natural): to modify a saying of Virginia Woolf's, they have valued those varieties of art where, in the rhapsody, one can still hear the babble, the chuckle of the infant.

One may think in this connection of visual artists who have particularly valued child art (the German expressionists and Mark Rothko are examples). Among contemporary theorists of the arts Julia Kristeva is a notable example of someone who identifies and values the presence of the infantile in the adult. In her book, *The Revolution in Poetic Language* (1974), she advances a theory which can be read as a development of Virginia Woolf's insight. Kristeva argues that in numerous experiments with language — symbolist poetry, surrealism, Russian futurism, the prose of Celine, Joyce and Beckett, in the theatre of Artaud — what we encounter is language which has heterogeneous sources. In some of its aspects it belongs to the symbolic order of pre-existing, conventionalized phonology, syntax and semantics: if you like, the language of the Father, or of what Kristeva calls 'the semantic'. But in others it harks back to and reactivates the rhythmic pre-linguistic babble, cries and moans through which the infant expresses its desires, and specifically its (incestuous) desire for the mother. Kristeva (using the word in its Ancient Greek sense) calls this use of sound 'semiotic', meaning that it is an *index* of desire (q.v. 'Icon, Index, Symbol'). Her theory allows us to talk about ways in which in poetry, rhythmic sound may make an independent contribution to sense, yet to sense thought of not as literally, propositionally expressible, but rather to sense as experienced, let us say, psychosomatically. This is a use of language which, for example, the Russian futurist poet, Khlebnikov (1885–1922) would have called 'transrational language'. For example, Khlebnikov writes of glossolalic incantations and chants as using words which can bypass 'the government of the head' and address themselves directly to the 'people of the feelings' (see Raymond Cooke, *Velimir Khlebnikov*, pp. 82–99).

It is easy to think of other examples of poetry, apart from Kristeva's, which lend themselves to treatment using her contrast between the semantic and the semiotic. For example, I have taught Sylvia Plath's poem, 'Daddy', using Kristeva's approach, highlighting the insistent play on the sounds 'oo' and 'u'. But a distinction needs to be drawn between the semiotic as something at work willy-nilly in our language, and the conscious echoing of the infantile in highly wrought literary works, like the poem by Plath just mentioned. (For a discussion of women's writing in a framework influenced by Kristeva, see Deborah Kelly Kloepfer's *The Unspeakable Mother: Forbidden Discourse in Jean Rhys and H.D..*)

It is not just as a critical tool that claims such as Kristeva's have implications for teaching. They may also inform approaches to creative work. For example, they can lend support to techniques which emphasize autobiography, regression to infantile states, and exploration of material, sensuous properties of artistic media, whether (say) sound or paint. One way, for example, of understanding the difference between fine art and graphics or design is that in the former it is central to the activity that properties of the medium (oil, pencil, charcoal) are explored and used expressively (q.v. 'Medium', 'Communication' and Robin Morris's contribution to Peter Abbs (Ed.), *Living Powers*).

'I'

It is a common view that in art (more than anywhere else perhaps) we can express ourselves, or can represent ourselves to ourselves. I write a lyric poem, expressing the love I feel for someone; I paint my own portrait, representing myself to myself. As other volumes in the Falmer Press Library on Aesthetic Education emphasize, progressivism in education has championed art as a, or the, principal means of self-expression.

It is only a slightly less common view, however, that the notion of the self is extremely elusive, and perhaps that the concept designates nothing. Consequently, whatever art is, it cannot be the expression of a self or the self's representation of itself to itself, or at any rate it cannot be these things in any straightforward way (q.v. 'Expression', 'Representation', 'Self-Expression').

Doubts about the self arise (1) from thinking directly about it and about consciousness of self; (2) from the theoretical critique of the unity of the self which is given by psychoanalysis (q.v. 'Unconscious'); and (3) from thinking about the way the personal pronoun 'I' is used in speech and writing. Consider these sources of doubt in turn.

First, what is the self? The philosopher David Hume begins a modern tradition of scepticism about the self (the *moi*) in his *Treatise of Human Nature* (1739). Trying to locate the self by introspection, Hume finds that he 'never can catch *myself* at any time without a perception, and never can observe any thing but the perception. When my perceptions are remov'd for any time, as by sound sleep; so long am I insensible of *myself*, and may truly be said not to exist' (Book 1, Part 4, section 6). From this he infers that he — his self — is 'nothing but a bundle of different perceptions, which succeed each other with an inconceivable rapidity, and are in a perpetual flux and movement.' On this view the self is not elusive, it is non-existent. There is no substance to it — it does not function to support the perceptions which pass before the theatre of the mind. Rather, it is the successive perceptions which alone constitute the mind.

Yet we cannot accept this view. It flies in the face of our sense that what makes a perception mine is that I have it, not that I am my perceptions. One way of indicating what is this self is to say that it is the person, the agent who acts in the world: I am an agent, rather than a perceiver, and my sense of self derives from doing rather than perceiving. Making art is one variety of such doing. But then the follower of Hume might say: a bundle of doings is no more a self than a bundle of perceptions. We still want to know: what ties the bundle together? One answer is that the unity of the self is to be sought in the unity of a life, and 'the unity of a human life is the unity of a narrative quest' (Alasdair MacIntyre, *After Virtue*, p. 203; see also Richard Wollheim, *The Thread of Life*).

Second, psychoanalysis puts the self in question in the quite different manner of a scientific critique of the unity of the mind. In place of the self we are offered id, ego and superego; or alternatively the unconscious as something existing beneath and out of the control of the conscious mind, (q.v. 'Unconscious/The Unconscious'). Though art may well be expression, it cannot be guaranteed as expression of the conscious self and may well and even necessarily contain elements deriving from the unconscious self — elements which are unconscious, elements which are not controlled by the conscious self and which threaten the unity of an artist's work, conceived as a self-conscious expression of conscious self. Thus it becomes a standard form of psychoanalytic criticism to tease out elements in a work which express unconscious thoughts and desires, often enough disrupting the work as intended by its author. For example, in his introduction to the Penguin edition of Edmund Gosse's *Father and Son*, Peter Abbs concludes:

> The manifest intention of the work is to end with the Victorian panegyric to the eminent patriarch: unique and noble. At this critical and falsifying moment in the book I suggest that the unconscious thrust of the whole volume broke through the surface and made itself dramatically visible. The deeper purpose of the book was to justify the son's act of freedom. (p. 29)

Third, of greater current critical interest are those post-structuralist critiques of the self and the unity of the self which, crudely summarized, derive from reflection on the first person pronoun 'I' — its acquisition and use by speakers and writers. It is on an introduction to these ideas that I shall concentrate in the remainder of this section.

Suppose I write, as an apparently autobiographical statement. 'I was a happy child.' The man who writes this (me) is a man in his forties and it is he who is writing (or speaking). Yet the purport of the utterance is to express or represent the happiness of a child, somehow identical with the man, such that the I who speaks here in 'I was a happy child' is somehow the same as the I spoken of, the child, and hence an I which can speak authoritatively, without being asked for evidence (How do you know?) about that child. (Compare 'I was a happy child' with 'He was a happy child'.) But how so?

Suppose one says that it is my memory which allows me to write authoritatively of myself as a child: I remember being a happy child. Do I? It can readily be conceived as an objection that I remember no such thing. I certainly don't remember thinking, 'What a happy child I am!', which is not at all a childish thought, and in any case would licence me only to say, 'I thought I was a happy child', not, 'I was a happy child.' In fact, 'I was a happy child' is an *adult* assessment of a childhood, my own, as I remember its incidents and my feelings about them and so on: the bundle of experiences I had. Not only is it an adult assessment; the criteria for applying it to myself are in an important sense initially preconstructed for me: I know what (other) people think makes a happy childhood, and that I know this is immediately clear when I seek (if I do) to cancel the application of one or other of the standard components or criteria of a happy childhood, as when I say, 'I was a happy child, despite my family's poverty.'

The upshot of this little discussion is to leave 'I was a happy child' as a here–and–now adult assessment in socially constructed terms of a childhood which happens to have been mine. I don't really seem to be anywhere near capturing my childhood or expressing my childhood sense of self: we deceive ourselves if we think 'I was a happy child' gets any closer to my childhood than a third person's 'He was a happy child.' No wonder (though for other reasons as well) post-structuralists end up saying things like, 'I is nothing other than the instance saying I' (Roland Barthes, 'The Death of the Author', p. 145) — a sentiment which derives from a formulation of the linguist, Emile Benveniste, who wrote, 'Est ego qui dit ego' — a self is whatever calls itself a self (which one does using the word 'I').

We can further undermine the credibility of our little autobiographical attempt by introducing an account of language development which attributes a psychologically constitutive role to language as such. There are certain kinds of psychological predicate which cannot be ascribed to the languageless infant. For example, though most people would agree that we can truly say of languageless Sarah that 'She's missing her mother' or 'She hopes her mother will come back', no one supposes we can truly say of her 'She hopes her mother will come back on Wednesday.' Sarah clearly doesn't have a concept of Wednesday and you only get a concept of Wednesday by learning that it is one of the days of the week, and you learn that by learning the names of the days of the week and learning that they are the names of the days of the week.

In similar vein there are post-structuralists who think that you are not born an I, a self, but that you become one, or at least acquire the illusion of becoming one. Very roughly, they think you do this by learning to use the first-person pronoun, 'I'. Even if they think you already have to have some sense of self in order to be able to acquire the use of 'I', they argue that this equally comes from outside (e.g. from the way your parents construct you as a self, by giving you a name and relating to you through it, or from sight of your 'self' in a mirror-image), and imposes a (spurious) unity on an organism and mind which is intrinsically split, divided or multiple, as psychoanalysts have urged.

It might objected at this point that there must be something *given* in the organism or mind which is not learnt and which allows a sense of self or the ability to use 'I' to be assumed. There must, for example, already be a self to recognize the self reflected back in a mirror-image. This issue might be pursued by contrasting what the psychoanalyst Jacques Lacan says in a famous essay on 'The Mirror Phase as Formative of the Function of the I' (1936/1949) with what the psychologist Colwyn Trevarthen says about un-learnt subjectivity in such essays as 'Communication and Cooperation in Early Infancy: A Description of Primary Intersubjectivity' (in M. Bullowa (Ed.), *Before Speech*).

However, to return to the line of thought previously being pursued, we can say that what is emerging is the idea that, as organisms or minds, we are in some sense other (or alien) to the sense of self and to the concepts which we inhabit but which derive from 'outside' and, specifically, from language. In this context it becomes an intelligible and interesting idea whether we can, and in art whether we should, seek in some sense to *regress* to those parts of ourselves which are other or alien to the culture which has constructed us to be what we are and to possess the sense of self which we (habitually) do possess. These parts may be thought of as the unconscious, which is made up of all that culture has repressed (so in art we can talk about the return of the repressed — something aimed at in surrealism). Or they may be thought of as what preceded the entry into language, so that (for example) the rhapsody of music or poetry is thought of as connected at a deep level with the babbling and chuckling of infancy. One French post-structuralist, Julia Kris-teva, in *The Revolution in Poetic Language* (1974) pursues such an argument, seeking in symbolist poetry linguistic evidence for the continuing presence and efficacity of pre-linguistic modes of expressing desire. (Her approach is summarized in the essay, 'From One Identity to Another', in her book, *Desire in Language*; and q.v. 'Human Nature' for a discussion.)

Icon, Index, Symbol

Within semiotics (q.v. 'Semiology/Semiotics'), defined as the science of signs, it is usual to distinguish three non-exclusive categories of sign, or more accurately, aspects of a sign's relation to what it is a sign of. This tripartite categorization originates with the American philosopher C.S. Peirce (1839–1914).

A sign is iconic if it resembles what it is a sign of. Figurative paintings are an obvious example of signs which signify by resemblance. However, because it is hard to define 'resemblance' non-circularly, some writers prefer to elucidate what an icon is by saying that the structure of an icon provides information about the structure of what it signifies. The structure of the word 'dog' contains no information about the structure of a dog, but a figurative drawing of a dog does — we can map from parts of the drawing to parts of the dog. Put this way, it is possible to see that there are iconic aspects to language. The order in which I say, 'I came, I saw, I conquered' maps onto the order in which I actually did those things. The structure of the utterance provides (iconic) information about the structure (the unfolding) of events.

A sign is indexical (an index) if it is causally linked to its object. Spots are a sign of measles, clouds a sign of rain: the spots and the clouds are indexical signs. So too is a photograph, as the effect of light on a light-sensitive medium (q.v. 'Photography'). Of course, the photograph is *also* iconic: Peirce's tripartition is of aspects, not of mutually exclusive types of sign.

By symbol, Peirce means simply any sign which has no intrinsic relationship to what it is a sign of — in other words it is an *arbitrary sign*. Normally, it is by *convention* that an arbitrary sign is used to signify something, and language is usually regarded as a matter of conventional use of arbitrary signs (see David Lewis, *Convention*). (Onomatopoeic words are conventional but have iconic aspects.) Because of the connotations of the word 'symbol', it is common to use 'sign' instead, to talk about arbitrary and conventional signification. This is Saussure's practice in the famous *Course in General Linguistics* (1916), one of the inaugural texts of contemporary structuralism (q.v.) and semiology (q.v.). Saussure also uses semiology (q.v.)

where Peirce spoke of semiotics (q.v.). Saussure's usage creates the problem that we then have no superordinate term to talk about icons, indices and signs together, unless we use 'symbol' as the generic! But 'symbol' has its own connotations, discussed under 'Symbol'.

Missing from the account so far is any reference to the *user* of signs (or symbols). Yet Peirce realizes that there is no sign without a user and so defines a sign in general as something used by someone to signify something to somebody. The branch of semiotics which considers the relations between signs and their users is called pragmatics, and contrasts with syntax and semantics. All signs can be studied in pragmatics, but it is disputed whether all signs have a syntax or a semantics. It is commonly said that painting has no syntax and music (except 'programme' music) no semantics. This amounts to saying that there is no *language* of painting and music if 'language' is defined by reference to the properties of the spoken and written languages which distinguish human beings from other animals. This issue is explored in the section 'Language' (q.v.). On musical semantics, see Peter Kivy, *Sound and Semblance*.

The category of iconic sign has been of interest to theorists of art, to some of whom it has seemed central to art that its signs are analogues of, and have resemblances to, what they are signs of. A useful distinction can be made between iconic signs which are *transparent* and those which are *translucent*. The former are those where the audience is able immediately to recognize what the sign is a sign of, even in ignorance of the conventions according to which the sign is built. Thus prehistoric cave paintings, Chinese paintings, Japanese prints and so on are generally transparent signs. Even the most naïve spectator can tell what is represented in the painting or the print. In contrast, an icon is translucent when the spectator needs some information, some guidance to see the way in which the sign maps onto what it is a sign of. Much music and dance is iconic, for example, of the forms of human feeling, but translucently so. However, once we are told where the iconicity is to be found — through a title or a programme note, for example — we see it in a flash, all at once. The same is true of some paintings, for example Mondrian's *Broadway Boogie-Woogie*. (For more discussion see my 'Transparent and Translucent Icons'.)

Imagination (q.v. 'Creativity')

What's your favourite animal? asks the child and you reply, say, 'A sheep'. What's your favourite colour? ('Red') What's your favourite number? ('Five'). The child then declares, triumphantly, 'I've never seen a red sheep with five legs!' I assume this little game is widely played; my own children have found it — like 'knock, knock' — an endless source of pleasure. But in terms of a distinction central to romantic thought, and specifically attributable to Coleridge, the game exemplifies the use of *fancy* rather than *imagination*. For what the child does is to combine merely mechanically items drawn from different domains (animals, colours, numbers) to produce a novel but (in this case intentionally) absurd fictional, non-being (q.v. the idea of novelty sketched in the section on 'Creativity'). As Coleridge expresses it, fancy

> has no other counters to play with, but fixities and definites. The Fancy is indeed no other than a mode of Memory emancipated from the order of time and space; while it is blended with, and modified by that empirical faculty of the will, which we express by the word CHOICE. But equally with the ordinary memory the Fancy must receive its materials ready made from the law of association. (cited in M.H. Abrams, *The Mirror and the Lamp*, p. 168, from Coleridge's *Biographia Literaria*)

In the associationist philosophical and psychological tradition (Hobbes, Locke, Hume, Hartley), against which Coleridge was reacting, recombination of existing real elements into new fictional entities was itself taken as the characteristic operation of the imagination. But Coleridge will have none of this: 'Fancy' is his name for associationist imagination, and Fancy is decidedly inferior to what is really involved in the exercise of imagination when that is properly understood.

Imagination works holistically, as we would now say, or organically, as Coleridge said. It does not take discrete components as input and yield a novel assembly of them as output. Rather, it yields 'at once' a whole image (verbal, visual or enacted) which is intended as the adequate realization of an emotion or idea. This whole image will not be illuminated *as* such an attempted realization by any efforts at decompositional analysis. The imagination may well yield us, on appropriate occasion, the image of a five-legged red sheep, but it does not do so by abstraction and re-combination. And it yields us such an image only because it forms itself out of the 'living power' — that is, the *activity* — of 'the spirit of poetry' — that is, of the imagination. (The first volume of the series in which this book appears evokes the Coleridgean heritage in its title, *Living Powers.*)

In the romantic tradition, and specifically in Coleridge and Wordsworth, the active power of the imagination requires further characterization beyond the point at which it is said that imagination forms images as wholes. It is also said that imagination creates images which have what one might call a feeling tone or emotional charge. That is, imagination is not merely cognitive but also affective, though one might want to say that there is a scientific imagination which forms cognitive images as wholes in the shape of conjectures, hypotheses, paradigms or patterns; see, for example, T.S. Kuhn, *The Structure of Scientific Revolutions*. In addition, it is said that the images created by the artistic imagination instantiate the universal, the particular image exemplifying or standing for some general idea. In German idealist philosophy, notably in Hegel, this thought is expressed as the idea, as Roger Scruton puts it, that 'art seeks to arrive at an order in experience through the achievement of an embodied concept' (*Art and Imagination*, p. 189). The full scope of the romantic idea of imagination is summarized by Mary Warnock, who writes in her book on *Imagination* that the imagination is something,

> working actively from within to enable us to perceive the general in the particular, to make us treat the particular, whether something we see or something we call up as an image, as symbolic, as meaning something beyond itself. Ideas of imagination cannot be called up by *mere* association, nor by mere likeness to one another or to what is seen. The imagination is not merely passive; it is an active combining power which brings ideas together, and which is at work to create the forms of things which seem to speak to us of the universal, and which at the same time necessarily cause in us feelings of love and awe. (p. 84)

Two further perspectives on the imagination deserve attention. First, the concept of imagination as aiming towards or intending an *adequate* image for some reality implies that the idea of imagination is a normative one, as it is in everyday speech where 'more imaginative' means something better than 'less imaginative' and 'unimaginative' (mechanical fancy or simple literal-mindedness). It is a separate question whether and how the imagination is educable, but it is already implied in the concept of imagination that it is worth educating. We do, it is true, have the notion of someone's having an overactive imagination, where this means something like being too quick to imagine possible but counterfactual scenarios in contexts where there is evidence pointing to a probable plain truth.

Second, in this century the romantic theory of imagination reappears in

Gestalt psychology and Wittgenstein's philosophy as the idea that imagination is exercised in our ability to see one thing as another. In Gestalt psychology this is illustrated by our ability to see a trick drawing in two different ways: to see it as a drawing of a rabbit or of a duck. In philosophy this idea is generalized over all instances of our ability to see one thing as another, and in particular our ability to see one thing as another without *believing* it to be that other thing. In imagination we entertain thoughts, ideas and emotions without necessarily asserting them to be true. This approach to the study of imagination is developed at length in Roger Scruton's *Art and Imagination*, where he also sketches an account of imaginative activity:

> Doing something imaginatively means doing it thoughtfully, where one's thought is not guided by the normal processes of theoretical reasoning, but goes instead beyond the obvious in some more or less creative way. In doing X imaginatively one does more than X, and this additional element is one's own invention, added because it seems appropriate to X. It goes without saying that there is a normative sense of the adverbial construction: some actions may be judged to be truly imaginative, while others might be thought of as whimsical or foolish. On this basis we can see how the concept of the imaginative becomes extended to apply to a plan, an hypothesis, a work of art or a person. (pp. 99–100)

In linking imagination to creativity, Scruton may make us think that the question of the teachability of imagination is not different from the question of the teachability of creativity (q.v. 'Creativity').

But in both cases there is a problem which rapidly threatens to turn into a paradox, analogous as it happens to that identified for another context in Karl Popper's *The Poverty of Historicism*. The paradox is that if we could see what, in a particular situation, would count as an imaginative or creative leap, then we would have had to have already *made* that leap. But it is of the essence of imagination and creativity that the imaginativeness or creativeness of a leap can only be seen *after* the event. Of course, a teacher may guide a pupil into re-inventing a move which the teacher has already made. That does not deprive the pupil of the chance of being imaginative or creative. The tact of the teacher then consists in giving enough clues but not so many as to simply give the game away.

Intention and Convention
(q.v. 'Interpretation', 'Text and Context')

Few words have caused such barren discussion in aesthetics as the word 'intention' (Richard Wollheim, *Painting as an Art*)

Works of (human) art are always produced intentionally, unlike objects of natural beauty which may nonetheless display an 'as if' purposefulness — purposefulness without purpose, as Kant expresses it in *The Critique of Judgment* and as over a century of evolutionary theorizing has made intelligible. But to say that all works of art are intentionally produced in human actions guided by thoughts which define the relevant intentions ('He did such-and-such intending to produce a painting', etc.) is not to say that for every discriminable element of a work there was some corresponding thought involved in its production, such that it was produced with *that* intention. This is obvious when artists choose to work with various chance (aleatory) techniques, ensuring that the work will contain elements which though they may be aesthetically important are not the product of separately assignable intentions. Thus surrealist automatic writing, the drip-painting technique of Jackson Pollock, chance techniques in choreography or musical composition and computer-generated forms (visual, verbal or musical) are all examples of ways in which discriminable elements of a work can be produced without being the product of discriminate intentions. Nonetheless, the work as a whole is produced under the guidance of some higher-level thought or thinking which defines the intentionality of the work: 'I am going to choreograph a dance by picking numbers out of a hat', and so on.

This higher-level generic intention guides the artist, and assumptions about it guide audiences. For example, for the artist it may define the boundaries of the work — what is inside and what outside it. It may be that I intend to produce a painting by riding a bicycle across a wet canvas following a route defined for me by some random route-generating device. The marks on the canvas thereby produced are part of the work. If my 3-year-old decides to get in on the act by riding her trike across the same canvas, that is definitely not part of the work. (Unless at this point I change the defining generic conception I have, and decide that she is doing something other than spoil the painting.) It is in virtue of the controlling generic intention that artists feel entitled to sign their names to works the content of which may have been produced without specific intentions.

From the audience's point of view the knowledge that they have to do with a work of art, rather than, say, an object of natural beauty, guides the approach to the work in a variety of ways. If the question, 'What is it?' can be answered by reference to some controlling generic intention ('It's a music-al composition', as opposed to 'It's a hum from the loudspeakers'), then this not only defines the object, but suggests a relevant mode of attention. In particular, it holds out the promise of some reward. It may or may not be possible to locate an interesting or pleasing pattern in the hum from the loudspeakers; to present something to an audience as a work of art just is to claim that attention will be rewarded with the perception of some interesting or pleasing pattern, or lack of pattern. When a film for which a film-maker claims credit (the word 'credits' is interestingly apposite) is projected to an audience, a promise of some rewarding experience is extended, but there can be no guarantee that the promise will be fulfilled, since in this case it is the audience and not the film-maker who fulfils the 'promise'. The right thing to say about, say, some of Andy Warhol's experimental films is that they make a promise which no audience has yet found a way of fulfilling. They are very boring films; and no amount of theorizing will alter this fact.

There are other ways in which assumptions about generic intention are always and appropriately deployed by audiences. For example, when we see what appears to be an advertisement but without any brand name present, we assume in virtue of what we assume about the preparedness of adverts that the name hasn't been left out by accident. We assume it has been left out intentionally, and that the intention is that we discover the name for ourselves on the basis of clues provided by the advertisement before us. Even an artist using chance techniques may make slips in transcription or perform-ance which are legitimately discounted or corrected by an audience, relying on an understanding of the guiding generic intention.

However, most theoretical and critical interest has focused not on the idea of generic intention (as I have called it), but on the idea of intentions (thoughts) attached to and accounting for discriminable elements in the content of a work, and that this interest is located within the framework of concern identified by such typical questions as: Can (the meaning of) such-and-such be understood without knowing or making an assumption about the artist's intentions in producing (saying or doing) such-and-such? In con-crete terms, can we understand (the meaning of) Blake's line in *The Tyger*, 'Did he who made the Lamb make thee?', without knowing or assuming something about Blake's thoughts/intentions in writing *that* line, and not some other possible line?

Now in one sense to know what Blake meant (thought, intended), all we have to know is what the words mean and then add the assumption or knowledge that Blake used the words to mean what they normally mean. What they 'normally' mean is what they mean 'by convention' — conven-tionally, the words here are being used to ask a question, and the question is whether lambs and tigers are the creatures (creations) of the same God. Unless Blake was using a code, or playing Humpty Dumpty, or not fully competent in English, Blake must have meant what the words mean. So it is not a problem that we have no other means of access to his specific thoughts/ intentions in composing and selecting that line. One might say: we have conventions of language (or conventions of pictorial representation and so on) precisely as a means whereby we can make publicly available our thoughts/intentions in action, and nothing more is needed than knowledge of the conventions in order for an audience to recover (to understand) some-one's meaning.

It is not that simple. What the critic wants to know is whether Blake wrote, 'Did he who made the Lamb make thee?' intending that the reader should answer 'yes' or intending that the reader should answer 'no', or neither, or either, or both. And the words (the conventions of meaning) do not answer this question about Blake's meaning; nor could they, since now we are interested in what *Blake* meant by using these words which mean such-and-such. What are the possibilities?

1 Blake wrote the words intending that readers would answer 'yes', 'no', or whatever. Either we do or do not have a record of or a way of reconstructing his intentions, more or less plausibly.
2 Blake wrote the words *thinking* that he intended one answer, when *really* he intended another. His unconscious 'got the better of him', and readers can tell what is going on (as when someone damns with faint praise, while thinking they are simply praising).
3 Blake had no definite, discriminable thought/intention which accom-panied the writing or acceptance into the poem of the line in ques-tion. He accepted it because it seemed appropriate, but he didn't have a view of *what* the appropriateness was or what it was appropriate to. He didn't, for example, accept the line *because* it would lead or oblige readers to answer the question 'yes', 'no', or whatever. In other words Blake (like many artists) could not and would not have been articulate about his artistic choices.

Now surely all three are real possibilities and show that while it is always *relevant* to understanding (the meaning of) a work that we ask for the artist's specific intentions in relation to discriminable elements, it is by no means always going to be the case that we can say what the intentions were, or that they are decisive in establishing what the meaning is (this is the import of 2), or that they existed (the burden of 3). Does this mean that we could always read poems and approach other art works *as if* the artist's specific intentions were irrelevant, since if sometimes there are going to be no knowable or given intentions, yet there is still going to be the work of art, why not act as if this were always the case?

Why not, indeed? And sometimes we do. For example, there is a great deal of Western art produced in the context of a general intent to glorify God, and in which specific elements are constructed to glorify God in particular ways. But it seems entirely possible for audiences to listen to such music, enjoy it, appreciate it, be moved by it, yet not approach it as religious music intended for the glory of God. One listens to it 'as music'. So also one might read poetry 'as poetry'. In neither case is one's listening or reading arbitrary since it is controlled by or attentive to the music as played or the words as written or spoken. To use a key distinction of E.D. Hirsch's in *Validity in Interpretation*, one can attend scrupulously to the *meaning* of a work while bracketing off consideration of its *significance*. One could go further in justifying such an approach by saying that though one kind of significance is set by an artist's intentions, this is not the only context of significance. There are other contexts given by wider cultural and historical settings. To hear or read a work as portending the crisis or collapse of a culture is precisely to give it a significance which could not have been intended by its author. Likewise, though there are self-consciously revolutionary works, it is only in retrospect that the revolutionary significance of a work can be confirmed, that is, properly heard, seen or read.

One could go on indefinitely: q.v. 'Interpretation', 'Meaning', 'Text and Context'; and for further reading: David Newton-de-Molina, *On Literary Intention*; G.E.M. Anscombe, *Intention*; John Searle, *Intentionality*. The classic essay, 'The Intentional Fallacy', in W.K. Wimsatt's *The Verbal Icon* (1954) is still frequently read and relied on, but it can no longer be taken as a helpful piece, since it was written in the context of peculiarly mistaken views in the philosophy of language and mind, particularly the then influential behaviourism.

Interpretation (q.v. 'Meaning', 'Intention and Convention', 'Text and Context')

Interpretation is the revenge of the intellect upon art (Susan Sontag, 'Against Interpretation')

If I went to talk about interpretation in China, I should need an interpreter. An interpreter translates what I say in one language into what one would say in another language if one wanted to say the same thing as I have said. Here 'say the same thing' means 'express the same thought, proposition or meaning'. So an interpreter is adept at saying the same thing in different ways (languages). This is one concept of interpretation: that of rendering afresh, in different terms, what has already been expressed. One question that immediately arises is whether interpretation in this sense is ever or often achievable. This general question has specific forms: Can poetry be translated from one language to another? Can what a painting expresses be expressed in words? Can one form of words mean exactly the same as another?

There is another concept of interpretation. I say, 'That's only my interpretation' or 'It's all a matter of interpretation' or 'Stick to the facts. I'm not asking for an interpretation.' What I mean is a variety of things: that my interpretation is of something's *significance* or its *motivation*; but also that it's an attempt at stating the *meaning* of something when this is arguably unclear. This second concept of interpretation has its own difficulties. What (collateral, contextual) information do we need to *make* an interpretation? What is the difference between a reasonable interpretation and a wild guess? Is there such a thing as an exhaustive interpretation, such that we could truly say, 'Professor X has said the final word about Shakespeare.'

Questions, questions. What are the answers? Consider the first concept of interpretation. There has been no shortage of people willing to take up the challenge of translation or of writing about work in a non-linguistic medium. The translator of poetry may well aim to do more than provide a literal or word-for-word translation, and instead provide a rendering which will afford the (say, English) reader an experience equivalent to that offered by the original to the (say, German) reader. With this as an aim, the 'translation'

85

may depart substantially from a 'literal' rendering (whatever a literal rendering is: q.v. 'Meaning', 'Figurative and Literal'). It is not only poetry which is subject to free translation; so too are novels. Compare, for example, Camus's *L'Etranger* with the Penguin translation (*The Outsider*) to which, for example, whole phrases have simply been added. There have been art critics who have thought that it is their task in interpreting a painting to a reader (who may not have seen the painting) that they should offer the reader an experience analogous or comparable to the experience the critic had looking at the painting.

These examples are enough to cast doubt on the project of what one might call 'true interpretation', even while indicating that it is a project which, for various motives, we are constantly driven to attempt and to assume the possibility of. The academic discipline of anthropology is perhaps our culture's outstanding monument to its belief in the possibility of rendering the life of one culture into the language of another.

So interpretation in the first sense inevitably connects to and merges with interpretation in the second sense. For some there *is* only interpretation in the second sense. Put differently, for some there is no gap between giving the *meaning* of something and indicating its *significance* (q.v. 'Meaning'; and see E.D. Hirsch, *Validity in Interpretation*).

The literary theorist Stanley Fish thinks there is *only* interpretation. Thus he writes, in a highly readable book 'Interpretation is not the art of construing, but the art of constructing. Interpreters do not decode poems, they make them' (*Is There a Text in This Class?*, p. 327). This is immediately threatening. After all, if there is no (stable) text to be decoded, what is there to distinguish a reasonable interpretation from a wild guess? Fish's answer is that there is a distinction, but that it exists not because the text exerts some kind of control over interpretation, but because interpretation is a historically and socially situated activity which is undertaken within traditions, conventions and norms which the apprentice interpreter has to learn, and which provide the basis for discriminating the sensible from the crazy. Interpretation is the work of interpretive communities, and these exert control, not the text. As Fish puts it, 'while there are always mechanisms for ruling out readings, their source is not the text but the presently recognised interpretive strategies for producing the text' (p. 347). These strategies can, of course, change and it is part of the job of literary critics to produce upheavals in the world of criticism by seeking recognition for new strategies, for example deconstruction (q.v.), of 'producing the text'.

In philosophical terms, what Fish is doing is collapsing the real object (the putative text outside and before interpretation) into the object of knowledge (the text as constructed by interpreters). This position has a respectable enough pedigree in several philosophical traditions, including British empiricism and German idealism. Whether it is true is another question (q.v. 'Meaning'; 'Text and Context').

In the classroom pupils need to be constantly recalled to the content of the work of art before them — the words on the page, the disposition of image, sound or movement. For there is a standing temptation to use works of art like Rorshach ink-blots and to project onto them fantasies and idio-syncratic concerns. But when that happens, the work of art can no longer work to extend and deepen experience and the articulation of experience.

Judgment (of Beauty, of Taste)

'There is no arguing about taste', says the old maxim (*De gustibus non est disputandum*). In other words, though we may sometimes *say* things like (1) below, there is nothing more we can or do mean by this than what is represented in (2): apparent judgments of taste reduce to self-validating declarations of personal, subjective experience:

1 Beethoven's *Pastoral Symphony* is a beautiful composition.
2 Beethoven's *Pastoral Symphony* seems to me a beautiful composition.

Ruthlessly, one might then go on to claim that (2) has no more content than (3) or (4):

3 It pleases me to listen to Beethoven's *Pastoral Symphony*.
4 I like listening to Beethoven's *Pastoral Symphony*.

Now it is clear that I may like doing something that you don't like doing, and there is no arguing about who is right or wrong. I may find it strange or curious that you don't like what I like ('Really, you don't like strawberries?'), but there's nothing I can do about it; nor is there any obvious right or means I have at my disposal to try to change you: So, you don't like strawberries; can I offer you something else?

But to claim that something is beautiful *is* to stake a claim, to commit oneself to engaging in argument with someone who does not accept the claim. It is to suggest that there are grounds on which the claim can be defended, and to suggest that anyone who disagrees with the claim is mistaken, plain wrong. You don't think the *Pastoral* is a beautiful composition? But, surely — just listen to this passage, and this . . .? It leaves you cold? Well, of course, there is no arguing with philistines. In our post-liberal culture where everyone has a right to their own opinion, a right to their own taste — however stupid, cruel or vulgar — it becomes worse than bad taste to suggest that someone might be wrong in not finding beautiful what I find beautiful. It is elitist and intolerant. Who wants to be thought elitist and intolerant when it is so much easier to go along with the crowd, smilingly observing, '*Chacun à son gout*' — everyone to their own taste.

The trouble is, however, that judgments of taste won't go away, even in post-liberal culture. It is not only that criticism continues to offer discriminations between the good and the bad. It is also that no one really finds it possible to talk about the arts without using terms which implicitly commit the user to the possibility of an argument, and hence to the supposition that you may be right and I may be wrong and vice versa. No one actually abandons judging things to be beautiful; no one actually abandons talking about the arts in favour of talking about themselves. (A companion who can say no more than 'I liked it' in exiting from the concert, the cinema, the theatre, is pretty dull company.)

The problem of the validity of value judgments about art has haunted and preoccupied aesthetics since its eighteenth century inception. It is entirely analogous to the problem of the validity of moral judgments, the problem of demonstrating that a moral judgment is something more than (not reducible to) an expression of (personal) approval or disapproval. For example, it is central to Kant's enterprise in *The Critique of Judgment* (1790) that he demonstrate not only that judgments of taste *claim* to be universally valid, and *demand* assent regardless of whether everyone actually agrees with them — but that he demonstrate that such judgments can indeed be rationally grounded. This involves, centrally, showing that the concept of beauty does have application to objects, and is distinguishable from the (merely) subjectively pleasing, and that it makes sense to speak of the discernment (perception) of beauty by means of (the faculty of) taste. Hence the understanding of what an artistic or aesthetic (value) judgment is depends on the account given of beauty and taste (q.v. 'Beauty', 'Taste').

Intelligent opponents of the elitism and intolerance they see masquerading as objective judgments of artistic or aesthetic value can go half way with the Kantian at this point, but resist the final conclusion. Yes, they can say, we do try to talk about works of art and evaluate them using grounds and criteria which give us the possibility of rational argument. However, in the end there is no reason to suppose that a particular set of grounds or criteria must be selected at all times and in all places, nor that they be ordered in the same way. In the last analysis there is always a culturally or individually variable component and it is this, in the end, that undermines the pretensions of the critic to judge for all of us. That this is so is most obvious in relation to those works appreciation of which is inseparable from an audience's ability to engage with the religious, political values or world-view they express.

But the last analysis is not the first analysis. There is no reason why children should not be schooled in making judgments of art works, and encouraged to be articulate about those judgments. Equally, they should not be bullied into making judgments of approval or disapproval which they do not really feel ('You don't *really* like Top of the Pops, do you?'). Nor can teachers avoid selecting what their pupils encounter as representative works of art. This does not imply that they are free to be narrow-minded about what they choose to represent: for example, pop music has its high moments just as much as classical music, and both should be present in any balanced music curriculum.

Language

Is music a language? Is there a language of images? Does dance notation suppose the existence of a language of dance? Such questions are not merely verbal, since they are connected to possible answers which tell us quite a lot about the nature of music or painting or dance. But what we understand by 'language' is neither clear nor agreed. For example, in some definitions language is presented as essentially a medium of communication. In others language is conceived to get its distinctiveness from being a medium of thought or representation. So what is *language*? And what is *a language*? I'll take the second question first.

A language might be defined as anything for which a grammar can be written, and a grammar defined as a set of rules which takes as input a vocabulary and delivers as output all and only the well-formed (grammatical) expressions (sentences) of the language. So now we have three key concepts: an inventory of words, a set of rules and a set of (well-formed) sentences. Put like this, it does not seem to be stretching things to say that a *style* of music constitutes something like a language: there is a vocabulary of notes, a set of rules of composition (which can be taught) and at least some scope to apply the concepts of well- and ill-formed: in some styles a composition which does not end on the tonic note is ill-formed. Equally, it is hard to see a style of painting as constituting a language, since there does not appear to be anything analogous to a set of notes in music which might constitute the vocabulary of a painting style.

We could push this analysis to a greater level of sophistication, for example, by introducing a distinction between syntactic rules and semantic rules — roughly, a distinction between rules which yield well-formed expressions and rules which yield meaningful expressions. At this stage it will appear that most Western classical musical styles can be analyzed by using fairly clear analogues of syntactic rules, but that the semantic rules are weak or non-existent. Musical sound is not linked by rule to extra-musical meaning, or so it is commonly argued. (For contrary arguments see e.g. Peter Kivy, *Sound and Semblance*.)

To see what the components of a fleshed-out grammar of a language look like, and to see what a grammar is supposed to do, it is worth consulting the original source for most of the work done in linguistics over the past thirty years: Noam Chomsky's *Syntactic Structures* or, alternatively, John Lyons' *Chomsky*.

From quite a different perspective, a language can be thought of in relation to the people who use it. So we could say of English, French, etc. that these are the conventional means of spoken and written communication used in Britain, France, etc. The signs or symbols of English, French etc. are arbitrary in that there is no meaningful connection between sound (or letter shape) and sense, except in onomatoepeia. It is by convention that these arbitrary signs are used and used to mean what they do. One might go on to say that it is likewise by convention that composers, painters, etc. use particular styles and techniques in their time and place; sometimes these conventions and styles involve arbitrary signs, though more often they are non-arbitrary, iconic signs (q.v. 'Icon, Index, Symbol'). Thinking in such terms tends to represent the arts as media of communication (q.v. 'Communication') and to emphasize large-scale historical and geographical traditions rather than the individual artist.

Different again is an emphasis not on the idea of *a language*, but on the idea of *language* as characteristic of the species homo sapiens, and as imparting what is common to all languages. It is not unusual for a textbook of linguistics in answering the question, 'What is language?', to list a set of features (often called 'design features') which distinguish linguistic from other semiotic (sign) systems. Such a list is presented, for example, in John Lyons' *Semantics*, (Vol. 1, pp. 70–85). Such distinguishing features of language tend to point to the conclusion that the expressive powers of language are greater than those of any other kind of sign system, so that it is not by accident that language is, for humans, the dominant semiotic system, freely used, among other things, to talk about language itself and all other systems which do not themselves have such expressive or reflexive potential. The present book could not be recast in pictures — but pictures are significantly commented on in language.

Consider briefly some of the design features of language and their presence or absence in other sign systems. First, there is the *hierarchy* feature or *duality* of structure. Natural languages have a hierarchical organization: a small inventory of significant sounds, phonemes, twenty to thirty-five in number, is used to construct the thousands of word forms (morphemes, lexemes) which make up the vocabulary of a language. These in turn can be combined into phrases or sentences, indefinitely or infinitely large in number, the rules of combination forming the syntax of the language. Whether there is any significant hierarchical organization of language above the sentence level, governed by rules which might be formalized by a text grammar, is disputed. It does seem that combinations above sentence level are largely governed by human purposes and patterns of thinking. Nothing like this hierarchy of structure is found in painting or dance, though something quite similar is to be found in music, where we seem, however, to jump from note (phoneme) to phrase (sentence), without a level of vocabulary, but where there is at least one higher level of organization above phrase level (see also work in cinema semiotics, such as Christian Metz's *Language and Cinema*).

Second, language is not only a meaning system with a level of semantic organization, but meaning is created compositionally: by varying one discrete element in a sentence we can vary its meaning dramatically as in (1) and (2):

1 The cat sat on the mat
2 The dog sat on the mat

Now in painting there is no vocabulary of discrete elements which can be pulled out and plugged in like this: pictures do not have parts in the way that languages have parts. In dance, where there are arguably discrete elements, it is at least commonly the case that changing a step in a sequence of steps does not yield a well-defined change in the meaning of the movement accomplished. Steps in a dance do not build meaning compositionally in the way that words do. Paul Ziff, a philosopher of language, elaborates this claim. He thinks that our perception of the expressive movements of a dance is holistic, and resistant to decompositional analysis. We simply see whole chunks of movement as significant in some way, but we cannot say much about how we came to see them that way or how we justify seeing them that way. The role of the dance critic is not an analytical one, but rather has to do with putting us in the right Gestalt frame of mind to see a particular dance (see Paul Ziff, 'About the Appreciation of Dance', in Fancher and Myers, *Philosophical Essays on Dance*).

Third, in language there is a distinction to be drawn between the meaning of a sentence in abstraction from a context of use, and its situated meaning in a context of utterance. Thus the sentence

3 Visiting relatives can be boring

can mean either that relatives who visit one can be boring, or that going to visit relatives can be boring. What it means on an occasion of utterance will be settled on that occasion.

Analogously, there are ambiguous pictures, for example, the famous duck-rabbit:

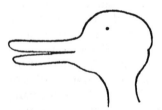

This can be seen either as a duck or as a rabbit. On an occasion of use, the drawing may be intended to be seen and actually seen in only one way. Likewise, one can write melodically or harmoniously ambiguous musical passages, which are 'resolved' one way or another in context.

Fourth, it is possible to prevaricate or lie in language: what is said does not have to correspond point-by-point to some feature of the world. In contrast, the camera cannot lie, though a photographer can (q.v. 'Photography'). For different reasons there seems no place for the idea of a deceitful piece of music or dance, since in music or dance no one is making assertions which might be insincerely made. On the other hand it does not seem to be stretching usage to say that a portrait painter lies when he or she paints an excessively flattering — an untrue — portrait of someone.

One could go on, comparing and contrasting semiotic systems against a checklist of features derived from an understanding of the nature of language. Such an enterprise belongs to semiotics (q.v. 'Semiology/Semiotics'). For a full and subtle discussion see Nelson Goodman, *Languages of Art* (1968), and, rather older but influential on thinking about the arts, Susanne Langer, *Philosophy in a New Key* (1942).

Literature in Education

A conception of literature in education founded on creative principles would put the notion of encounter at the centre of the enterprise. In the making of literature the artist encounters the world of experience, or significant aspects of that world. Out of that encounter literary works (as all the arts in their own distinctive ways) construe a sense of reality. The making of the work shapes, and in shaping discovers, what that reality might be through its symbolic presentation.

Through this creative act there is encounter too with memory: that which is recalled directly to the mind, and that which is subliminally held or tacitly apprehended in preconscious and unconscious awareness. The discovery of these states of knowing engages reciprocally with the need for form, since that which is formless subsists without definition in the flux of experience. Form here defines the particular organization of each work by which it is fashioned towards an internal correspondence with a unity; each work (poem, novel, for example) in this sense achieving its own elaborated *gestalt*. Through the need for form, however, the making of each work to lesser or greater degree engages with previous examples of form, and to those genres of writing to which they belong and on which they draw. Each individual writing connects with the literary traditions of a culture or cultures: traditions of disposing of the symbols of that art — against which each new work defines its own identity. Without tradition there can be no originality.

Interpenetrating and mediating all of these dimensions of the literary encounter there is language itself, the art medium. Language, in literary writing, becomes the agent of discovery. Through the symbolization of language the experience is confirmed. Through language used towards artistic shaping, the agencies of the human psyche — thinking, feeling, intuiting and sensing — achieve a realization which explores a personal sense of being, and that sense in relation to others.

It is a movement by which, through the active shaping of language, one comes to know personally one's own world of experience and that of others. The advantage of literature is that through its processes of making, the aesthetic mode of apprehending reality attends to evidences of experience which are not bound to the exclusively intellectual, not to discursive forms of representing that reality. Through rhythm, image, symbol, contiguities and patterns of association, literature may work via the implicatory as well as the fully-expressed. In part this is so because words are themselves 'saturated with sense' (in Vygotsky's phrase) and 'can mean more than they say'. Thus in literature one may dwell within experience, using the medium of expression, the systems of language, as the means of researching what that significance may be.

A programme of literature in education would, therefore, concentrate upon artistic making as a prime experience for its students. In connecting with personal experience students would construe that experience, to arrive at a sense of meaning. In so doing their writings would become powerful means towards self-realization or self-actualization, thus serving a purpose central to educational development itself. In the process of this making, however, students would also be working within certain forms belonging to a range of genres. Their own writing would lead them into previous examples of form, and various modes of that presentational form — autobiography, short story, lyric poem, dialogue (drama or novel), myth and so on. The prime making of their own literary writings would thereby connect at all points with the study of literature, their readings within other texts. The study of those texts might also issue in literary writings which take further their explorations of those texts. Thus the programme would include additionally activities founded on creative re-making: the design of presentational modes and forms of writing and performance which would embody the student's responses to a text. Some of these activities might work through transposition, from one mode or form to another. The study of a story, for example, might prompt personal responses shaped as poetry, or collaborative improvisations which led to play-scripting. Such responses would thereby seek out further literary forms for their expression and presentation (q.v. 'Aesthetic Field'), rather than be confined simply to the essay.

In the practice of teaching founded on these principles of literary making and re-making, there would be three principal sets of creative activities, those aimed at:

connecting a student *to* a text;
enabling a student to explore *within* a text;
and encouraging reflections leading *from* a text.

Such procedures would not replace the practice of literary criticism — and the sharing of responses through talk would remain a key process of engagement. But expressive writing and presentation would supplement the activities of textual analysis and appraisal by working creatively within and through the forms and modes of the literary texts themselves. This approach to literature 'from the inside', as it were, enables recognitions to be formed which can by-pass objective scrutiny. The 'detached evaluative response' (D.W. Harding) to which traditional criticism is directed would proceed through personal response, the making and re-making of individual contexts of perception and knowing, towards more discursive understanding and judging. To work within the poetic mode, for example, would include an exploration of those associations of image which, to begin with, are personal — these connections then being re-located within the text to be tested, modified or rejected as they apply to the network of the poem itself. A poem would be explored, too, for its aural effects — the poem viewed as organized speech, not scanned as print symbol, so that one may hear what may be easily overlooked — just as the voices of dialogue, through expressive improvisation, would animate dimensions of meaning which print symbol alone cannot enact. Such ways of working with and from and to a text pay regard to the aesthetic means of responding, immediate perceptual apprehensions by which literary works move from sensuousness to sense.

Within these terms of reference literature unites the subjectivism of the reader with the objectivity of the text — an extension of self into the experience projected by participation in the making of meaning; thus replicating the processes of making which themselves produce the art.

For further reference see Peter Abbs, *English within the Arts* and 'The Aesthetic Field of English', in *A Is for Aesthetic*; also Edwin Webb, *Literature and Education: Encounter and Experience* and 'English as Aesthetic Initiative', in P. Abbs (Ed.), *Living Powers: The Arts in Education*.

EW

Mapping Some -isms: Expressionism, Impressionism, Naturalism, Realism, Surrealism

The study of 'movements' in art, has always seemed a pretty deadly business. No sooner has one put some dates around an -ism than precursors and 'late' representatives of the movement obtrude themselves to spoil the periodization. One pins down an archetypal, paradigm artist representative of the -ism only to become aware of how the other supposed 'representative' artists are actually very different.

Of course, certain -isms are easier than others, especially when a limitation by country and artistic medium is added. So, yes, there *is* a movement *in painting in France* which we can reasonably call 'Impressionism'. But even in this (paradigm) case the 'official' self-ascribed distinguishing feature — faithful reproduction of the play of light on the surface of visible objects — is accompanied, in the real historical movement, with a challenge to the hierarchy of subjects considered paintable, with landscape and still life being promoted and the 'history' painting consigned to oblivion. And that seriously complicates the picture.

Again, we know that most if not all -isms — certainly the important ones — focus beliefs, energies and visions which are recurrent across history and cultures. For example, romanticism is not (just) a movement in *English* poetry, best exemplified by Wordsworth — indeed that makes out romanticism to be a very small thing indeed — rather it is a recurrent, if often inhibited, way of relating to the world, oneself, artistic or cultural traditions and artistic media. Thus anyone is well on the way to romanticism who believes in the existence of a non-trivially specified human nature, conceived as essentially good or benign, but often cramped and perverted by society — by education and social relations. One has arrived at romanticism in art when one looks upon making art as a way of finding one's own nature and putting others in touch with theirs, even in adverse educational and social conditions.

If movements, -isms, are then thought of as high points, crystallizations of recurrent ways of being and believing, they can be appropriated pedagogically not as inert facts of history but as living entries into educational practice. Here it is helpful to map some -isms in terms of whether their emphasis is on the inner (subjective) or the outer (objective), and whether they are attached to how things appear or to how they are — in philosophical terms the distinction here is between appearance and essence.

For example, impressionist painting was certainly perceived as working from outer appearances. In opposition (German) expressionist painting of the period 1910–1933 is certainly a reaction to both the concern with the outer and with appearance. Expressionists thematise the *inner* and the *essence*, as is evident in their attitudes to the use of colour: 'Their crucial move was to associate colour not with visible reality (as had been the case with orthodox impressionism) but with the artist's affective responses . . . the painted forms may be viewed as externalized emotions: colour no longer designates optical facts, but psychic values' (Roger Cardinal, *Expressionism*, pp. 114–15). Earlier Eduard Munch wrote: 'I do not believe in the art which is not the compulsive result of Man's urge to open his heart.' In a teaching programme this contrast could be developed systematically, with students brought to an understanding of the different demands made by 'painting from the outer' and 'painting from the inner'. Looking at impressionist and expressionist works would be central to developing such understanding. Dance proves to be a medium which is peculiarly adapted to expressionist ideas, whereas the novel is not.

On a broader canvas, the objective attention to appearances places impressionism within the context of nineteenth century naturalism, to which twentieth century modernism (including expressionism) is (or was) a reaction. It is common to single out as defining modernism the concern with the inner, the subjective, at the expense of the outer, the objective. The 'stream of consciousness' novel, as in Virginia Woolf, would fit this schematism.

Before addressing the possibility of pedagogic practices in this area, it is as well to draw a further distinction between *naturalism* and *realism*, terms which the impressionists used interchangeably. However, there is a long philosophical tradition which wants to distinguish between appearances (which may be misleading) and essences (which, as it were, cannot be misleading), and this philosophical tradition has been annexed by literary critics — notably Gyorgy Lukacs — and converted into a distinction between naturalism and realism in art, especially in the novel. So it is said that Balzac and Thomas Mann are realist novelists, and Zola a naturalist (q.v. 'Politics and Art'). It might also be said that the impressionists are naturalists, whereas Cézanne (and pre-impressionists like Millet and Courbet) are realists (of rather different kinds).

The naturalist is impressed by, and pays attention to, the surface of things — whether it be the play of light on water or the effects of poverty on the daily detail of life. The realist is, in effect, a scientist who probes beneath appearances in search of essences — the causes of things, the heart of the matter. Between 1930 and the 1950s a great deal of ink was expended in left-wing debates on who was and who was not a realist, and whether modernist practices were compatible with realism — realism being taken to be a good thing. These debates can be followed in Lukacs' books and in the collection, *Aesthetics and Politics*. Often overlooked was the simple point that someone might be or try to be a realist but get things wrong (and is it better to have tried to be a realist than never tried at all? — see below on surrealism).

Pedagogically, the contrast between naturalism and realism could be explored in reading the novels singled out for attention in the debates mentioned above. In another domain one might explore the contrast through comparing photography and painting, for example, in the genre of portraiture. Can a photograph capture the essence of a personality — a character — in the way that a painted portrait can aspire to show a sitter's soul? Well, yes, a photographer can try to catch a subject at a moment of self-revelation: a moment at which appearance and essence coincide. The painter may use many such moments or no moments at all to represent a character made manifest in the painted image. In both cases the contrast between appearance and essence is being used, and value is being attached to the essence — or, less grandly, something other than the fleeting or passing moment. It would make a good practical exercise in photography to ask students to produce a photograph of someone which does *more* than show the fleeting moment, though one could still ask: What's wrong with the fleeting moment?

The energy which powers a search for essences can show up in *abstraction* and, more generally, *formalism*, both of which can be discussed in terms of the contrast between appearance and essence. After all, when one abstracts, one is generally trying to abstract what is (really) important, though there is also a kind of abstraction which is 'mere' formalism. The nature of mere formalism is nicely captured by Brecht when he writes, 'if someone makes a statement which is untrue — or irrelevant — merely because it rhymes, then he is a formalist' (quoted in *Aesthetics and Politics*, p. 72), though this dictum is tongue-in-cheek to the extent that it lets off the hook virtually all those who would have been denounced as formalists by Brecht's comrades. (Even in nonsense poetry, where mere rhyme appears to take over, it is often the case that the supposed mere rhyme sets up pathways of (humorous) association, and so contributes to the sense as much as to the nonsense of the poem.)

Many artists in the twentieth century have been impressed by Freud's theory of the mind — very much a theory which distinguishes essence (the unconscious) from the appearances (consciousness and self-consciousness) in which we are misled and mislead ourselves about our true nature. The surrealist movement sought consciously to realize a Freudian project within the arts, looking for techniques which would permit essence to break through the illusions of appearance. In this surrealists sought to act like realists, but realists of the inner rather than the outer world. The technique of automatic writing, which André Breton described as a 'true photography of thought', clearly illustrates the nature of the surrealist project. However, one has good reason to suppose that the technique did not and does not work to bring to light the reality of the unconscious. Rather, what it produces is material which illustrates what the automatic writer *thinks* is or ought to be in his or her unconscious, not what is actually there. Thus one may also understand Freud's devastating remark to Salvador Dali apropos of the latter's paintings, 'It is not your unconscious mind which interests me, but rather your conscious mind.' This is not to say a lesson devoted to automatic writing or to painting 'the surreal' would be wasted. The cautionary tale is simply that those committed to realism do not necessarily succeed in being realists. (On surrealism, see sympathetically, F. Alquié, *The Philosophy of Surrealism* and Michel Foucault, *This Is Not a Pipe* — this is on Magritte.)

In some ways the writers known as 'magical realists' (Gabriel Marquez, Angela Carter, Salman Rushdie) have been more successful as realists than the surrealists. In effect, they have combined a commitment to exploring concrete, historical circumstance with a fantastic moment in which the unpredictable escape of individual consciousness from reality is charted and made to deepen our understanding of how characters (real individuals) respond to circumstance.

The idea that one might find techniques to release an (inhibited) imagination is not peculiar to surrealism. Artists influenced by Jung rather than Freud have also been inclined to the notion of techniques for gaining access to the hidden, techniques which include meditation, exercises and free association. The painter Cecil Collins as a teacher of art made regular use of such techniques such as playing music and eliciting free dance movements. Elsewhere in this book classicism and romanticism, modernism and postmodernism, and formalism are considered. All of these -isms, and many others besides, can be approached in a pedagogic rather than historical spirit as exemplifying permanent possibilities of human engagement with the world. It is part of the task of the teacher of the arts to enable students to encounter and explore a full range of such possibilities.

Marxist Critical Theory

In Marxist theory, art and literature are treated as social and material practices which are produced by and within specific historical conditions. Crucial to Marxist thought is the question of class relations within production. Literature and art are not created in isolation by the individual writer or artist, as romantic theories of art might suggest, but are the product of the labour of a number of workers, for example, printer, stage hand, pupil painter and picture restorer; nor are they value-free. Marxists are concerned with the extent to which the received beliefs of groups and classes within society, especially those of the dominant class which controls the means of production, are reproduced in art and literature. This raises the central issue of art and ideology which is discussed below. The reception of works is also important. Why are some works suppressed or 'lost'? Why are some texts and works of art 'rediscovered' and some plays 'revived' in later periods, and what are the ideological reasons for the 'rediscovery' and 'revival'? Then there is the role of criticism. How does criticism mediate our reading of literature and the way we see art and drama?

Although discussions of art, literature and cultural practice can be found in the work of Marx and Engels, they did not formulate a coherent cultural theory; we need to turn to later Marxist theorists for an overview of Marxism and the arts. However, if we want to place the arts within a social and political structure, then we need to consider the concepts of base and superstructure formulated by Marx. The base can roughly be defined as the economic foundation on which the superstructure rests. Exactly what constitutes the superstructure is more difficult to decide. Marx refers to 'legal, political, religious, aesthetic or philosophic — in short, ideological — forms' (1859 'Preface' to *A Contribution to the Critique of Political Economy*), and Engels writes of 'political, juristic, philosophical theories, religious views and their further development into systems of dogma' (letter to Bloch, September 1890).

Art and literature, like other intellectual activity, would appear to belong to the superstructure which is separate from the base, although the relations between the two are important in theory and practice. The superstructure is in the realm of the ideological, but the term 'ideology' is open to more than one meaning. Generally, in Marxist criticism it refers to a system of beliefs of a given class or group; these beliefs are often illusory (false consciousness) and can be opposed to knowledge or science which is based on reality (see Raymond Williams, *Marxism and Literature* for a fuller discussion of ideology). Art and literature are related to the dominant modes of production in society and hence to the dominant ideology.

Marxism is often contrasted with formalism, the Russian formalists (q.v. 'Form, Formalism' and 'Structuralism') having been condemned by the Soviet social realists for their emphasis on literary language and structure and allegedly ahistorical approach to art. In Marxist aesthetics, as in the aesthetics of Hegel, form is determined historically by the content it has to convey, and changes in form occur when content itself changes. Form and content are, however, distinct, and the relations between them form a dialectic. Trotsky sees new forms developing when there is a 'collective psychological demand', but he also acknowledges that literature has a degree of autonomy (*Literature and Revolution*). Fragments of earlier forms may remain within a new form because literary tradition is available to the writer, but whether old forms can be reworked to create something which is new depends on whether there is an ideological change. If art reflects reality, then it reflects the base, not merely in the sense of the base as an object, but also in the sense of movements behind events. This, according to the critic Lukacs, was what the realist novel was able to do. Balzac is a great writer, although conservative in ideology, because he depicts the typical, and it is this which demonstrates the forces in society which will lead to change. Lukacs saw realism as a revolutionary form which was concerned with a totality, a total representation of reality, which would look at underlying causes and work towards reconciling contradictions. He opposed realism to naturalism, an inferior movement at the tail-end of realism which described only the surface of the everyday world and in its quasi-scientific descriptive method failed to consider historical forces (an example would be the novels of Zola). He also regarded modernism as inferior, seeing it as a formalist movement, which in showing private despair and alienation, cannot be dialectical (an example would be the novels of Kafka) (q.v. 'Modernism and Post-Modernism').

Following Lukacs, Lucien Goldmann has argued that the great artist presents a unified vision or world-view of the class or group to which she or he belongs. The historical conditions of a given group or class can be transferred to a work of literature through the mediation of their world-view. In his study of Pascal and Racine, *The Hidden God*, Goldmann shows the relationship between the *noblesse de robe* (a group at the French court who were unable to challenge the monarch's absolutism) and the movement of Jansenism and how the Jansenist vision was expressed in the plays of Racine. What is important in Goldmann's theory of genetic structuralism is the relationship between the historical conditions, the world-view and the literary work. An alternative to the concept of totality can be found in the work of Louis Althusser and Pierre Macherey. Althusser has argued that art has a specific relationship with ideology, just as it has a specific relationship with knowledge, but that that relationship is one of difference. In art we 'see' the ideology from which it is born and the reality to which it alludes, but there is a distancing from that ideology. We 'perceive' by an internal distance the ideology in which works are held, but we do not know it in the sense of having a full knowledge of its specificity or of the mechanisms which produce its aesthetic effect ('A Letter on Art in Reply to André Daspré', in *Lenin and Philosophy and Other Essays*).

In his essay on the little-known Italian painter Cremonini, Althusser argues that the animals and men created by Cremonini are distanced from the nature fixed for them by the dominant ideology because Cremonini searches for an origin which contains 'the true meaning of things'. Cremonini's representation of men in the form of inanimate objects such as stones and bones returns them to their primordial origins and, according to Althusser, produces an absence, not a presence. The deformed faces of Cremonini's human beings remove subjectivity, and the humanist function of art is absent ('Cremonini, Painter of the Abstract', in *Lenin and Philosophy*).

For Macherey, like Althusser, it is the absences or 'silences' in art which matter, not a unified concept such as totality. In his critique of reflection theory Macherey takes issue with Marx's analysis of how the epic form could have been developed in an undeveloped Greek society and of why we appreciate Greek art which was produced in material conditions so different from our own. Marx's answer that it is the memory of a past to which we shall never return does not grapple fully with the problem. Macherey asks a wider question: if art is absolutely determined by its material conditions, then what can be 'left' of it? Macherey's reply is that works of art are processes not objects. The *Iliad* that we know is not the *Iliad* of the Greeks because it was not a book or a myth for the Greeks in the way it is for us. In reproducing the work in new material conditions, we give it a new meaning and significance. Macherey also argues that literary works are incomplete and incoherent and contain conflicting and contradictory meanings. The writer gives shape to what Macherey calls 'illusion' through form. The form of art — its 'fictionality' — is what allows the writer to transform illusion or ideology by distancing it from the work of art and revealing its limitations through the contradictions it expresses (see *A Theory of Literary Production* and 'Problems of Reflection', in Francis Barker, *et al.*, *Literature, Society and the Sociology of Literature*).

Renée Balibar has provided an example of how the reproduction of a work in a different form can give it a new significance. She shows how the school as institution mediates literature in her study of the way in which George Sand's novel, *The Devil's Pool*, has been adapted for use in French primary schools. Balibar argues that the democratization of linguistic practices which occurred in France at the time of the Revolution has been lost because of the established practices of the education system. An adapted and simplified course is given to primary school children which separates their study of the French language from that offered to children in secondary schools, where the historical development and complexity of the language is studied. When texts such as *The Devil's Pool* are read in school in an abbreviated form as 'model texts', students are denied access to the revolutionary potential of the language and are left in a position of linguistic and social subordination which allows the reproduction of existing social relations ('An Example of Literary Work in France: George Sand's *La Mare au Diable/The Devil's Pool* of 1846', in Francis Barker *at el.*, *1848: The Sociology of Literature*).

If we move away from the idea of art as product and see it, in the words of Raymond Williams, as a 'formative process within a specific present' (*Marxism and Literature*), then there may be a tension or displacement between practical experience and consciousness and formal meanings and systems. Literature and art cannot be fixed categories as they are open to new meanings. It is then possible for alternative cultural practices which challenge the dominant ideology to emerge. However, what is not clear is where these practices stand in relation to hegemony, Gramsci's term for the whole of the lived social process in which one group or class exercises control over another. In a situation where there are dominant and subordinate cultures and languages, is it possible for oppositional practices to remain outside the hegemonic and have an independent existence, or is it inevitable that they will be neutralized or incorporated? This unresolved debate has implications for anti-racism, women's and gay liberation.

Ernst Fischer maintains that art challenges ideology by finding new areas of reality through making visible what had previously been hidden (*The Necessity of Art*), but a revolutionary practice goes beyond this and attempts to alter the social relations between author or producer and audience. These altered relations are made apparent in the work of Walter Benjamin and Bertolt Brecht. For Benjamin it is the new or 'mechanical' forms of art, for example, photography, film, records, which create new social relations between producer and spectator as they reduce the authority or 'aura' of a work of art by removing it from tradition (q.v. 'Originals, Copies, Performances and Reproductions'). In a film the actor cannot relate to the audience in the way that he or she can on stage as the camera continuously changes its position and the editor selects from what remains of the performance. The actor is left in an estranged position, but the audience takes the position of the camera and assumes the role of critic in a more participatory role than in conventional forms of art.

The movement away from the known and the fragmentary distanced form of the new result in a sense of shock which leads to the disintegration of the 'aura' and a questioning, critical response on the part of the spectator ('The Work of Art in the Age of Mechanical Reproduction', in Benjamin's *Illuminations*). Benjamin believed that a similar effect was achieved in Brecht's epic theatre (q.v. 'Alienation Effect'). Through the use of montage, song, posters and other distancing or alienating techniques, Brecht required the audience to think about what was being represented on the stage in contrast to their passive reception of the bourgeois theatre of illusion. The interrupted actions of epic theatre allowed the audience to see that what was presented could be different, that change was a possibility (see Benjamin's *Understanding Brecht*). Latin American Third Cinema, consciously or not, appears to have adopted this theory.

Terry Eagleton has pointed to the emphasis on the body in Benjamin's concept of the *flâneur* in his study of Baudelaire and in Brecht's emphasis on gesture and laughter in epic theatre. He links this to the work of the Russian critic Mikhail Bakhtin (*Walter Benjamin or Towards a Revolutionary Criticism*).

Bakhtin, in *Rabelais and His World*, describes how medieval carnival provided an alternative and separate ideology from that of the Christian Church, whose practices it inverted. In *Gargantua and Pantagruel* Rabelais brought the irreverent laughter of folk humour into contact with the dominant ideology by formalizing it in literature. By using bodily images of defecation, sexuality and eating in an unfamiliar context, he 'made strange' or defamiliarized (in formalist terms) medieval ideology and made way for its replacement by a new ideology, that of Renaissance humanism. Clearly there were external developments which determined the replacement of the ideology of the Middle Ages, for example, the breakdown of feudalism, the diminishing power of the Pope, the change from Latin to the vernacular and the development of printing, but Rabelais' work does more than reflect material contradictions; it suggests that a new practice of writing can be one of the historical determinants which lead to a change of ideology. Bakhtin's study of Rabelais also considers the later reception of Rabelais' work and its marginalization in the seventeenth and eighteenth centuries as a comic work (see Tony Bennett, *Formalism and Marxism*).

Ironically, Bakhtin was considered a Marxist when he wrote under the name of Valentin Volosinov and a formalist when he wrote as Bakhtin. There is now a renewed interest in Bakhtin's work, in the literary representation of the body, in the dialogic principle and in the concepts of carnival and *heteroglossia* (the existence of different languages and codes in the same work) as these concepts have been used to energize feminist critical theory (q.v.) and post-colonial discourse theory. Volosinov's work on language has been used by Hazel Carby in her critique of multiculturalism (*Multicultural Fictions*) (q.v. 'Death of the Author').

The strength of Marxist critical theory lies in its insistence on the social and ideological context in which art is made. Its weakness lies in its tendency to ignore the nature of the creative process and the specific dynamic or aesthetic experience which would appear to have its own autonomy and the power, at times, to transcend the dominant values of any period; see Herbert Marcuse's *The Aesthetic Dimension*. For a good introduction to Marxist critical theory see Raymond Williams' *Marxism and Literature*.

PD

Meaning (q.v. 'Interpretation',
'Intention and Convention', 'Text and Context')

Only a sadistic teacher would assign a student the task of writing a 1000-word essay with the title 'Meaning'. Only a masochist assigns the task to himself.

The word 'meaning' and its cognates occur in a diversity of contexts. Central debates in the theory of interpretation and in criticism itself have focused on whether to give a statement of meaning is to give 1) *the artist's intended meaning* or to give 2) *the meaning of the text* (or its analogue in other art forms). This has sometimes missed the possibility of giving 3) *the meaning of the text as produced by this artist on this occasion.*

In everyday situations of conversation we might similarly distinguish 1) *speaker's meaning*, 2) *sentence meaning* and 3) *utterance meaning*. So I utter the words, 'This is a game of tin soldiers!', intending thereby to express my disgust with or disdain for the activity referred to by 'This': speaker's meaning is here given by citing intention and describing the action performed by the utterance of such words. Sentence meaning is given by giving the meanings of the words which comprise the sentence uttered: the sentence has a literal meaning in which it can be used to refer to and describe what someone is doing when they play with certain scale-models of soldiers, made out of tin. But as uttered on this occasion, the sentence does not have its literal meaning. It is used metaphorically: I indicate my disdain for an activity by likening it to a childish activity. So the utterance meaning is not the literal sentence meaning, though it might incorporate that meaning or incorporate a reference to it.

None of this, unfortunately, is uncontroversial. For example, it is disputed whether there is something which can be called 'sentence meaning', derived by invoking the rules of an independent and context-free system of meaning. Stanley Fish denies there is any such system (*Is There a Text in This Class?*, p. 321), and even those sympathetic to the idea find it difficult to give an account which is actually context-free. Thus, in giving the (literal) meaning of 'The cat sat on the mat', one will make such background assumptions as that the laws of gravity obtain so that a cat sits on (top of) a

106

mat, not on the underside of a mat floating in mid-air. That there is a problem might be indicated by asking for the literal meaning of the sentence, 'The fly sat on the ceiling.' Does this mean that the fly sits on the underside of a ceiling suspended in the normal way, or on the top side of a ceiling which has (e.g.) fallen down and turned over in the process? (For discussion of such problems see John Searle, 'Literal Meaning'.)

Likewise controversial are both the very idea of speaker's meaning and, relevant to the arts, the possibility of giving any content to the idea. Thus it is not only queried whether we can (ever) know what a (dead) artist's meaning was, but also doubted whether there is any sense to 'artist's meaning'/'speaker's meaning' which is not derivative from what the artist produces or what the speaker says. For we cannot play Humpty Dumpty with words and make them mean what we wish. Of course, I may utter, 'This is a game of tin soldiers!' as a password, intending thereby (say) to signal my co-membership of an organization. But this coded utterance is a password not because that is how the *speaker* means it, but because the speaker is party to a *convention* to signal co-membership by means of these words (cf. 'Intention and Convention'): intention goes to work through what is already convention, and we discover intention only in and through conventions of meaning. In other words our best or only evidence for what the speaker/artist meant is what the speaker/artist did: we do not have to fill empty marks on a page with artist's meaning; artist's meaning is in the already full marks on the page (or the canvas).

But if we are cautious about the very idea of sentence meanings, we might also be cautious about the idea of 'the meaning of the text', as if that existed independently of any context (q.v. 'Text and Context'). Rather, just as we have the notion of what someone meant by saying, 'This is a game of tin soldiers!' on a certain occasion (what I called 'utterance meaning'), so we might make more use of the sense contained in such expressions as 'Shakespeare's text' and 'Cézanne's painting'. The sense contained here is that the sentences on the page are not just any old text, from any time or place, but that they are sentences produced by *Shakespeare*, and that that fact is a central part of the context to which reference has to be made to determine their (occasion) meaning. This is very clear in the case of irony, as E.D. Hirsch points out. Two speakers can utter the same words, one ironically, and one not. In terms of the words nothing alters — but the *meaning* alters. What we are normally interested in is not the invariant (sentence) meaning, but the variant (occasion) meaning; and what makes the difference in the meaning is the speaker or artist and what they are doing with the words they utter: *Swift's* text is ironic; Swift's *text* is not.

One implication of this idea is worth bringing out: contrary to some notions often found in stylistics, *meaning* cannot be inferred from *form* (alone). Satire, irony, metaphor even may not be transparent in the words themselves, and, indeed, often are not. They have to be inferred from the words with the help of contextual information. Central to this contextual information is knowledge of whose words they are — which is a shorthand way of referring to the purpose, time and place of 'utterance' of the words.

Medium

'The medium is the message', says a well-known slogan of Marshall McLuhan, applied especially to television, our response to which is inseparable from its existence as part of the furniture of the ordinary domestic living room.

In the arts our beliefs or knowledge about the medium in which someone is working affect our response, entirely appropriately and often in ways intended by the artist. The following provide examples.

1   A sculptor chooses to work with a particularly difficult stone, say granite. Our knowledge or beliefs about the stone's resistance to human shaping affect our sense of what the artist is about, what the work is about. In virtue of the knowledge or beliefs the artist can expect us to hold, he or she can use the stone *itself* as an expressive medium/a medium of expression.

2   A composer writes notes for a singer, knowing that they are at or near the limits of the human voice, and knowing that we are likely to know. Mozart does this in writing 'Der Hölle Rache kocht in meinem Herzen' for the Queen of the Night in *The Magic Flute*. Hearing this sung live, we are (if we know the piece) *excited* as we anticipate the difficult feat the singer is about to attempt, and *exhilarated* if she succeeds in pulling it off — feelings just like these we might have watching a high-wire act at the circus. In both cases applause is an appropriate response. But it would not be appropriate if the 'singer' were merely ventriloquizing to an electronic voice which could produce the high notes effortlessly without risk of failure.

Some would say that this response to the exploitation of the human voice 'for effect' is essentially non-aesthetic. If so, there are many non-aesthetic or non-artistic elements in classical music. Consider: 'the energy and brilliance of a fast violin or piano passage derives not merely from the absolute speed of the music, but from the fact it is fast *for that particular medium*. In electronic music different pitches can succeed one another at any frequency up to and including that at which they are no longer separately distinguishable. Because of this it is difficult to make electronic music *sound* fast' (Walton, 1970, p. 250) — one might add at the end, 'to anyone who knows how electronic music is produced.'

3 It is a commonplace of all writings on photography that our response to photographs is conditioned or determined by our beliefs or knowledge about the way in which photographs are produced, as the product of a causal-mechanical process in which an image is produced as the effect of light on a light-sensitive medium (coated glass or paper). Reflection on this fact has often led to the conclusion that photography is a non-artistic medium, and our responses to photographs non-aesthetic — at least that photography as a medium is *resistant* to being used and responded to artistically or aesthetically (q.v. 'Photography').

These three examples not only illustrate how our understanding of the artist's medium enters into our response to a work, but also they are examples of the interaction between *knowledge or belief* and *response*. In the examples, the knowledge and belief are not readily dismissable as extraneous, irrelevant or improper. For example, in the case of the sculptor, not knowing the character of the stone with which he or she is working could result in an impaired or incorrect response or understanding of the work. The work is not merely 'in stone', but in a stone of a particular sort, characterizable not only by its visible or tactile properties (grey, rough, ...) but by its resistance to human shaping. Since we cannot there and then seek to shape the stone (as we can look at and probably touch it), then its malleability is something we have to *know* about. Our senses are not enough to provide an adequate response to or understanding of the particular piece of sculpture imagined.

In traditional or classical aesthetics it was a main preoccupation to consider what could or could not be done, or what ought or ought not to be attempted, using a particular medium, once the character of that medium was properly understood. Thus to characterize painting as making use of a *spatial* medium, and music and/or poetry as a *temporal* art, creates a framework for the discussion of such issues as whether painting can or should represent action (which necessarily occurs in time), and this in turn provides the space for such concepts as the pregnant moment (q.v. 'Space and Time, Arts of'; and Lessing's *Laocöon* (1766)).

Mimesis and Katharsis

My readers, like me, are likely to have little Latin and less Greek, but enough general education to know that many of the concepts in which we describe and appraise works of art come to us, ultimately, from Ancient Greece, from Plato and Aristotle. So it is, for example, with the place given to genre concepts (epic, tragedy, comedy, lyric, . . .) in aesthetics and criticism, and to normative concepts of artistic rightness (e.g. unity of time, place and action in drama). So it is also, and evident in the words themselves, with *katharsis* (or catharsis) and *mimesis*.

For Plato and Aristotle and for the traditions of classical or neo–classical criticism later created from their work, works of art are representations of an actual or possible world, and as representation are mimetic of it. Sometimes but by no means always 'mimesis' does have the sense of 'illusion' and of creating an illusion, as in trompe l'oeil painting, a genre which exercises a considerable fascination for Greek authors. In contrast, there is little interest shown by the Greek philosophers and critics in those genres, like lyric poetry, where it is less the relation of work to (possible or actual) world than of work to artist which is central. It is only in romanticism that the lyric 'I' is privileged (q.v. 'Classicism and Romanticism'). Aristotle indeed, in the *Poetics*, takes the view that poets should not speak in their own voice, but should represent or show others speaking or acting, and this is because he thinks a first-person use of language can only be one which asks us to evaluate it in terms of truth (as an assertoric use of language) whereas artistic mimesis is not assertoric. It shows fictional possibilities; it does not make claims to truth. (This idea appears in contemporary aesthetics, notably in work on the logical status of fictional statements. See, for example, Roman Ingarden's *The Literary Work of Art* and Käte Hamburger's *The Logic of Literature*. Dostoyevsky is a stock example of a novelist who always shows and never speaks in his own voice.)

In stressing fictionality, Aristotle is reacting against Plato's assumption that the poet is a truth-teller who tells lies, and hence is to be condemned and banished from the ideal republic. This is the famous theme of Book 10 of Plato's *Republic*. For Plato, poetic mimesis does indeed capture the apearance of things — this is the poet's skill — but these appearances may render persons and actions attractive and acceptable which are ethically repugnant. Hence they are dangerous and ought to be controlled or proscribed. This is doubly so because the encounter with poetry takes place in the context of performance (oral recitation or dramatic enactment), the theatrical qualities of which may effect a bypass of the audience's understanding and make direct connection with the audience's (baser) feelings. A painter's trompe l'oeil effects are of relatively trivial ethical concern; the poet's ability to mislead the heart is, to Plato, of enormous ethical moment since it threatens the role and effectiveness of a properly philosophical education aimed at an understanding of reality, the forms manifest in the appearances of life.

Consider, notably, that tragedy is a genre which represents extremes of human suffering and invites us somehow to accept and take pleasure in them. In response to this, says G.R.F. Ferrari, 'Plato banishes tragedy from the stage for fear that it will prevent us coping with the drama of life' ('Plato and Poetry', p. 141). Aristotle's *Poetics* may be read in large part as an attempt to find a positive conception of tragedy and of our response to it. One result is a strongly normative conception of how tragedy ought to be constructed, which eventually results in neo-classical ideas of unity of time, place and action. Another result is an influential, if obscure, conception of katharsis.

A well-constructed tragedy shows individuals better than ourselves, but not so different that we cannot identify with them in the unmerited afflictions which overcome them. We experience sympathetic pity for their suffering, and a kind of terror arising from the thought or recognition that such suffering could befall us ('there but for Fortune'). The experience of pity and fear is the katharsis effected by the play. Katharsis is not pure emotional release, still less discharge of pathological emotions — though this is how the concept tended to be understood in the nineteenth century (for example, by Nietzsche) — rather it is, according to Stephen Halliwell, 'a powerful emotional experience which not only gives our natural feelings of pity and fear full play, but does so in a way which conduces to their rightful functioning as part of our understanding of, and response to, events in the human world' (*The Poetics of Aristotle*, p. 90).

Mimesis and katharsis are connected in that it is the mimetic (representational) qualities of the well-made play which allow the identifications and elicit the emotions of the katharsis. The normative requirements of unity (of time, place and action) are consequences of the idea of a mimesis which aims to represent a possible reality. Unity is made, not found, and mimesis should not be equated with any kind of 'slice of life' naturalism. Nor is the idea of mimesis of a possible reality the idea of verisimilitude or *vraisemblance* insofar as these are concepts of the representation of the typical rather than of the simply possible. Nonetheless, there is a clear line of intellectual descent from Aristotle to classical and neo-classical norms for tragedy and for the theatre more generally.

In the present century these norms were contested, notably by Brecht, who connects them explicitly to Aristotle. Thus early in Brecht's *Messingkauf Dialogues* (written 1939–1942) we find the Dramaturg summarizing and endorsing the conception of tragedy he thinks is found in Aristotle's *Poetics*:

He defines tragedy as an imitative representation of a self-contained morally serious action of such-and-such duration; in heightened speech whose different varieties are employed separately distributed among different parts; not narrated but performed by the persons taking part in it; stimulating pity and terror, and thereby bringing about the purging [katharsis] of those same moods. In other words, it's a matter of imitating your events from life, and the imitations are supposed to have specific effects on the soul. Since Aristotle wrote that, the theatre has gone through many transformations, but not on this point. One can only conclude that if it changed in this respect it would no longer be theatre. (p. 16)

Brecht challenges this Aristotelian conception of theatre in a way which might reasonably be described as quasi-Platonist. At one level he takes issue with the Aristotelian emphasis on unity of time, place and action, preferring the epic (episodic) mode to the tragic privileged by Aristotle. For example, Brecht's *Life of Galileo* (written in 1938) has fifteen scenes representing events spread over more than thirty years in a variety of settings, some of them precisely located temporally, others not. Brecht says that 'the *Life of Galileo* is not a tragedy' (p. 117), yet it is not optimistic with respect to Galileo (scene 14), and the 'happy ending' (scene 15) is not debarred by Greek rules of tragedy (Halliwell, *op. cit.*, p. 138). It is reasonable to compare *Galileo* with a 'classical' tragedy. The obvious point then is that though the play is not held together, unified, by time, place or — in any obvious sense — action, it is held together by the character of Galileo whose *Life* the play, episodically, represents, and whose life could in principle and may in practice inspire pity and terror.

However, as everyone knows, Brecht does not value positively the empathy created in Aristotelian theatre as the precondition of katharsis. Brecht may be wrong to think that such empathy is importantly uncritical and merely emotional. Interpreting Aristotle, for example, Stephen Halliwell writes that for Aristotle, 'Pity and fear presuppose and involve ... a fundamental sympathy for the tragic agents, and a sympathy which is not purely spontaneous or unreflective, but one which engages us imaginatively in understanding the causal nexus of the tragedy' (p. 125). Nonetheless, it is understandable that Brecht took the view he did, since important strands in nineteenth century German thinking about theatre — including Wagner's avowedly Greek-inspired *Gesamtkunstwerk* — did emphasize the spontaneous, unreflective character of empathy and empathetic response. Brecht wants to break with this in order to introduce thinking into the theatre, to make the audience think. So in *The Messingkauf Dialogues* (First Appendix) he summarizes the idea of a theatre where 'empathy would lose its dominant role' (p. 102), a goal to be achieved by the use of what Brecht calls the *Verfremdungseffekt* — the Alienation (A) or Estrangement effect. This 'consists in the reproduction of real-life incidents on the stage in such a way as to underline their causality and bring it to the spectator's attention. This type of art also generates emotions; such performances facilitate the mastering of reality; and this it is that moves the spectator. The A-effect is an ancient artistic technique; it is known from classical comedy, certain branches of popular art [e.g. *commedia dell' arte*] and the practices of the Asiatic [e.g. Noh and Kabuki] theatre, (p. 102) (q.v. 'Alienation Effect').

Plato would have approved of the idea of 'mastering reality', in contrast to the idea of wallowing in illusion, and he would have understood Brecht's reasons for reviving the chorus, an aspect of Greek theatre which Aristotle ignores but both Plato and Brecht emphasize.

Modernism and Post-Modernism

The term 'modernism' is far from easy to define for it has been used to refer to a whole variety of movements which would often seem to have little more in common than that they have taken place in the twentieth century. The now highly fashionable word 'post-modernism' in a matter of a few years has come to share a similar fate, many diverse movements contending to hijack the word and to wear it as their own distinctive badge. Yet both concepts can be used to define fairly accurately a certain orientation towards experience most tangibly expressed and codified in the arts and crafts, and in particular in architecture. The shift from modernism around 1980 to post-modernism, beneath all the paraphernalia of fashion and trendiness, does mark a profound shift in sensibility which this entry will explore and try to formulate.

A clue to the understanding of modernism is provided by the word itself. It derives from the Latin *modo* meaning literally 'just now' and has obvious links with such related concepts as modernity, modernization, modish, *à la mode*. The desire to be fully contemporary without reference to the cultural past, and particularly the immediate past — the desire to be *just now* and fully of the moment — would seem to constitute the central commitment of most modernists. The philosopher Anthony O'Hear has written:

> If anything is characteristic of modernism, in whatever field you look, it is the assertion of the validity of the present experience or thought of the individual. Present experience is a fundamental given: something historically pristine, against which all that is past is to be judged, and from which one can move on to create a future free from what will no doubt be regarded as the dross of history. (*Salisbury Review*, July 1987, p. 4)

O'Hear is right to point to the Modernist's belief in the primacy of the present experience (and in this modernism was at one with educational progressivism, the two meeting in the influential work of Herbert Read), yet, as it will be argued here, there is a strong link between modernism and the historical process as it was formulated by both Hegel and Marx in the nineteenth century. By a curious paradox, deriving from a progressive view of historical development, the ahistoricity of much modernism is based on a distinctive historical sense of its own need. Above all, the various avant-gardes claimed to be serving 'the spirit of the time' (Hegel's term) as it moved into a necessary future.

This insistence on a contemporaneity without reference to the past can be found in most of the manifestos and polemical declarations of the self-conscious modernists. Marinetti, for example, directing the futurists (a revealing title) wrote in 1919: 'but we will hear no more about the past we young strong Futurists'; Walter Gropius, founding father of the Bauhaus, that seminal centre of visual modernism in design and mass production, urged his students to 'start from zero'; while Ezra Pound, the indefatigable pioneer of new forms of poetic formulation, was emphatic about the need 'to make it new'.

The insistence on iconoclastic originality, on continuous artistic experimentation, on the systematic disruption of the received codes created in the first flowering of modernism an extraordinary vitality and arresting urgency. It gave birth to a series of memorable works: the dances of Isadora Duncan (between 1900 and 1920), Picasso's *Les Demoiselles d'Avignon* (1907), Matisse's *Dance* (1910), Stravinsky's *The Rite of Spring* (first performed in 1913, choreographed by Nijinsky and put on by Diaghilev's Russian Ballet Company), James Joyce's *Ulysses* (1922), T.S. Eliot's *The Waste Land* (also 1922), Kafka's *The Castle* (1926), then Virginia Woolf's *To the Lighthouse* (1927) and *The Waves* (1931). At the heart of much of this urgent and disturbing art was a crucial re-evaluation of the function of language in the arts, which was, in turn, a further extension of romanticism (q.v. 'Classicism and Romanticism'). Artistic language was no longer seen as a received tool for a conventional and therefore confirming mimesis (q.v.), but, rather, as a dynamic agent able through its own creative powers to explore and open up unconscious levels of reality and, therefore, human possibility, from nightmare unreality to visionary perception. The surrealist movement encompassed both possibilities — possibilities which were not open to the formal and collective codes of classicism (q.v. 'Mapping Some -isms').

The imperative to keep it new meant that one movement was destined to follow another, often with extraordinary rapidity. This was particularly true of the visual arts whose history provides us with the most unambiguous case of modernism. Much of the restless desire to experiment, to leap frenetically from one style to another, can be discerned in the prolific work of one great artist alone, namely in the eclectic opus of Picasso; but it can be detected with little effort across the span of the century in the sudden flowering and quick fading of a plethora of schools, manifestoes, movements. In the two decades between the two world wars it gave birth to Dadaism, Fauvism, cubism, futurism, constructivism, vorticism, to name only some of the more prominent movements. As the century moved on, so the iconoclastic spirit became more frenetic and self-conscious. The desire for revolution remained, but artistically and culturally there was less and less to rebel against. The last movement, as it were, had done it all before.

The notion of perpetual revolution in the arts must lead, inexorably, to exhaustion. This is the story of modernism. It depleted itself; it systematically destroyed its resources and ended impoverished and infertile. As time passed, it became not an authentic individual task but an international habit of mind, a kind of mind-set, a series of conventions against conventions, a tradition against traditions. As early as 1930 the American poet Hart Crane was telling his contemporaries that 'revolution as an all-engrossing programme' was over, calling poetry an architectural art 'based not on Evolution or the idea of progress, but on the articulation of contemporary human consciousness *sub specie aeternitatis*' and invoking in his argument Dante's *Commedia* and Milton's *Paradise Lost*. By the 1960s some of the more alert modernists were aware of a kind of exhaustion. The poet Octavio Paz, for example, declared that the 'avant-garde of 1967 repeats the deeds and gestures of those of 1917. We are experiencing the end of the idea of modern art.' If the systematic disruption of the received artistic codes engendered, in the first instant, a remarkable act of aesthetic exploration and vitality, it yet led, by a kind of inevitable self-depleting logic, to a state of anaesthetic exhaustion and a thin state of cultural extremity. Deprived of any tradition for the best part of five decades, the dominant work in the visual arts became either purely formal or dependent on what Peter Fuller called 'the anaesthetic practices of the mega-visual tradition' (photographic montage, etc.) or gave itself up to exhibitionistic antics amorphously named 'happenings'. For a critical documentation of these 'movements' see Giles Auty's *The Art of Deception* (1977). Fashion, it has been proposed, is the mother of death; Auty demonstrates the truth of the proposition in relationship to the last two decades of visual modernism. It is also pertinent to notice that many of the great achievements of modernism formed, as it were, symbolic cul-de-sacs, rather than bridges. No one was able to follow with any success the very peculiar achievement of T.S. Eliot's *The Waste Land*, Joyce's *Finnegan's Wake* or the extreme atonal music of Schoenberg, not to mention the more questionable examples of Duchamp's *Urinal* or John Cage's *4'33"* or whatever was the first example of autodestruct 'art'. Their perverse extremity precluded any worthwhile emulation. They represented, in quite different ways, ends: culminations, denials, implosions.

If this highly schematic account of modernism has any virtue, it would suggest that it is necessary to differentiate between two stages of modernism: its first highly creative substantive phase (from, say, 1900 to 1940), followed by its second decadent and rhetorical phase (from, say, 1940 to 1980). If the First World War marks the dramatic development of the first phase (it is interesting that in November 1914 the poet Rilke wrote: 'the past is left behind, the future hesitates, the present is without foundation'), then the Second World War marks its demise and the emergence of the formulaic phase. The case for such division has been argued by Frank Kermode who in Bernard Bergonzi's *Innovations* (1986) proposed two terms: 'paleo-modernism' for the first phase and 'neo-modernism' for the second. A similar division was suggested in *Living Powers* (1987), where the term 'late modernism' was used to designate the second phase.

Doubtless, we are still too close to modernism to define with objectivity its achievements or the reasons for its disintegration as *the* international twentieth century movement in the arts. This entry is deliberately polemical and far from definitive, if any account of such a labile and multifaceted movement can ever be definitive. Yet we need to ask, at least, two further questions. Why did modernism collapse around 1980? And what is the phenomenon of post-modernism which has claimed to take its place as the dominant cultural orientation in our own time?

It can be argued that international modernism had to collapse because of its own tenets; the seeds of its own destruction lay within the womb of its own assumptions. It is not the place here to locate all those assumptions. In an earlier volume in the series they were named as historicism, functionalism, scientism and literalism (see *Living Powers*, pp. 22–31). To those fallacies others could be added; for example, conceptualism and 'relevantism' — to coin a word for that position which adopts an absolute reliance on the contemporary need to justify or cancel any cultural proposal. However, the key fallacy, from which most of the others derive, is the fallacy of historicism and has been defined by Karl Popper in *The Poverty of Historicism* (1957).

What is meant by historicism in relationship to the modernist movement in the arts? It entails an extrapolation of categories in which dubious historical terms are transferred into aesthetic terms and seen to justify various artistic movements and specific forms of art. The fallacy can be understood best by taking some examples. Schoffer, a self-consciously modernist painter, has claimed:

Contemporary painting and sculpture don't interest me. Can you imagine anyone nowadays building a factory for the construction of horse-drawn carriages? Of course not! Well it's the same with art: brushes were all right for painting and mallets for sculpture between the fourteenth and seventeenth centuries. (quoted in Parmelin 1977, p. 61)

The argument depends upon a developmental view of history which is used to validate or invalidate and generally determine the form of artistic work. That is precisely the fallacy of historicism. The supposed meaning of history is invoked to justify or disown values relating to the aesthetic and ethical domain. Here are two further recent examples taken from the columns of *The Independent*:

In literature we have gone beyond Dickens and Tennyson, and in medicine and nursing beyond Joseph Lister and Florence Nightingale. Why should architecture alone among the arts and sciences turn its back upon innovation and change? (William Rodgers, 7 September 1989)

We live in a post-Freudian age, the nuclear age.... Modern Society must and should support the art of its time; and that means supporting experiment and change. Where would medicine or technology be without research? After all, we use jet aeroplanes, body scanners and fax machines, not stage coaches, leeches and pigeons. (Leslie Waddington, 21 January 1989)

In both quotations it is categorically and uncritically assumed that the artist has to be at the service of an inevitable historical development which both parallels and can be unambiguously measured by reference to stated technological advances. But it is fatuous to suggest that an author can go 'beyond Dickens' in the same way that medicine can be improved. Because it is modern, Centre Point is not aesthetically superior to the Parthenon; the fact that we now use body-scanners and fax machines tells us absolutely nothing about what should be the content or style of any of our art forms.

Yet modernism has relied heavily on this conception of historical advance. The very notion of the avant-garde — one of the key terms in the lexicon of the international modernist movement — entails the idea of being at the vanguard of the historical process and of serving 'the spirit of the age'. This preoccupation with progressive time is deep in Western culture, but in the case of modernism it is derived largely from Hegel (1770–1831) and his subverting disciple Marx (1818–1882). Debunking Hegel and his influence on art critics and art movements, Ernst Gombrich has described modernist artists as the 'business managers of the world spirit', having 'to be aware of the necessary next step to be taken....They represent, as it were, the next species which had already been prefigured internally.' The same criticism can be made even more cogently concerning the influence of Karl Marx, who saw the role of the intellectual and artist as the quickening agent of the revolution, which was nonetheless historically determined by the iron laws of the historical process. The unclouded historic optimism of both Hegel and Marx fed the international modernist movement with a sense of power and inevitability — for who, in the age of withering religious faith, could possibly set themselves against the meaning of history? To be modern was to be on the crest of historic time; the task was to be loyal to the moment, to the 'just now' of imminent historic realization of 'the world spirit' (Hegel, in fact, thought history had ended in his own time, in 1806 to be precise) or the triumph of the proletariat and the subsequent withering away of the state.

The international disintegration of communism in the last few years can be seen in this light, as the final withering of the modernist esprit. History bears no predetermined meaning, and even if it did, it carries no absolute right to determine ethical or aesthetic principles. One can, for example, paint beautifully *against* 'the spirit of the age' — as our best British painters have done during the whole course of the modernist age (think of Paul Nash, John Piper, David Bomberg, Cecil Collins). With this realization, dramatically confirmed by the failure of Marxism as the science of history, we find ourselves now laying the spectre of late modernism and entering, it would seem, the emerging ground of post-modernism; for post-modernism is a movement which consciously opens itself to the past and to the inexpungable plurality of things and their expression as metaphor and ornament in our diverse human lives and plural cultures. It rejects any utopian sense of the future and advocates a kind of self-conscious solidarity with the past and the public memories and associations it carries. In a sense post-modernism negates modernism by reversing that arrow of time. It is concerned to make playful connections with the whole of the cultural continuum and has no faith in geometrical visions or singular necessities. It tends to be eclectic rather than uniform; conservationist rather than revolutionary; conciliatory (even wanting to include its opponent through quotation) rather than iconoclastic.

Post-modernism as a movement is most dramatically clear in the realm of architecture. It is a spirited reaction against the international functionalism which through the various powerful exponents of modernism, from Le Corbusier to Nikolaus Pevsner, had been widely seen as the necessary architecture of all advancing industrial and technological societies. The post-modernist architects advocated against the monolithic style of rectangles and glass a self-conscious and ironic return to the classical traditions. As early as 1966 Robert Venturi in *Complexity and Contradiction in Architecture* had urged a return to historical sources, proclaimed the values of elaboration, ambiguity and irony, and demanded an inclusive recognition of all previous cultural manifestations, both 'high' and demotic. This case was developed by Charles Jencks in a stream of books, pamphlets and articles. According to Jencks, no 'present-tense architecture' was possible for there can be 'no escape from the historicity of language'. In essential agreement, J. Mordaunt Crook (1987) has written in relationship to the reality of post-modernist architecture: 'the quest for objectivity in design has been very largely abandoned. We have had to re-learn what the nineteenth century painfully discovered: architecture begins where function ends' (p. 270). Such architecture, given the heterogeneity of beliefs and communities, has for all post-modernists to be eclectic in character. From this perspective post-modernism could be cogently represented as a self-conscious cultural eclecticism.

The post-modernist spirit, as manifested most visibly in contemporary architecture (in pitched roofs, in decorative motifs, in the use of local materials, in the affirmation of primary colours, in the eclectic use of the classical orders), is clearly at work in most other areas of our culture; in the making of music (one thinks of the work John Adams), in the visual arts (particularly in the return to figurative and narrative art), in drama (where the proscenium arch has been reaffirmed) and in much literature (where the practice of retelling and juxtaposing earlier narratives in the tradition — including, for example, fairy tales — has become almost the new literary orthodoxy). In the teaching of the arts one also finds a growing recognition of the need to impart traditional expressive techniques and of the need to include more comprehensively the demanding artistic work from the cultural continuum. Indeed, the teaching of the arts, in the series of which this book is a part, is largely seen as an initiation into the aesthetic field (q.v.). Such a commitment could be interpreted as being post-modernist in conception, as could also the current nostalgia for earlier forms of culture and the obsessive development in our society of theme-parks and cultural heritage exhibitions and displays, together with the obvious popularity of faithful period reconstructions on film and television.

It is at this point that some definitions and qualifications become necessary. In as much as post-modernism is used as a tag to denote the end of modernism, to indicate a certain style in architecture and, more broadly, to refer to a complex (often ironic) orientation to the past, it has a certain shorthand use. However, in as much as it defines a new movement in the arts *based on the new spirit of the age*, it is guilty of the same crime as modernism, namely historicism. *And what must come after Modernism in the arts?* This is a question predicated on the historicist fallacy. Is it a false question? For no more than modernism can the term 'post-modernism' confer aesthetic worth or ethical value. At best it can define a set of practices and conventions which can be used well or badly. The self-conscious and ironic elements in the intellectually advanced versions of post-modernism, which celebrate 'pariodic imagination', 'pastiche' and 'fun', almost ensure that, most often, the art works lack spiritual power and substance. Under post-modernism we are in danger of having a society based purely on simulacra, an image-culture of reflections, without interior significance, without depth or symbolic power; an echo-chamber without a meaning.

Charles Jencks has written that 'the characteristic fact of life in an age of information processing is a reworking of previous traditions.' The post-modern age, he claims, depends on the advent of organized knowledge, world communication and cybernetics. Because our age is plural, 'no orthodoxy can be adopted without self-consciousness and irony'. As we listen to the phrases and demands, we begin to hear the drum-beat of the characteristic modernist manifesto committed, once again, to the spirit of the age. We encounter a theory linked to a historical unfolding which is seen to determine the nature and the mood of art-making. Post-modernism, in brief, is the avant-garde after modernism. It is the next fashionable movement after it had been said there could be no more 'nexts'. Although much in the general movement of post-modernism represents a necessary reaction, particularly to the excesses of late modernism, as a philosophy for the arts it must be stringently queried. It is for individual artists, in relationship to their gifts and their own particular visions of the world, to create significant art, *for or against or beyond the spirit of the age*. It is for the critic and for the audience to evaluate them. What we need is not a fashionable theory based on a questionable reading of history, and merely fitting the present consumer society, but a better recognition of the primacy of the aesthetic and ethical. We need to recognize the profound freedom of the artist to embody his or her apprehensions of meaning and value. Once again, the artistically liberating position outlined by Hart Crane in 1930 that the artist exists to articulate through the power of metaphor the nature of human consciousness *sub specie aeternitatis* needs urgent attention.

For further reference see Peter Abbs, 'Towards a Coherent Arts Aesthetic', in *Living Powers* and 'Art and the Loss of Art in an Age of Science: The Demise of Late Modernism', in *A Is for Aesthetic*; Arthur Danto, 'Approaching the End of Art'; Peter Fuller, 'Aesthetics after Modernism';

Ernst Gombrich, 'The Father of Art History: On the Influence of Hegel', all in P. Abbs (Ed.), *The Symbolic Order;* Robert Hughes, *the Shock of the New;* Charles Jencks, *What Is Post-Modernism?;* Gabriel Josipovici, *The Lessons of Modernism;* Frank Kermode on 'Modernism', in B. Bergonzi (Ed.), *Innovations;* Norbert Lynton, *The Story of Modern Art;* J. Mordaunt Crook, *The Dilemma of Style;* J.F. Lyotard, *The Post-Modern Condition;* Karl Popper, *The Poverty of Historicism.*

PA

Morality and Art

It is immediately clear as one reads the opening chapter of *The Great Tradition* (first published in 1948) that F.R. Leavis does not think there can be great (literary) art without serious moral purpose. So Flaubert and Turgenev, for example, are not the equal of George Eliot as writers because they lack her moral seriousness, and there was less that Henry James could, in consequence, learn from them than from her. Likewise, Dickens does not enter the Great Tradition of the novel in English — defined by the line from Jane Austen through George Eliot, Henry James and Joseph Conrad to D.H. Lawrence — because his genius was merely that of 'a great entertainer' (p. 19). Except in *Hard Times*, says Leavis, he assumes for the most part 'no profounder responsibility as a creative artist than this description suggests' (p. 19).

For Leavis, if a work of art is to alter the tradition to which it belongs, reshaping and giving a new meaning to the past from which it emerges (q.v. 'Tradition'), then it must possess qualities of 'form' or 'style' which mark it out as 'technically' original. But it can only have these if its content is informed by serious purpose. So of Jane Austen, Leavis says that 'without her intense moral preoccupation she wouldn't have been a great novelist' (p. 7), and goes on, 'when we examine the formal perfection of *Emma*, we find that it can be appreciated only in terms of the moral preoccupations that characterize the novelist's peculiar interest in life' (p. 8). Of course, though he asserts that it is a *necessary* condition of artistic greatness that the art be informed by 'a vital capacity for experience, a kind of reverent openness before life, and a marked moral intensity' (p. 9), he does not assert that it is a sufficient condition: there are evidently morally intense authors who have written dreadful novels: after all, D.H. Lawrence did write *Lady Chatterley's Lover*, a book which in any reckoning of his work ought to be held against him.

Leavis's approach invites comparison with his near contemporary, Gyorgy Lukacs (1885–1971). In works which appal Roger Scruton 'not only for their horrifying bigotry but also for their total lack of grace, charm, irony or percipience', Lukacs sorts novelists and their novels according to whether they are able to penetrate beneath superficial appearances to the real structures of social reality. The possibility of formal achievement is made dependent on the quasi-scientific abilities of the writer. In other words Lukacs pins onto social scientific sense the burden which Leavis hangs on moral sensibility. Both end up, for example, with a negative evaluation of James Joyce. For Lukacs, Joyce compares unfavourably to Thomas Mann. For Leavis, Joyce is no match for D.H. Lawrence. A paragraph in which Leavis makes the comparison does so in terms — including the hostile use of 'cosmopolitan' — with most of which Lukacs would have heartily agreed. It is worth quoting at some length:

> It is this spirit, by virtue of which he [Lawrence] can truly say that what he writes must be written from the depth of his religious experience, that makes him, in my opinion, so much more significant in relation to the past and future, so much more truly creative as a technical inventor, an innovator, a master of language, than James Joyce ... there is no organic principle determining, informing and controlling into a vital whole, the elaborate analogical structure, the extraordinary variety of technical devices, the attempts at an exhaustive rendering of consciousness, for which *Ulysses* is remarkable, and which got it accepted by a cosmopolitan literary world as a new start. It is rather, I think, a dead end, or at least a pointer to disintegration.... (pp. 25–6)

Two questions obtrude themselves regarding Leavis (and Lukacs). Is he *just* a moral policeman (or a political commissar), or does he really have something to say about the preconditions of greatness in art? Can what is said in the context of the novel be said generally — not just for poetry and drama, but for painting, dance and music?

In relation to the first question, I suppose that someone who has nothing to say is unlikely to say it well, nor are we likely to be interested by what someone says when they have nothing to say. There *is* obviously a correlation between shaping a vision and having a vision to shape. But Leavis's idea of an art-enhancing vision is extremely limited, and in particular he allows no place for the comic, the grotesque (the carnivalesque). Indeed, except in moderation the carnivalesque repels him. So Dickens can be accommodated as an entertainer, but Sterne is merely an 'irresponsible' and 'nasty' trifler (p. 2). In always giving preference to the po-faced, Leavis certainly misses the possibility that a 'serious' vision is appropriately expressed in the carnivalesque — in what apparently 'does dirt' on conceptions of life which may, despite their self-proclamations, actually be life-denying. The carnivalesque is exemplified by Rabelais' *Gargantua and Pantagruel*, by Joyce's *Ulysses* (which ends with a life-affirming 'yes'), and — let's say — Angela Carter's *Nights at the Circus*. The relevant theoretical reference point here is Mikhail Bakhtin's *Rabelais and His World* (and Bakhtin's indebtedness to Russian Orthodox conceptions of the Holy Fool, etc.). See also Stallybrass and White's *The Politics and Poetics of Transgression*. One might also usefully compare Leavis on the supposedly life-affirming Great Tradition with what has been found in it by feminists, like Kate Millet in *Sexual Politics* and in Angela Carter's 'Alison's Giggle', a fine contemporary essay.

One may also get Leavis into perspective by considering whether there is such a thing as moral seriousness in music, and whether it is a precondition of musical greatness. No one doubts the seriousness of Bach or Beethoven; but what about Mozart? I suppose that Leavis, prompted by R.G. Collingwood (see *The Principles of Art*), would sit down to *The Magic Flute* and end up declaring 'Genius, but the genius of an entertainer.' Yet *The Magic Flute* contains passages of as transcendent beauty and sublimity as one could wish, created out of (at least apparent) playful irresponsibility. From music one could go on to painting, where Picasso might be taken as a challenge to Leavis. Yes, Picasso is 'open to life', but for Leavis — one suspects — too open.

This entry has introduced the enormously broad topic of morality and art through the narrow focus of F.R. Leavis. Leavis's attraction for teachers was in large measure connected to the fact that any arts teacher is likely to believe that the arts can help children (and adults) *develop*, and development is an ethical notion insofar as we have a normative (standard-setting) conception of what it is to be a (developed) person. The teacher of the arts is likely to share Wordsworth's faith that 'poetry by sensitizing, purifying and strengthening the feelings, directly *makes* us better.' But no one ought to hold this belief uncritically (q.v. 'Politics and Art').

Multicultural Arts Education

In cultures all over the world people sit and tell stories. These stories hold the listener for a moment in a spell, reinforce the continuing sense of tradition, sometimes offer advice to someone who has a problem to resolve or who is about to embark on a journey. Stories are a way to make personal and communal meaning out of human experience. Stories may be similar; they differ in their structure, sense of aesthetic, and experiences re-told. Personal experiences — today's news — become communal consciousness.

A story which needs re-telling is how arts teaching can contribute to multicultural/anti-racist education. In the last twenty years there has been active use of the arts to explore a variety of cultures. This exploration may have taken the form of handling artifacts, reading, listening or speaking in dialects, or engaging in workshops with artists from different cultural traditions. More recently there has been a shift to ensure that multicultural arts work becomes embedded in the curriculum and therefore becomes mainstream.

This perspective of mainstream multicultural arts education is not easily achieved or common practice. Many arts educators work within two arts constructs: one sets the plot, while the other plays a subsidiary role. The first is concerned with perpetuating a 'European' ideology which places European philosophy at the root of all understanding. Many arts educators have trained and practised within this framework of understanding and consequently view other arts perspectives as marginal. Often the curriculum content is contained within traditional perspectives, rarely acknowledging that 'European' arts have always been receptive to and influenced by the arts of other cultures. The National Curriculum Art Working Group Interim Report illustrates this point in Attainment Target 2 'Making' for Key Stage 4: '...examine the influence of Cameroon sculpture on German Expressionist wood-carving.' Another example is the 'Paisley' which traces its history to the Indian Orissi pattern. It is this missing knowledge, a philosophy built on omission, which hampers the 'European' arts model and places educators at a disadvantage when trying to present multicultural arts work.

Ethnomusicologist Curt Sachs, in *The Wellsprings of Music*, recalls 'the days when ancient Egyptian art was disdainfully judged as a not yet matured precursor of Greek and Roman classicism, and Romanesque architecture a somewhat lowly preparatory step towards the dizzying Gothic cathedrals, which in due time led the way to the noble perfection of Renaissance building.' He notes that 'there cannot be a steady, straight evolution from childish beginnings to an ever more perfect art as evolutionists once dreamed. There is rather a bewildering sequence of sudden changes by leaps and bounds, indeed, a constant reversal to older, new and foreign ideals.'

The second construct is the 'ethnic' one, often justified because of the number or lack of visibly different racial groups within an educational environment. Practice reflects the intentions of educators to integrate everyone into a community ethos celebrating the notions of difference, tolerance and mutual respect. The activities selected to explore difference are often based on skin colour, geographical location or religious festivals. It may be that in order to understand ourselves we need to experience being different or being a 'stranger' elsewhere. Being a 'stranger' can be used effectively to challenge assumptions, and drama, because of its facility to engage through metaphor, presents itself as a powerful medium to explore this concept.

Many artists have commented on working within the 'ethnic' framework, where they have participated in an activity which suspends the normal curriculum: '. . . I often find myself the unprepared cog in the working out of a grand scheme'; and again,' . . . a one-off session in Indian classical dance is only the tip of the iceberg in the constant fight to gain credibility for a different movement aesthetic in a predominantly insular culture', writes Shobana Jeysasingh in K. Owesi (Ed.), *Storms of the Heart.*

In some environments, educators shape their curriculum content around their population in the belief that some arts belong and are more easily understood by particular groups. This artistic colonization is problematic not least because it limits perceptions and opportunities, the very things which the arts are able to explore and develop. The ethnic construct can be interpreted through Aesop's fable: 'A wolf peering through a window saw a company of shepherds eating a joint of lamb. "Lord!" he exclaimed, "what a fuss they would have raised had they caught me doing that."'

Arts Education for a Multicultural Society (AEMS) is the only national arts curriculum development research project currently in Britain. The project works on the principle of partnership between Local Education Authority and Regional Arts Associations, between educator and artist. Its major aim is to fuse the 'European' and 'ethnic' models by working with black artists who practise outside the Western European tradition and educators in schools and colleges. Through action research, where educator and artist research, design, implement, record and evaluate their work together, new perspectives in arts education can emerge. Many arts educators have worked closely with a variety of arts providers, be they agencies or individual artists, to enrich curriculum content and practice. AEMS has contributed to this process and has tried to promote black artists within an arts rationale. This rationale is based on the view that the arts are inseparable from daily life. The physical, cultural, social, psychological, economic and political dimensions of society are all bound up with the arts. The artifacts produced are not only functional and decorative but are also symbolic of complex relationships within British society. The work reflects the structures, aesthetics, process of creativity, values and traditions of contemporary Britain.

In more recent years there has been a trend in education to combine a variety of arts subjects under one umbrella. There is a belief that combining the arts is more likely to reflect a multicultural arts understanding and lend itself to cross-curricular work. Many AEMS artists, born and trained in Britain, have a specialist knowledge within an arts subject but are also able to present their work within a cultural framework, drawing on a variety of arts disciplines. Pitika Ntuli (in K. Owesi (Ed.), *Storms of the Heart*) reminds us: 'It is more than a fusion of arts forms; it is the conception of a reality, of a total view of life. It is a capsule of feeling, thinking, imagination, taste and hearing.'

The enriching resource and perspective have challenged arts educators to re-examine their own beliefs. AEMS research has highlighted that black British-based artists share a philosophy in which basic experiences unite them into a communal collective. They use symbols which have a history, which have communal significance, that may have travelled in time and space. This contrasts with the training of arts educators which seeks to examine the purity of a genre and isolates individual achievement. In search of purity, information selected can often make assumptions which become universal truths. Individuality becomes concerned with formulating and rendering experiences in a personal response.

Unity and singularity, however, are allied concepts, and it is the arts which help make communal meaning out of individual experiences. What is significant to a person, what enables them to transcend everyday concerns, is largely culturally determined. However, it is the imagination, the aesthetics of personal experience which can be valued within a community. New experiences are woven into existing traditions for personal experiences to become communal experience. What differs, however, is the respective community's sense of the aesthetic and how a society of conflicting aesthetics can work towards a common reality.

Arts educators have a responsibility to understand the arts from a variety of perspectives and to use the arts to work towards a common reality. It is only when this is recognized as a serious pursuit that the arts in education will be multicultural and anti-racist in policy and practice.

This contribution began by using the analogy of a story to discuss cultural diversity and arts education. It ends with a story which might strike resonance with some arts educators:

A wise griot summing up his message for an audience reminded them of the old saying: one hand cannot clap. A young boy laughed loudly and shouted 'of course one hand can clap but it needs the assistance of another'. The griot turned slowly and smiled. He surveyed the hushed audience and paused on the two shining eyes of the impetuous speaker. 'You are right my friend, when a hand of one and the hand of another meet they signify respect and harmony. It is

127

when one hand only is portrayed and part of a message told that we see a limited view of reality.'

For further reading see Frances Aboud, *Children and Prejudice*; R. Arora and C. Duncan, *Multicultural Education: Towards Good Practice*; Arts Council of Great Britain, *The Arts and Cultural Diversity*; J.A. Banks, *Multi-Ethnic Education: Theory and Practice*; Martin Bernal, *Black Athena*; M. Craft (Ed.), *Education and Cultural Pluralism*; A. James and R. Jeffcoate (Eds), *The School in the Multicultural Society*; Kwesi Owesi, *The Struggle for Black Arts in Britain*; Maud Sulter (Ed.), *Passion Discourses on Black Women's Creativity*; K. Owesi (Ed.), *Storms of the Heart*.

MS

(Maggie Semple is currently Director of the Arts Education for a Multicultural Society project. Further details of AEMS work and publications can be obtained from AEMS, Commonwealth Institute, Kensington High Street, London W8 6NQ.)

Music in Education

Although there have been frequent references to the educational significance of music since Greek times, the foundations of modern school music programmes were laid during the nineteenth century. A number of influential Victorian churchmen and educational reformers advocated musical instruction in the elementary schools; music was valued for religious, social and moral reasons, and the class singing lesson became a regular and popular feature of the curriculum. But it was imaginative educators like John Hullah, Sarah Glover and John Curwen who formulated coherent systems of teaching which combined choral work with the development of musicianship skills. They thus established the principle of music 'study' and the idea of music as a curriculum 'subject'.

Class music lessons today reflect the wide variety of methodologies that have been devised by musicians and educationists during the past hundred years. Some teachers favour 'traditional' approaches based on performance activities, the acquisition of conventional aural and literacy skills and acquaintance with the works of the great European masters. Others have been influenced by more 'progressive' ideals. They tend to concentrate on the 'exploration' of sound materials and compositional activities; this is for the purpose of promoting creative self-expression. It is most unlikely that these two 'types' of music teaching ever exist as pure forms, but it is not difficult to identify programmes and published 'courses' which incline towards one or the other.

The limitation of traditional and progressive styles of music teaching is that both can become narrow and exclusive. This is recognized by teachers who are usually interested in drawing on ideas that 'work' in the classroom. However, in recent years we have witnessed genuine attempts to unite different methods and practices within a systematic framework. These moves have led to what I shall call an eclectic approach to music education. This is more than a reconciliation of alternative methodologies. Underpinning eclecticism in music education there is a view of the arts as realms of meaning which are just as significant in their own ways as other branches of educational knowledge. Such a view owes much to the aesthetics and epistemology of John Dewey, Susanne Langer and Louis Arnuad Reid. Music is justified as a way of knowing and an important aspect of a liberal education which aims to introduce all children to the full range of human meanings and forms of discourse.

The eclectic rationale rests on four main principles. First, the focus is on supporting the growth of musical understanding and musical intelligence. This is to be achieved by initiating pupils into the techniques and expressive procedures of the discipline through the interrelated experiential modes of performing, composing and listening. Second, it is recognized that music, like any art form, is an evolving discipline. Understanding depends on a proper awareness of musical traditions. It is against the background of these traditions that experimentation and innovation become significant within what is a musical continuum. Third, eclecticism in music education incorporates the principle that there is no one 'world' of music. In a pluralist society there will be a rich variety of musical styles and genres which are valued by particular groups but unfamiliar to others. These will be represented on the curriculum but not in a tokenistic manner. Rather, they will be united by those deep structures which are to be found in all musics and which ultimately transcend cultures. The content of the curriculum will be essentially inclusive. Fourth, music is regarded as part of the 'community' of arts disciplines. Accordingly, close links across the arts are to be encouraged in both curriculum planning and practice.

Music is now a foundation subject of the National Curriculum; this is some 'official' recognition of its value as part of a broad and balanced education. However, the position of the arts subjects is neither clear nor secure. In a system which is dominated by propositional views of knowledge and utilitarian aims, fine arts have often been regarded as 'extras' and therefore of only marginal concern. The principles underlying the eclectic rationale present a major challenge to this conception of education. If music and the arts are to be taken seriously, they must be valued for what they are. No longer can they be regarded as hobbies, pastimes or leisure pursuits to be fitted into education as 'luxuries' or 'options'. They require proper provision in terms of staffing, accommodation and time allocation.

It is well-known that music curricula vary considerably, in content and style, from school to school. No doubt some educationists support the view that a coherent national framework will lead to better classroom practice and more continuity and progression in school programmes. Whether or not greater conformity will improve the quality of teaching and learning remains to be seen. For however well constructed programmes of study might be, their effectiveness is entirely dependent on teachers. Rationales, frameworks or guidelines have to be translated into workable practices. This is never a matter of straightforward application. It is certainly essential for music education practice to be founded on secure principles; but teachers also need to be able to utilize principles, or theory, for the purpose of critical reflection on practice. Information arising from this process can then contribute to decisions about future action. Curriculum development in the field of music education depends very much on identifying strategies which will assist teachers in bringing theory and practice together in meaningful ways.

To talk about music *in* education raises questions not only about musical studies within the context of a general education; there are also issues to do with the importance of musical activities within the corporate life of the school. Most schools have their choirs, orchestras and other ensemble groups. These activities were originally encouraged in the independent sector and valued for their contribution to the social and cultural life of the institution. Children do not attend school simply to acquire prescribed skills and knowledge. Schools are communities with their own characters, traditions and customs. Teachers, parents, governors and members of the public recognize and value the contributions music and the arts make to the quality of the educational environment. Concerts, musical productions and other events permeate an institution in a very special and powerful way; they provide for social bonding, cohesion and solidarity. Indeed, without arts activities schools would be dreary and impoverished places. They would lack that sense of vitality so essential to the life of any educational community.

For further reference see J. Blacking, *How Musical Is Man?*; DES, *Music from 5 to 16*; H. Gardner, *Frames of Mind: The Theory of Multiple Intelligence*; S. Langer, *Philosophy in a New Key*; M. Metcalf, 'Towards the Condition of Music', in P. Abbs (Ed.), *Living Powers;* J. Paynter, *Music in the Secondary School Curriculum*; L.A. Reid, *Ways of Understanding and Experience*; K. Simpson, *Some Great Music Educators*; K. Swanwick, *Music, Mind and Education.*

CP

Obscenity and Pornography

When *is* something obscene or pornographic, and when, in particular, is a work of art obscene or pornographic? (From now on, I'll abbreviate to 'obscene'.)

A piece of instrumental music might be described, metaphorically, as obscene, but only literally so if the music were 'programme' music, that is, representational of something in the world. A piece of music might conceivably mimic the rhythms or sounds of sexual intercourse and in an obscene way. One can only produce actual examples from songs: some readers may be old enough to remember the controversy aroused by the sounds of arousal which punctuate Serge Gainsbourg's and Jane Birkin's *Je t'aime*. So, 'No obscenity without representation' (q.v. 'Representation') — but representation of what, and representation how?

Roger Scruton, no friend of liberalism in these matters, writes, 'Anything can be represented without obscenity, even the genitals' (*Sexual Desire*, p. 12). This is obviously the case with the representations in, say, a medical textbook and, for many, equally obviously true of most representations of the genitals in the Western tradition of painting the nude. Conversely, it appears that there can be an obscene representation of things which are not human. For example, there is a minor genre of photography which consists in photographing inanimate objects to make them look like human bodies or parts of bodies. It is easy to photograph the crotch formed where one branch of a tree forks from another or from the trunk so that it looks like a human crotch. The result may be perceived as obscene for a reason to be suggested below.

Suppose, then, we grant that obscenity lies not in *what* is represented, but somehow in *how* it is represented. How *how*? One answer is to suppose that the representation is obscene if it causes or is intended to cause sexual arousal in someone. There are objections to this approach as baldly stated. A fetishist watching a film in which a woman puts on or takes off shoes or stockings may be aroused by what he sees, but this is scarcely a satisfactory index or criterion of obscenity. In other words, who is the 'someone' who is supposed to be aroused? One answer might be, 'a typical or normal male or female'. Suppose that one added that whether there is an intention to arouse is also a relevant factor. Pornographic magazines are constructed with the intention to cause arousal in some identifiable category of purchasers: foot fetishists, 'normal males', lesbian sado-masochists. But against this one might say: to suppose a representation obscene if it is intended to arouse (someone) — and where 'obscenity' is supposed, an obstacle to perception of the representation as art or to an aesthetic experience of it — is to suppose that sexual arousal is, in some sense, an inappropriate response to a representation.

But why? If tears and laughter are appropriate responses — some have doubted it (q.v. 'Tears and Laughter') — then why not sexual arousal? If crying is not incompatible with experiencing a work as a work of art or with having an aesthetic experience, why should sexual arousal be thought incompatible? (Of course, someone might disapprove of sexual arousal or of anything likely to cause it. Tight jeans and short skirts have been disapproved of for such reasons. But disapproval of sexual arousal needs to be discussed in its own right.)

At this point a different approach needs to be introduced. The idea now to be considered is that a representation is obscene if it is constructed from an obscene point of view. Some systematic suggestions as to what such a point of view is have been made. Interestingly, these suggestions show a convergence of thinking between people of otherwise very different persuasions: for example, the anti-feminist Roger Scruton's views in *Sexual Desire* are very similar to views in feminist writings on pornography, for example, Susan Griffin's *Pornography and Silence* and Suzanne Kappeler's *The Pornography of Representation*.

The shared idea is that representations of human beings and of human relationships, especially in their sexual part, are obscene if they depersonalize persons, fragment their wholeness, or encourage a voyeuristic ('third-person') experience of people and relationships. Thus someone is depersonalized if they are represented as a mere body or part of a body, and human relationships are emptied of meaning if they are represented in such a way that we do not engage with the experience of persons but merely (say) with the interaction of bodies: the voyeuristic perspective of the key hole or the peep show. A photograph of the crotch of the tree is obscene if it invites us to see in it a fragmented, depersonalized human crotch. On this view it is possible (for example) for a literary representation of a sexual encounter to be sexually arousing but not obscene if we are led to experience the encounter from the (first-person) point of view of a character (that is, a representation of a whole person) and not to experience it as a (mere) curious (scatalogical) observer or spectator. Likewise, for visual representation, both in film and on canvas.

It may well be difficult to decide in an individual case whether or not a representation is obscene, but there is no reason why the proper test for obscenity should be easy to apply. Of course, the 'test' which I have been outlining is by no means agreed by all who have thought about obscenity and pornography. Some people would see it as embodying an unduly restrictive (excessively Kantian) view of how people should relate, and would argue that human sexuality has at least as a component the desire to thematize (to objectify) the body of another, and even one's own body. Nor does the 'test' tell us what to do when we have found an obscenity. Do we pass by on the other side, or stop to seek the legal suppression of what we have found? That is an area of controversy the main outlines of which are probably familiar to readers; I shall not reproduce them here.

Originals, Copies, Performances and Reproductions

Suppose someone says: 'All, or at least most, of the aesthetically relevant features of a painting can be reproduced in a good copy. It is only an aesthetically irrelevant historical aura and an equally irrelevant price tag which attaches our interest to the "authentic" original.' Suppose they advance in defence of the claim that paintings can be successfully copied the evidence that great forgers have always had considerable success in passing off their own works as those of great artists — that forgeries have fooled acknowledged experts, whose powers of discrimination are certainly above the average. Suppose they conclude: 'What a pity it is that the great forgers have not been usefully employed in making copies of great paintings, so that we would not have to travel the globe in search of overrated originals, but could see everything we could wish for in an enlarged National or Tate Gallery.' Is the person who says such things a philistine, a vulgarian? What, if anything, is wrong with their argument?

In practice, of course, copies and originals are distinguishable, often easily, and they are distinguished by aesthetically relevant features, like the quality of brush work or colour, and not just 'invisible' features like the age or provenance of the canvas. The important thing to recognize about forgeries, one might go on to argue, is that once they are unmasked, it is possible to see the works of the original artist with a fresh eye, picking out features as aesthetically relevant which had previously escaped attention. Thus, while to begin with no one could tell a van Meegeren from a Vermeer, now even those with modest expertise can see the differences — and see that the Vermeers are better paintings. But suppose forgers became better at their art, and that copying techniques improved to the point where we could legitimately speak of the perfect forgery or the perfect copy. Would any *aesthetic* value then attach to the original? Would the specific interest still attaching to originals be any different from the interest attached, say, to the author's manuscript, the holograph of a novel or — perhaps a more appropriate example — the photographer's or print-maker's original print from a negative or a plate?

It might be argued that our aesthetic interest in a work extends beyond or is conditioned by more than its painted surface. For example, it is part of the interest of Picasso's *Les Demoiselles d'Avignon* (1907) that it was the *first* cubist painting, and when we look at it, our interest is (partly) in the evidence the painting provides of *Picasso's* struggle to *create* cubism. It is relevant to our interest in the painting that it is dateable (1907) and attributable (to Picasso). A subsequent copy cannot be looked at as the first cubist painting, but merely as a copy of it. Though we may know (externally) that it is a copy of the first cubist painting, we cannot see a copy as we can see the original. But could one not say that the interest in *Les Demoiselles d'Avignon* as the first cubist painting is an *artistic* interest (an interest in it in the context of an interest in art and its history) whereas the *aesthetic* interest we have in a work is strictly in its surface, such that dating and attribution are irrelevant?

Compare our interest in a literary text or a piece of music. Here any correctly printed copy of the text is as good as any other in affording us access to the work, as an object of either aesthetic or artistic interest, or both. Likewise, any non-faulty performance of a piece of music (one which follows the score and uses the prescribed instruments) gives us access to the musical work, as aesthetic or artistic object, and in this case even though performances may be of variable quality. But to this it might be replied that the analogy is not between a copy of a painting and the original, on the one hand, and different copies of the same literary text or performances of the same musical work, on the other. Rather, the idea of a copy of a painting indistinguishable in point of aesthetic interest from its original is analogous to the idea of two *identical* but independently composed works of literature or music. If Ash and Beech produce identical works, unknown to each other but a century apart, is there any ground for thinking one work better than the other? Are they aesthetically indistinguishable?

Once again the answer depends on what we take to be an aesthetic interest. Suppose Beech composed a piece of music note for note identical to Ash's. Listening to Beech's music, I can hear in it the influence of Chopin, and that enters into my appraisal. But if Ash composed his work a hundred years earlier than Beech, I cannot hear Chopin's influence, for Chopin was not alive to influence Ash. Might I not conclude that Ash's is the more remarkable composition, and listen to it with more pleasure than to Beech's — even though they are ex hypothesi identical?

One might reply: there seems to be a confusion here between the achievement of the *artist* and the achievement of the *work*. Only one work can be Chopin-influenced and that affects a differential assessment of Ash and Beech as composers. But both works must be Chopin-like and in exactly the same ways. So there is no basis to discriminate in our assessment of the compositions, only in our assessment of the composers. Aesthetic and artistic are different categories. Aesthetic interest and relevance concern only what is available in the surface or structure of a work, even though in some cases that surface or structure may only be accessible to those with quite definite knowledge (q.v. 'Text and Context').

In the literature of aesthetics Nelson Goodman, in *Languages of Art*, sharply distinguishes between autographic and allographic arts. The former, exemplified by painting, are arts where aesthetic interest attaches to an original defined by a history of production (typically indexed by an artist's signature or autograph). The latter are arts where the 'original' has no aesthetic status, and can be lost without affecting the availability of the work, as original manuscripts and scores of many literary and musical works have been lost. Only in autographic arts is forgery, as opposed to imitation or pastiching, possible. Rather surprisingly, in a later work, *Problems and Projects*, Goodman undermines the autographic/allographic distinction when he says that he has

> not maintained that painting is inalterably autographic. For an art to become allographic depends upon establishment of a practice of classifying instances (copies) into works in a manner independent of history of production. If and when reproductions of a picture come to be accepted as no less original instances than the initial painting, so that the latter has only the sort of special interest or value that attaches to the manuscript or first edition of a literary work then indeed the art could become allographic. (p. 136)

This concession leads other writers to the view espoused by Gregory Currie, in *An Ontology of Art*, that 'no art form is either autographic or allographic ... however we understand the distinction, it turns out not to distinguish any art form from any other' (p. 125).

In quite another tradition of thinking about art Walter Benjamin speaks of the 'aura', closely linked to art's involvement with ritual, which surrounds the 'original' work of art, and looks forward to its loss in a world of secular 'post-auratic art' made possible by mechanical reproduction. His views are to be found in the essay, 'The Work of Art in the Age of Mechanical Reproduction', in his book, *Illuminations*. They are popularized in John Berger's *Ways of Seeing*. Benjamin contrasts the *manual* reproduction of one person's work by another, and the mechanical or *process* reproduction of sound and image made possible by the advent of new recording media (the record and the photograph), and says:

> that which withers in the age of mechanical reproduction is the aura of the work of art ... the technique of reproduction detaches the reproduced object from the domain of tradition. By making many reproductions it substitutes a plurality of copies for a unique existence. [One might say that printing had already done this centuries before for literary works.] And in permitting the reproduction to meet the beholder or listener in his own particular situation, it reactivates the object reproduced. These two processes [multiplication of copies, reactivation of the object] lead to a tremendous shattering of tradition.... Their most powerful agent is the film. (p. 223)

Photography

Not so long ago I went to an exhibition at the Royal Academy in London: 'The Art of Photography 1939–1989'. At the same time the RA was exhibiting prints and paintings by Gauguin and his associates at Pont-Aven. I walked round both exhibitions on the same afternoon. To see photographs framed and hung in an art gallery is an unusual context for looking at them — we usually encounter photographs in newspapers, magazines and snapshot albums — but it does allow me to pose the question: How, if at all, does looking at a photograph differ from looking at a print or painting? That is to say, do we — or ought we — to bring different expectations to an encounter with photographs? Does the photograph itself affect us any differently from a print or a painting?

Consider the question of belief or expectation. Most photographs are not taken with a view to being framed and hung as 'works of art', nor do we often look at them in that way. (Whether we *can* look at them in that way is an issue I'll come to.) Most photographs are taken to provide a record, a document, a proof, an aid to memory, that something once happened, that someone looked like this (as they look in the photograph), that somewhere you can encounter that (that which can be seen in the photograph). Of course, a sketch, a drawing, a painting can be made with a view to showing how someone or somewhere looked; but the documentary value in this case is intrinsically less than in the case of the photograph. This is because it is the case (and we know that it is the case) that the sketch or painting can show something which never actually existed — that it can be drawn out of the artist's imagination — whereas a photograph at least is evidence that there was something in front of the camera when the photograph was taken and, ambiguity aside, the photograph also shows what that something was. In other words a drawing is the product of the intentional activity of a person (an artist) using a drawing medium, whereas a photograph is the causally explicable effect of light falling on a light-sensitive medium. We (normally) know this when we look at paintings and photographs. Knowing what we do accounts for at least part of the difference in the ways we look at paintings and photographs, and the ways we respond, attributing to the latter an evidential or documentary value quantitatively much greater, and perhaps qualitatively different from that we attribute to the former.

It is because photographs are particularly credible in this way as documents or evidence that it is worthwhile for the person intent on deceiving us (1) to set up and photograph as 'real' a scene which is merely representational, or (2) to interfere with a photograph by cropping and painting in or out to show as real what is merely ideologically preferred. Thus the RA exhibition I saw included a famous much-reproduced photograph by Robert Capa entitled 'Loyalist Soldier, Spanish Civil War, 1938', which at the time was purported to show the soldier at the moment of being struck and fatally wounded by an enemy bullet. It is now thought by many that Capa posed the scene with the loyalist soldier, who is merely pretending to be shot. If that is so, the photograph may become of 'aesthetic' interest, but loses its documentary value and loses whatever affective response belief in its truth-value would have elicited from us. There is also a famous photograph from the Russian Revolution of Lenin addressing a crowd from an improvised rostrum. In the original the photograph shows Trotsky standing close to Lenin. In the version of the photograph reproduced in Russia under Stalin and subsequently, Trotsky has disappeared from the photograph: he has been painted out — visually unpersoned.

For many critics, the way in which photographs are produced has other consequences for how we can and do look at them. First, it is argued, photographs — which are often taken for 'sentimental reasons' — encourage an essentially sentimental response. Second, knowing how photographs are produced, it is — despite the efforts of the photographer — difficult for us to look at them as works of art, or to respond to them aesthetically.

Photographs looked at here and now are necessarily photographs of something, someone, somewhere there and then. They are a present means of access to something past. We can carry *here*, in our wallet or handbag, a souvenir, a memento, a keepsake, of the look of someone *then*, all the more valuable because (unlike a miniature painting) the photograph is a trace, a remainder, of the actual light which fell on that person and was reflected through the eye of the camera. Photographs, in virtue of how they are made, encourage nostalgia, sentimentality. So it is argued, and so it is evidenced (for example) in Roland Barthes' *Camera Lucida*: see notably Barthes' reponse to Andre Kertesz's 1931 photograph of a boy called Ernest (p. 83) and the whole of section 28 of the book, on a photograph of Barthes' mother.

Against this view it can be pointed out that the film medium is identical to the photograph, but that we do not look at films as the present evidence of something which occurred in the past: film has a *here-now* rather than a *here-then* character. We wince because the blow falls now, not because it once fell — and perhaps after all we wince at some photographs in exactly the same manner.

Photographs are necessarily photographs of something, and knowing how they are made, we tend to look through the photograph to what it is a photograph of. This, it is argued, stops us looking at the photograph, especially where the subject-matter is such as to play on whatever is prurient, morbidly curious or voyeuristic in our minds. Opposition to the display of photographs of the nude is stronger than opposition to display of paintings of the nude because it is felt that in the former we (in some sense) have to look at the nude, but in the latter (in some sense) at the painting. In an important essay, 'Photography and Representation' (in his *The Aesthetic Understanding*), Roger Scruton ends a critique of photography as a possible artistic medium by declaring, 'The medium of photography, one might say, is inherently pornographic' (p. 126). At the very least, the photographer of the nude who wants to avoid pornography is driven to use devices which seek to pull the spectator's attention away from the subject-matter and towards the photographer's art: for example, by securing a distorted image of the body (Bill Brandt), or exploiting the possibilities of close-up (Edward Weston), by etherealizing the image with soft focus, coloured lenses (David Hamilton). Some would say these activities only compound the original inherent pornography. Others would say that it is mistaken in the first place to suppose that we 'see through' photographs to what they are photographs of: see Nigel Warburton, 'Seeing through Seeing through Photographs'.

Much could be said on this topic; a little more is said in the section on 'Obscenity and Pornography'. The general interest of the discussion is that in pursuing questions about if and how photography can be an art form (a medium for art), much light is thrown on what we think we understand by art and medium (q.v.). Scruton's essential point in this connection is that because photography is a causal-mechanical process (not an intentional practice) the photograph is consequently just a trace or index (q.v. 'Icon, Index, Symbol') of that process, resistant to being used as a medium of art. That resistance may (to a greater or lesser extent) be overcome by the intentional activity of photographers in their ingenuity in using this resistant medium. For other critics photography is no more 'resistant' to art than is a tube of paint. They might go on to say that photography, like the microscope, has allowed new ways of seeing things. 'The camera introduces us to unconscious optics as does psychoanalysis to unconscious impulses', says Walter Benjamin in 'The Work of Art in the Age of Mechanical Reproduction' (*Illuminations*, p. 239). Benjamin also says, 'much futile thought has been devoted to the question of whether photography is an art. The primary question — whether the very invention of photography had not transformed the entire nature of art — was not raised' (p. 229). See also John Berger and Jean Mohr, *Another Way of Telling*.

Play

Teachers and parents like to think that they approve of children playing, that they believe children learn and develop through play, even — in the old dictum — that a child's play is its work. Yet, equally, children's play is a source of anxiety to these same teachers and parents. They may have come to terms with Doctors and Nurses, but Cowboys and Indians or more contemporary versions of violent shoot-outs leave them uneasy, not to mention the unease created by children's apparent resistance to accepting non-sex stereotyped toys and ploys for their play.

The unease might be relieved if we saw more clearly what play (play proper) is, appreciating its particular unreal (fictional, symbolic) character. For play is twice removed from reality, not once removed, as the following example illustrates. A boy who points an imaginary gun at the object of his anger and fires ('piaow, piaow'), is using a representation (of a gun) in expressing the anger he feels. His action is once removed from reality, in the sense that it represents an attack on the hated object rather than being an attack (with stones or fists). But it is still located very much within a (real) relationship with the person who is the target of the aggression, and is rightly liable to response within the context of a real relationship (so the target of the aggression might meaningfully say, 'You need to learn to control your temper' or some such).

But when a boy points an imaginary gun at a playmate and fires ('piaow, piaow'), there is no anger, and there is not a real relationship but a symbolic relationship between aggressor and victim. It is not appropriate for the victim to say, 'You need to learn to control your temper.' In a rather complicated formula of Gregory Bateson's (*Steps to an Ecology of Mind*, p. 152), playful actions are twice removed from reality in that they do not denote what those actions for which they stand would denote if they were not playful actions. That is, pulling the imaginary trigger in Cowboys and Indians does not denote the anger or the act of killing which is denoted (or, better, represented) when the angry boy points the imaginary gun at his frustrating parent.

Of course, the line between playful and non-playful representation is often transgressed: play can go wrong, and conversely a real dispute can turn into a playful one. In an essay on ritual insults William Labov has indicated that ritual insults are liable to be taken as real insults, and a playful bite may go wrong and be taken as a real bite. Conversely, a marital argument may turn into an exchange of ritual insults, and dissolve in laughter. That a line can easily be transgressed does not show that it does not exist, nor that it is unimportant.

Play in the sense of action and representation twice removed from reality resides in the fact that it exists in a realm (of fiction, imagination or symbolism) where it would be misguided and mistaken to evaluate it with respect to the kind of moral, political, commonsense or scientific criteria always relevantly applicable in everyday life. No moral condemnation can properly be attached to shooting dead your best friend in a game, and no teacher should be alarmed by the sight of a playground full of dead bodies. It's only a game, Miss.

But it is in being 'only a game', existing in a realm bracketed off from real-world appraisal, that play can function as a potential space for development, learning and creativity. This is the view of D.W. Winnicott, who in *Playing and Reality* writes that, 'in playing, and perhaps only in playing, the child or adult is free to be creative' (p. 62), indicating that among the adult games he includes psychoanalysis which, he says, 'has been developed as a highly specialised form of playing in the service of communication with oneself and others' (p. 48). Here 'playing' is being used in a technical or semi-technical sense, but to mean more or less what I have been using the term to mean. In psychoanalysis, the analyzed can, for example, say things which in the real world might fairly be rebuked as aggressive or depraved but which in the psychoanalytic situation are not taken to denote what they would denote if they were spoken elsewhere. But also in psychoanalysis, and in play more generally, Winnicott has in mind that suspension of rules makes possible the creation or invention of fresh meanings. Play is linked to creativity specifically via the idea that in play no holds are barred — all rules can be broken, new rules can be invented. This network of connections deserves some discussion (q.v. 'Creativity').

In play we do not have to aim at 'literal truth'. We are free to invent non-existent entities and treat them as existing for the purposes of the play. We are free to improvise, using our imagination to turn a broomstick into a hobby-horse (to take E.H. Gombrich's example; see his 'Meditations on a Hobby-Horse'). We are free to associate senses and symbols as we wish, and to create nonsense. The test of good play is not whether it mimics the world or conforms to pre-existing rules, but whether it satisfies the participants (and sometimes, of course, mimicking the world or conforming to rule may be necessary to satisfaction). So there is a connection between play and the 'free play' of the imagination, which is set at liberty in play.

However, one might well ask what *motivates* play, and what drives the imagination in play. Reflecting on these questions may cause a modification of the picture of play so far presented. For an 'obvious' answer to the question of play motivation is that it in some sense satisfies perfectly real desires, whether conscious or unconscious, and these desires give shape to the play, dictating the choice of Cowboys and Indians, Doctors and Nurses, or Mothers and Babies. Likewise, it is desires, and also anxieties and fears, which drive the imagination along particular pathways, producing (for example) narratives of abandonment or loss or happy endings. If this is at all the right way to think about the motivation of play and the shaping of the imagination, then it suggests that though in one sense twice removed from reality, in another sense play is not removed from reality at all. That, of course, is consistent with the idea that the line between play and non-play can all too easily be crossed, since the drives which produce play and fuel the imagination are the self-same ones which operate in the rest of our lives. We should then think of play, like art in the Freudian scheme of things, as involving something we might want to call sublimation.

A completely different approach would treat a 'play instinct' as sui generis. This is what we find in Schiller's *On the Aesthetic Education of Man*; in Huizinga's famous *Homo Ludens*; and perhaps also in Melanie Klein's idea of an epistemic instinct. Here one would simply say that there is a human drive to create symbols or representations — to play with words, images and actions — quite apart from any conscious or unconscious desires seeking an 'outlet'. Play would, on this view, be a self-sufficient activity with its own sources of energy. This is to make play even more opaque to the ordinary utilitarian understanding, since it is tantamount to saying that play is not *for* anything; it just *is*.

Understanding the nature of play is particularly important to drama in education, where children have been encouraged to continue their imaginative play as improvisation, both spontaneous and scripted. The problem for drama educators is to bring this recontextualized play into contact with the traditions of theatre. See David Hornbook's *Education in Drama* and Chris Havell's contribution to *Living Powers*, edited by Peter Abbs, and q.v. 'Drama Education'.

Politics and Art

There are artists who think they are political, and artists who think they aren't. The latter are suspicious of the former, suspecting them of prostituting their art to the service of extrinsic goals. The former think that the latter are, in fact, highly political, whatever they think about themselves.

In their work, political artists, even when not working directly to a commission, can aim at a number of things. First, they can aim to express their political position in an imaginative representation of events or states of affairs, so that audiences can see how it is that someone else sees the world. Second, they can aim to illustrate their position or a case through the example of an imaginative representation. Third, they can aim to convert others to their position through their art. This may amount to no more than engaging the sympathy of an (uncommitted) audience to a case, cause, person or group.

Consider these three aims. There are plenty of examples of contemporary theatre, including theatre in education, which aim to win the audience's sympathy for and secure positive belief in something or other: victims of racial discrimination, AIDS sufferers, striking workers. This is not incompatible with the production of work which is funny or moving and well-crafted. For presumably one can hold virtually *any* political position without being unfeeling, incompetent or humourless (though some religious enthusiasts have censured humour, and left-wing enthusiasts are often accused of humourlessness). Of course, it may be that the humour only appeals to those who already share the position being espoused, and that only those are moved who are already in favour, but that is another consideration. The point is that avowed didacticism is not necessarily incompatible with meeting at least some of the demands we place on works of art in the medium in question.

However, art which illustrates a thesis is often dissatisfying just because we experience the work as *merely* illustrative without intrinsic interest. Here it seems something has gone wrong. An artist must be interested in the particular and not just the general. Further, an artist must be willing to learn new things through the particular, not merely seeing the particular as an example of what is already known. So there is a difference between, say, painting a peasant or a worker, on the one hand, merely as illustrating the category 'peasant' or 'worker' and certain stock evaluations of peasants and workers (suffering, noble, ...) and, on the other, painting a peasant or worker as a person in whom one is intrinsically interested and from whose appearance or way of being in the world one may learn. In other words, to use art *merely* illustratively is to think one knows all that there is to be known and that there is nothing more to be discovered in and through the (real) process of artistic engagement with the world, using a specific artistic medium. But know-alls in art are just as tedious as know-alls in reality.

A merely illustrative novelist, for example, who knows in advance what ideas he or she wants to illustrate, and who is unable or unwilling to learn anything from his or her art, will not have the experience, which novelists often report, of the characters acquiring a life of their own — that is, leading the writer to think in fresh ways. As Brecht expresses it, literary 'production is the unforseeable. You never know what's going to come out' (*Aesthetics and Politics*, p. 97). In contrast the political artist who seeks to express something of a vision of the world through art actively embraces the idea that art is a way of knowing the world (afresh). Picasso's *Guernica* is a political artist's painting; but it is not an illustration of an idea about what happened at Guernica: it explores what happened in the artist's own exploratory medium. In this way it does not impose on the spectator, but accepts the spectator's sovereignty. It satisfies a norm laid down by Brecht, cited by Herbert Marcuse in *The Aesthetic Dimension*: 'A work of art which does not exhibit its sovereignty vis à vis reality and which does not bestow sovereignty upon the public vis à vis reality is not a work of art' (quoted, p. 32).

At this point one can see two rather different ways in which the work of a 'non-political' artist might be seen as political. First, through the process of exploration using their medium, 'non-political' artists may hit upon truths about their (social) reality, which they either do not (consciously) accept, or which they may not themselves see. Their art then transcends their own consciousness. Marxists have generally argued that it is perfectly possible for a self-consciously conservative artist to hit upon radical, critical insights into their social world, permitting their work to be legitimately read in a quite different way from that probably envisaged. In discussion of realism in the novel, Balzac is always cited as just such a conservative figure whose (artistic) integrity yielded in his novels radical insights. Thus Gyorgy Lukacs, invoking the authority of Engels writes, 'Engels showed that Balzac, although his political creed was legitimist royalism, nevertheless inexorably exposed the vice and weaknesses of royalist feudal France and described its death agony with magnificent poetic vigour' (*Studies in European Realism*, p. 10). Lukacs goes on, 'A great realist such as Balzac, if the intrinsic artistic development of situations and characters he has created comes into conflict with his most cherished prejudices or even his most sacred covictions, will, without an instant's hesitation, set aside these his own prejudices and convictions and describe what he really sees, and not what he would prefer to see' (p. 11). In other words Lukacs expects from the 'great realist' precisely the attitude we would expect in a scientist, but using artistic rather than scientific investigation as a means to discovery, to knowledge. Lukacs thus is at one with those who regard art as a way of knowing (cf. the positions taken by Peter Abbs in *A Is for Aesthetic* or by Louis Arnaud Reid in 'The Arts within a Plural Concept of Knowledge', in *The Symbolic Order*).

But, second, and more generally, 'non-political' artists are political just insofar as their work expresses a world-view, an ideological vision of the world, of which they may be wholly or partly unconscious, and which they might even disavow if it were synthesized and put to them in statement form. For example, Marxists have also sought to tease out the world-view of 'modernism' (q.v.), and especially in the work of those who would disavow political aspirations. Undoubtedly, for example, there is a vision of the world in Samuel Beckett's plays, a vision which he would not wanted to have stated in general, propositional form: 'the play's the thing', he might say. Or, as he is reported to have said when Billie Whitelaw told him she was to lecture on the meaning of *Waiting for Godot*, 'Damned if I know.' In a particularly interesting work in the (Marxist) sociology of art, *The Hidden God*, a study of Pascal and Racine, Lucien Goldmann seeks to show that the great artist is always at least the artist who, whether knowingly or not, succeeds in articulating a distinctive vision of the world, free of confusing elements drawn from other, and incompatible, visions of the world.

Is there a politics of non-representational art? Of course, one can claim that apparently non-representational art is not really so, and then treat it in terms of the ideas, etc. which it supposedly expresses. Thus Stalin thought that orchestral music expressed ideas and personally intervened to make sure that Shostakovich and others expressed in their music what Stalin thought they should express. There is a splended play about this: *Masterclass* by David Pownall.

But if a work is genuinely non-representational (abstract), can it have a politics? For some, the move into abstraction in painting is a political move: a flight from reality, an evasion of the challenge of meaning. (But those who might say this of abstract painting woulds not necessarily want to say this about 'abstract' music, which seems inconsistent.) Equally, for some, the *form* of all works is (politically) meaningful, hence at least as meaningful in abstract as in representational works. But here 'meaningful' can play fast and loose with us. Does it mean causally or intelligibly related to a social milieu, as chamber music is related to chambers and the triple-decker nineteenth century novel is related to Mudie's circulating library? Or does it mean that the form is, once again, expressive of an idea or a world-view so that certain forms (for example) express an elitist belief in 'art for art's sake' (whatever that may mean)?

In reality, art and politics increasingly meet each other across the tables of sponsoring and funding organizations. But that is another topic, which should be explored in relation to institutional theories of art (q.v. 'Art World').

Post-Structuralism

(q.v. 'Death of the Author,' 'Deconstruction,' 'I', 'Structuralism')

Anything which is merely 'post-' something else deserves little attention, and about 'post-structuralism' I shall be brief. Structuralism (q.v.) was and is a well-defined research programme in the human and social sciences, spanning linguistics, anthropology and analytical studies of all the arts. It has a seventy-year history in a number of intellectual centres and languages — Russian, Czech, French and English.

Post-structuralism is best thought of as the more or less sustained questioning of central structuralist assumptions or motifs, notably in French writings after about 1965. For example, in 'classic' structuralist studies of literary texts, like Propp's *Morphology of the Folktale*, there is a realist assumption that a correct analysis can and should carve reality at the joints, that there can be a naming of parts as scientific as that in, say, botany. The results make a claim on truth, but do not aim to be exciting, and, for example, give no insight into the pleasure we take in hearing tales told or in reading literature; nor do they address the question of artistic value.

In reaction and contrast, works like Roland Barthes' *S/Z* and *The Pleasure of the Text* claim to abandon the realist assumptions of structuralism and also to make the reader's pleasure a theme of critical reflection. In *S/Z*, for example, Barthes takes a short story by Balzac, *Sarrasine*, and cuts it into 561 passages (called lexias), the cuts falling just where Barthes feels the need to make them if he is to say what he will about the meaning of *Sarrasine*. These cuts are not an attempt to carve the story at its joints, to recover its truth — this would be to treat it as what Barthes calls a 'readerly' text (q.v. 'Death of the Author'). Rather, they are designed to allow Barthes to have his say, to have the pleasure of producing another text, of which *Sarrasine* is the provocation, functioning as what Barthes calls a 'writerly' text.

However, the procedure which Barthes adopts is less capricious than it may sound. In the way things strike us there are always idiosyncratic features, and there is something to be said for making a virtue of necessity. But there are also features which strike us the way they do because they strike others that way too, and that because they relate to a shared culture —

features which in *S/Z* Barthes classifies as referring to cultural codes. The gap between Propp's botanical sobriety and Barthes' hedonistic dismemberment of *Sarrasine* may be less great than is imagined by those who saw *S/Z* as a radically new departure in literary study. Barthes' main aim is to complement analysis of the level of *syntactic* structure — the strong point of structuralism — with analysis of semantic structure, and this is admirably achieved in *S/Z*'s coding and decoding of Balzac's short story, though one may reasonably wonder (as does Roger Scruton in 'The Impossibility of Semiotics') whether the result is very different from a traditional French *explication de texte*.

The reaction to structuralist realism is strongly marked in the scepticism and relativism of Derrida (q.v. 'Deconstruction'). But other aspects of post-structuralism can be read not as reactions but as more radical versions and sometimes inversions of structuralist claims. For example, the existentialism of a Sartre placed terrific emphasis on the world-making powers of the self, the 'I', whose essence was seen to be a product, not a precondition of human activity. But the structuralism of Lévi-Strauss insists on the way in which the human mind works independently of any conscious reflection or control by the 'I'. So Lévi-Strauss is able to say that it is not we who think in myths, but myths which think in us. However, the dynamics of the mind for Lévi-Strauss, as for Chomsky (whose views are very similar), are essentially inner or internally generated. They owe nothing to society. In contrast, the 'post-structuralist' psychoanalysis of Lacan, while it agrees with Lévi-Strauss in displacing the 'I' from centre-stage, sees the constitution of the mind, of the locus of human subjectivity, as the product of interaction, a view shared by Marxist post-structuralist theorists of the 'constitution of the subject' and the decentring of the 'I'.

For Sartre, human beings made themselves what they were, though they might in bad faith try to hide the fact — their responsibility — from themselves. For the post-structuralists, human beings are made what they are by family and society, though they also have the illusion that they are free and responsible agents who have created themselves (q.v. 'I'). In this aspect post-structuralism is simply at one with what one might call the suspicious theme in the thought of the past century, best represented in the work of Marx, Nietzsche and Freud. In these thinkers, things are not (ever) what they seem, and the task of the critic is to unmask and to demystify.

This is an appealing pedagogic stance, but it sits rather more easily with the realism of the structuralists than the relativism and scepticism of the deconstructionists. For scepticism is merely that position which (in a phrase of Adorno's about the sociology of knowledge) allows one to call everything into question, but criticize nothing. Post-structuralism does not have a name of its own when it calls everything (structuralism, but also existentialism and humanism) into question, but that is also to say that until it articulates alternatives with their own names it has very little to offer in their place.

Some Key Figures for Post-Structuralism

Gilles Deleuze (1925–) French philosopher who has written on numerous subjects, including cinema, schizophrenia, Sacher-Masoch, Nietzshe, Proust and Francis Bacon.

Jacques Derrida (1930–) French philosopher and writer, effectively the single-handed inventor of deconstruction as a method of reading literary and philosophical texts. Since the publication of three key works in 1967, he has exercised an enormous influence on French and American criticism, though some Angle-American philosophers regard him as little better than a clever charlatan. For an introduction see Christopher Norris, *Deconstruction: Theory and Practice.*

Michel Foucault (1926–1984) French historian of ideas and institutions, centrally concerned with intellectual systems and organizations as technologies of power. His main works fall outside the scope of the present book, though he wrote a text on Magritte, *This Is Not a Pipe*, which is worth reading. For an introduction see J.G. Merquior, *Foucault.*

Julia Kristeva (1940–) Bulgarian-born linguist, psychoanalyst and writer who has made her career in France, developing ideas from Mikhail Bakhtin and Jacques Lacan among others. Her *Revolution in Poetic Language* is a far-reaching, valuable study of symbolist poetry. For an introduction see the early essays translated in *Desire in Language* and Toril Moi (Ed.), *A Kristeva Reader.*

Jacques Lacan (1900–1981) French psychoanalyst who encouraged the systematic re-reading of Freud as a theorist of language, symbolism and imagination. Lacan had close personal and intellectual links with the surrealist movement. His flamboyant personality, controversial psychoanalytic practices and wilfully obscure writing have ensured a great deal of attention from academic writers. For an introduction see Anthony Wilden, *The Language of the Self*; see also Richard Wollheim, 'The Cabinet of Dr Lacan', and Malcolm Bowie, *Lacan.*

Jean-François Lyotard (1926–) French philosopher, for many years associated with the intellectually fertile political group, *Socialisme ou Barbarie*. A writer on aesthetics, he owes his current prominence to his contributions to debates on post-modernism. See his *The Post-Modern Condition* and, for an introduction, Geoffrey Bennington, *Lyotard.*

Paul de Man (1919–1983) Belgian-born literary critic, who emigrated to the USA and was posthumously identified as a prolific anti-Semitic journalist in Nazi-occupied Belgium. See Christopher Norris, *Paul de Man.*

Religion and Art

Art always and everywhere has been a medium through which people have sought to express their religious beliefs, or a vehicle through which societies have sought to have their religion represented. Probably the majority of European artworks produced in the past thousand years have had an overtly religious content, celebrating or representing biblical narratives or seeking to express a human sense of the divine. Of course, not all European religious art has been religiously inspired. Much of it is the work of artists working to church commissions, artists who themselves may have had no particular religious enthusiasms and who would execute a religious commission in no different a spirit than a secular one. Equally, European religious art continues to interest and to move people who think of themselves as without belief in the existence of God or the immortality of the soul.

Some significant contemporary art is religiously inspired or commissioned by churches. The names of Cecil Collins, T.S. Eliot, Eric Gill, John Piper, Stanley Spencer and Graham Sutherland come to mind. Not all of this religious art is orthodoxly Christian, and most contemporary art has no obvious religious aspiration. Even where an artist has firmly held religious beliefs, it may not be obvious that they are at work in his or her art. So it is, for example, not clear that one *should* read David Lodge's novels as illustrating a Roman Catholic vision of the world.

It is an arguable claim that all serious art is in some sense an attempt to articulate something ineffable, something which transcends everyday reality, and that it is consequently religious art, whatever the conscious beliefs of the artist or the audience. On this basis one may think that artistic creation is (in some sense) a religious act ('To reproduce is human, to create is divine', says Man Ray), that the art work is (in some sense) sacred, and that the experience of art is a (quasi-) religious experience. Anyone, for example, who feels shock or outrage at the destruction of an artistic work — the breaking of a sculpture, the destruction of a canvas, even the burning of a book — is probably not far from seeing such acts as literally sacrilegious.

In a widely publicized book, *Real Presences*, George Steiner has responded to the nihilism of deconstruction and, more generally, of post-structuralism (q.v. also 'I' and 'Death of the Author') by invoking the name and presence of God in defence of art. He believes that, 'on the secular level, on that of pragmatic psychology or of general consensus, the claims of nothingness cannot be adequately answered' (p. 199): art is not even meaningful without 'a wager on transcendence', a wager 'that there is in the experience of meaningful form, a presumption of presence' (p. 214) — where 'presence' alludes to the Catholic doctrine of the real presence of the body and blood of Christ in the bread and wine of the Mass. Embarrassed as we are to admit it, 'the entrance into our lives of the mystery of otherness in art and in music, is of a metaphysical-religious kind' (p. 178). The strongest claim that Steiner makes is that 'there is aesthetic creation because there is *creation*. There is formal construction because we have been made form' (p. 201). A much weaker claim is that there is, at least, in all art, 'a postulate of transcendence ... Plato's "aspiration to invisible reality"'' (p. 223).

Now the strong and the weak claims are significantly different. Slipping between these different claims, Steiner may well elicit in very different kinds of reader a vague sense that he must be right. Indeed, anyone who takes art at all seriously and who has ever asked themselves about the meaning of life, is bound to accord a hearing to someone who is as fervent as Steiner on behalf of the art-act and the aesthetic experience. But having once read Steiner's oracular prose (there is not a hint of his indebtedness to other writers, like Mikhail Bakhtin), one must read it a second, cooler time, and insist boringly and pedantically on some of the distinctions Steiner dazzles over.

Thus any claim for the real presence of a real God in art cannot be any stronger than the claim for the real presence of a real God anywhere. Even among Christians there are those who have been moved more by a sense of God's absence than of his presence (the Jansenists, for example). There are also those who would reject any (pantheistic) notion of God's omnipresence: after all, they might say, there is also art enacted against God and experienced as such: what else could have led the Bishop of Wakefield publicly to burn Hardy's (already bowdlerized) *Jude the Obscure* (1895). He didn't think he was burning a real presence! In other words, if you wish to understand art through theology, either metaphorically or analogically, or literally as exemplifying a theology — then you have first to sort out your theology. George Steiner does not appear to have any credentials as a theologian.

In contrast to the strong and literal claims which one might make, the idea that art is always, or at least, often, 'an aspiration to invisible reality' is a commonplace which carries no specific theological commitment. One might, for example, be thinking of 'invisible' reality in Kantian terms as the scientifically-unknowable 'thing-in-itself', and think of art as an (always-doomed?) attempt to grasp or express that of which we cannot have propositional knowledge. Again, one might come at 'invisible reality' as a Marxist and think of it as some non-existent but potentially realizable utopia, the character of which art can intimate. In *The Aesthetic Dimension* Herbert Marcuse writes of art as transcending its social determination and as invoking a beautiful image of another reality which has an 'overwhelming presence' just because the 'world formed by art is recognised as a reality which is suppressed and distorted in the given reality.' For Marcuse, as for his contemporaries (Walter Benjamin, Ernst Bloch, Theodor Adorno), the transcendence of art is placed and explained — as protest, aspiration and intimation — within a secular eschatology. Steiner might not wish to give such a vision house room, but, like the Kantian view, it is an alternative allowed by the weaker formulation of his own claims, and it is open to the reader to prefer the secular eschatology to Steiner's theology. One does not have to take one's Steiner whole.

Steiner is not the only contemporary writer on the arts to refer to a theological context for thinking about them. Peter Fuller does it in *Images of God*; Roger Scruton in various essays. Denis Donoghue does it in a book which parallels Steiner's, though in non-oracular style: *The Arts without Mystery*, where Donoghue distinguishes art and religion. Thus he writes:

> Even in a world mostly secular, the arts can make a space for our intuition of mystery, which isn't at all the same thing as saying that the arts are a substitute for religion, There is nothing in art or in our sense of art which corresponds to my belief in God. In religion, our faith and love are directed beyond ourselves. In art, faith doesn't arise. It's enough that the arts have a special care for those feelings and intuitions which otherwise are crowded out in our works and days. With the arts, people can make a space for themselves and fill it with intimations of freedom and presence'. (p. 129)

Representation (and Seeing-in)

If I dance for joy, I *express* my (feeling of) joy. If I dance someone dancing for joy, then I *represent* (iconically) that someone's joy. If instead of jumping for joy, I throw paint at a canvas, I express my joy and the canvas remains as a reminder, a trace, an index (q.v. 'Icon, Index, Symbol') of my joy. But if I try to paint in such a way that you will see joy or joyfulness in it, then what I try to do is to *represent* joy or joyfulness, even if the painting is an abstract one (that is, non-figurative). This sounds a bit odd; it would be more natural to speak of the abstract painting as expressive of (a state of) joy or of joyfulness. Yet if colours and forms have been chosen to convey a sense of joy, then it seems true to say that they *represent* it. The only hesitation is occasioned by the contrast we draw between original and representative existences (a contrast found in this form in the writings of the philosopher David Hume), and the thought that a colour (say) may not be so much representative of joy as (in itself) a joyful colour, that is, originally joyful. (A joyful colour is not an (arbitrary) sign standing for joy.) In other words *A* represents *B* when *A* stands for *B*, and it may stand for it either by some iconic resemblance such that *B* can be seen in *A* or by some convention such that *A* conventionally stands for *B*, or both.

This sounds like the beginning of a complex story, and indeed philosophers of art have offered complex analyses of the concept of representation — designed, for example, to explain why a screen print of Marilyn Monroe represents Marilyn Monroe while another screen print from the same screen does not in any sense represent the first screen print. (Why shouldn't it? One screen print is more like another screen print than a screen print is like Marilyn Monroe....) Such complex analysis can be found in Nelson Goodman's *Languages of Art* and Richard Wollheim's *Painting as an Art* (Ch. 2). One might also mention Ernst Gombrich's *Art and Illusion: A Study in the Psychology of Pictorial Representation*.

Wollheim's position is that representation is possible because we are naturally able to see one thing in another: to see the face in the fire, the man in the moon. The artist deliberately uses our ability to see one thing in another to create representations in which it is correct to see one thing in another. In the same way we can see expressive qualities or properties in things, and this can be built on by the artist, the composer as much as the painter, for, as Peter Kivy says, 'We tend to "animate" sounds as well as sights"' (*The Corded Shell*, p. 58), that is, hear them as having expressive qualities such as sadness or joyfulness (q.v. 'Expression').

From a teaching perspective the most important thing is probably to make clear to students the many different ways in which one thing can be represented, where the 'one thing' can be emotions as well as objects. This can be done using the distinctions between icon, index and symbol (q.v.) and requires that the distinction between expression (q.v.) and representation is clearly made. If this is done, it is possible to understand (for example) how a painting can be non-figurative but representational rather than abstract, since it can represent a mood without any figuration, yet equally without being a simple overflow of that mood.

Self-Expression (q.v. 'Classicism and Romanticism', 'Expression', 'I')

Would anyone bother with art if it were not, in some central way, a medium or an intrinsic form of self-expression? When all the debate between classicism and romanticism (q.v.) is over and all the distinctions drawn between expressing oneself and expressing a belief or a feeling (q.v. 'Expression') does it not remain true that without self-expression art is merely another form of alienated labour, a world we have made but in which we cannot recognize ourselves?

It is true that we can express ourselves in the way we deploy a tradition, rules or conventions — so that classicism is not incompatible with self-expression. Nor is it excluded that I express myself primarily through the imaginative expression of beliefs and feelings which are not (necessarily) mine — that I express myself in imagining the parts of other partners in a possible dialogue. One might say this of Dostoyevsky's novels; see M. Bakhtin, *Problems of Dostoyevsky's Poetics*. It is also true of Hume's *Dialogues Concerning Natural Religion*.

Let us suppose we can all agree on the presence and value of self-expression. But what is it to express one's self? Does everyone have a self to express? Are all selves equally worth expressing? What is the test for successful self-expression? Whatever it is, it is not plausible to suppose that our self is something we know antecedently to its expression. We discover our selves in our lives and in the works we produce, including our art works. But in doing this, we also place ourselves in a position to accept or reject our discovered selves, and (at least to attempt) to remake ourselves in our own image. Here we will be moved by whatever we take to be normative for a self, a self in which we can have self-respect, a sense of worth. If my work reflects a self which is trivial, or conceited, or mean, or sexist, or one-sided, I will not only reject the work but the self which produced it.

There will not, of course, always be a consensus on what ought to be accepted or rejected. The Marquis de Sade succeeded in expressing a self which by all prevailing normative accounts he ought to have rejected. E.M. Forster uses his posthumously published novel, *Maurice*, to express a self which could not (freely) be expressed in his lifetime. One expresses apostacy from Islam at one's peril. (In case that sounds smug, I have seen it written that the philosopher Anthony Kenny was not 'free' to give up the Catholic priesthood: 'for Catholics, Holy Orders are a Sacrament that, like matrimony, cannot be "left",' writes a correspondent in the magazine, *Oxford Today*.)

Children are often invited to express themselves, but adults often do not wish to accept the self expressed, for example, because it is 'immature'. But, then, are all children's selves immature or only some? At issue in this question are our notions of child development, and whether child art should be seen developmentally or, always and only, aesthetically. Are children invited to express themselves in order to accept what they see they have expressed, or to reject it? Does anything matter apart from (achieving) self-expression?

To this last question Peter Abbs answers, in *Living Powers*, with a critique of self-expression as a pedagogic demand made on arts education.

> Many children in 'free' art lessons may have expressed *themselves* only too well but produced, for want of technique and initiation into the symbolic medium, artistic non-entities. Good art is made out of a complex engagement, a reciprocal play between self and technique, between impulse and medium, between feeling and tradition. In the long term, the limited and limiting notion of self-expression could only lead to impoverished practice, the endless reproduction of the same minimal gestures, formulae, notations, brush-strokes, possibly *original* but not for that reason of any *artistic* worth. (p. 44)

For many thinkers, art is a *distinctive* medium or form of self-expression, which is distinguished by its capacity to enable us to reach parts of ourselves which other activities cannot reach. Personally, I work off minor irritations, bees in my bonnet, by writing letters to the press. Most of these, thankfully, remain unpublished. Half of those which are published cause me intense embarrassment. Writing to the press is self-expression, but it does not make contact with what I regard as really significant about the world or myself. If I wanted to express, say, my pessimism about human nature and human lives, I would not seek to do it in a letter to the editor. Rather, my pessimism is something only conceivably explorable, expressible as a 'deep' aspect of my 'personality' in the medium of art or philosophy. In that way I make sense of and accept the claims for the distinctive powers of the arts, where, in the words of the composer Aaron Copland, one can seek to satisfy 'the basic need to make evident one's deepest feelings about life'.

But 'making evident one's deepest feelings' is a rather more sophisticated conception of self-expression than that which has sometimes been articulated and practised in arts education, and which is criticized in other volumes of the Falmer Press Library on Aesthetic Education, for example, in *Living Powers*. It would be a careless assumption that it is *easy* to make evident one's deepest feelings, or that this can be done without simultaneous initiation into the techniques and traditions of the various arts disciplines.

Semiology/Semiotics

'Semiology' and 'semiotics' are alternative names (signifiers) for the same thing (signified): the science of signs. Both words have Greek roots, and the idea of a science of signs was conceived and practised in Ancient Greek philosophy. More recently the term 'semiology' was used by the Swiss linguist Ferdinand de Saussure (1857–1913) in his *Course in General Linguistics*, where, he says, 'A *science that studies the life of signs within society* is conceivable; it would be a part of social psychology and consequently of general psychology; I shall call it *semiology* (from the Greek *semieon* 'sign'). Semiology would show what constitutes signs, what laws govern them....' This notional semiology remained more or less undeveloped until the 1950s and 1960s, when Roland Barthes in France sought to make a reality of it in such books as *Mythologies* (1957) and *Elements of Semiology* (1964). Saussure's contribution is helpfully surveyed in Jonathan Culler's *Saussure*.

'Semiotics' was the term used to designate the science of signs by C.S. Peirce (1839–1914), the American philosopher responsible for the very useful tripartite classification of signs into icon, index and symbol (q.v.). The term has been taken up in more recent times, in preference to 'semiology', by such theorists as the Italian Professor of Semiotics, Umberto Eco, who uses it in the title of his textbook, *A Theory of Semiotics*.

Leaving aside any doubts one might have about a general 'science of signs', its potential scope is clearly vast, and embraces concerns discussed under numerous headings in this book: not only icon, index and symbol, but representation, symbol and symbolism, language, communication, intention and convention (q.v.) and others. In this section I present semiology/ semiotics as no more than a set of useful distinctions and instruments of analysis. Specifically, I look at:

> syntax, semantics and pragmatics;
> signifier and signified;
> form, sense and reference;
> language (*langue*) and speech (*parole*)
> denotation and connotation;
> paradigm and syntagm.

A language is the central example of a system of signs, used by convention. A grammar of a language will first of all comprise a *syntax*, that is, rules for permissible (grammatical) combinations of word forms. It will also comprise a *semantics*, which provides a method for determining the meanings of any combination of forms. Though not always thought of as part of the grammar of a language, a *pragmatics* will specify the means of determining the meaning of a combination of word forms on a particular occasion of use and, directly of indirectly, provide a specification of the rules governing the use of expressions in concrete situations of utterance.

A major part of the task of the would-be semiologist or semiotician is to show that grammars of sign systems other than language can indeed be constructed, or at least to show that it illuminates a sign system to show that a grammar or component of a grammar cannot be constructed for it. For example, there cannot be a syntax of painting, since painters do not use discrete forms, equivalent to word forms; and it is contested whether there is a semantics for much classical instrumental music. Such questions are of central concern in such works as Nelson Goodman's *Languages of Art* and Peter Kivy's *Sound and Semblance*.

But to talk of 'sign systems' supposes that we already know what a sign is. One of Saussure's most influential contributions has been his distinction between the two sides of a sign, at once *signifier* and *signified*. Thus 'cat' in English is the signifier for what in French is signified by '*chat*'. The forms, the signifiers, are different; the signified is the same. But what is the signified? Here Saussure's legacy has been unhelpful. Saussure equates the signified with something mental, an image, idea or concept — say, of a cat. This opens the way to supposing that in different languages the signifiers carve up the space of the signifieds in different ways, an idea developed independently of Saussure by anthropologists like Benjamin Lee Whorf, whose *Language, Thought and Reality* argues for the ultimate untranslatability and incommensurability of different conceptual schemes, different systems of signifieds. But there is only incomprehensibility and untranslatability if no appeal can be made to the real world of cats and dogs, the referents of 'cat' and '*chat*', 'dog' and '*chien*'. Such an appeal is made by Saussure and others, when they point out that (for example) 'rat' and 'mouse' in English carve up differently the semantic space occupied by the one Latin word '*mus*'. (The example is to be found in Eco's *A Theory of Semiotics*, p. 78.) It is only because there *are* rats and mice that we can say such things.

In another tradition, that of the German logician Gottlob Frege (1848–1925), one distinguishes sharply between the *sense* of a word (Saussure's signified) and its *referent* (the real-world object or state of affairs it is used to speak of). There are thus three things: word forms ('cat', '*chat*'), senses or signifieds, and referents, all to be taken into account in an adequate theory of signs.

If a language is a system of signs, it is a system put to use on specific individual occasions as speech or writing. Thus Saussure distinguishes between a language (*une langue*) and speech (*parole*). It should be reasonably clear that different methods of analysis and schemes of explanation are necessary for *langue* and *parole*, but this has sometimes been obscured in semiological work aiming to extend Saussure's approach beyond language, narrowly conceived. For example, a novel, a painting, and advertisement, a musical composition, a dance are not themselves like languages, but rather (and possibly) instances of the use of languages or language-like systems, that is, instances of *parole*. For example, in the case of spoken or written language one generally expects to be able to construe the meaning of an utterance at least partly through recourse to a dictionary, which correlates signifiers and signifieds for a given language. But it is, to say the least, doubtful whether there is a possible dictionary by reference to which the meaning of an advertisement could be construed, except — trivially — insofar as it incorporates linguistic material (cf. Judith Williamson, *Decoding Advertisements* and Trevor Pateman, 'How Is Understanding an Advertisement Possible?').

The pioneer of a semiological approach to advertising — and, more generally, of mass media imagery — Roland Barthes, clearly does see that advertisements can only be approached as *parole* rather than *langue*, and, indeed, that we quite possibly have to do with *parole* without any corresponding *langue* (see his essays, 'The Photographic Message' and 'Rhetoric of the Image'). His significant contribution, beginning in *Mythologies* (1957), was to find a way of talking about the fact that advertisements do not so much say one thing as mean another, but rather that they say or show one thing in order to suggest another. To talk about this fact, in the domain of advertising but equally in any other domain in which it occurs, Barthes distinguished between the *denotation* and the *connotation* of a text or image.

Thus an advertisement may denote (state or show) one thing (say, a beautiful woman), and by means of that same thing connote (suggest, imply) something else (say, sexual success). Barthes puts it like this: a sign at one level, comprised of its signifying and signified aspects, becomes the signifier, at a second level, of another signified, which is connoted by the first level of sign. Advertisements routinely connote a gamut of general values — the ideology of a consumer society: success (financial, sexual, social); satisfaction; security and so on. For Barthes, the task of the semiologist of advertisements (and, more generally, of mass or popular culture) is in large measure that of identifying and naming the connoted, suggested or implied values for which first-order, denotational signs are used as vehicles. However, in respect of some contemporary advertising (e.g. for cigarettes) it may be wrong to think of the advertisements as designed to suggest a definite set of associated values or as having a given meaning fully recoverable in a true interpretation. Rather, the advertisements are invitations to the construction of an indefinite number of narrative interpretation, none of them especially privileged. In this way some advertising now embodies practically the claims made more generally by post-structuralist and post-modernist theories.

How connotation is possible (how it is possible for people to hear and see connotations without being (fully?) conscious of them) is an important and difficult question. One mechanism which is involved is that of *association* of sound or sense. Saussure argued that every word in a language is linked by association to a *paradigm* of related words as well as linked *syntagmatically* (syntactically) to the words with which it co-occurs in any given sentence. Thus 'cat' is linked by sense to feline, kitten, animal, cattiness, ... and by sound or form to 'catch', 'catholic', 'Katrina', 'catheter', 'cattle', ... Poets do not need to be told any of this. The point relevant here is that paradigmatic association is (or, more modestly, could be) a standard way in which advertisements connote. If a lager refreshes 'the parts' other lagers cannot reach, there is a paradigmatic association to 'private parts' and hence to a connotation of sexual success. This despite the real-world incidence of brewer's droop. Paradigmatic association is very evident in dreams (q.v. 'Unconscious', 'Symbol, Symbolism').

The interesting research question which remains is to construct a full model of the mainly unconscious mental processes by which one thing can come to suggest in a non-idiosyncratic way a rich complexity of other non-stated things (see Dan Sperber and Deirdre Wilson's *Relevance* and my essay, 'How Is Understanding an Advertisement Possible?'). It does seem that mainstream post-Saussurean semiology has tended to settle down to the reiteration of the founding concepts and distinctions, despite the fact that it is now clearly possible to move beyond them. An exhaustive treatment of the scope of semiology/semiotics, with extensive bibliographies, can be found in Winfried Nöth, *Handbook of Semiotics*.

Space and Time, Arts of

In a famous work of neo-classical aesthetics and criticism, the *Laocoön* (1766), Lessing (1729–1781) argues that the starting point for an understanding of painting is that it is and can only be the organization of figures and colours in *space*, whereas poetry employs articulate sounds in *time*. Painting is consequently adapted to showing the visible properties of *bodies*, and poetry to representing *actions*. Poetry can properly suggest bodies through their actions. Painting, 'in her co-existing compositions, can use only one single moment of the action, and must therefore choose the most pregnant, from which what precedes and follows will be most easily apprehended' (*Laocoön*, Section 16). When much else in *Laocoön* has not survived, the doctrine of the pregnant moment is still very much alive, notably in writings on photography. It is found, for example, in John Berger's and Jean Mohr's *Another Way of Telling*, pp. 119–22. Also alive is the idea of thinking about the arts comparatively in terms of their relation to space and time. Lessing himself intended to extend his analysis to music, dance, mime and drama, and more recent writers have accomplished the extension.

However, we should now want to draw a clearer distinction than does Lessing between the mode of existence of a work of art (its ontology) and the manner in which we experience it (its phenomenology). For example, one could think of a musical composition as a (timeless) set of instructions for patterning a sequence of sounds and silence in real (clock) time, but the experience of listening to a musical performance is not adequately characterized in terms of the passage of clock time as one listens. Indeed, it is commonly said that in listening to a musical composition our sense of the passage of clock time is suppressed: music is a machine for the suppression of time, says Adorno; or, as George Steiner puts it in *Real Presences*, music is 'time made free of temporality' (p. 27).

Again, one could say that the literary work of art (poem or novel), like a mathematical problem, is out-of-time (non-temporal, timeless), but that it takes real (clock) time to read it, as it takes real time to solve a mathematical problem. Though we ourselves set the pace of reading a novel, in a way that we do not set the pace of a performance of a play (which gives the playwright an opportunity denied the novelist, fully exploited in, say, *Waiting for Godot*), it is the novel which sets the way we experience our relationship to time while reading it. This is not just a question of whether the novel is fast-moving or drawn-out. For example, in *Feeling and Form* Susanne Langer argues that narrative fiction orients us to an imaginary past, so that we experience a novel as in the past tense (whatever the actual tense of the novel), and in reading it are involved in the creation of what Langer calls virtual (that is, imaginary) memory. In contrast, says Langer, film orients us in present tense mode and involves us in the creation of a virtual history. Drama orients us to the future, and we experience it as virtual life.

Langer's phenomenology is not undisputed. In *The Logic of Literature* Käte Hamburger argues for the presentness, not the pastness, of our experience of the world of narrative fiction. Hamburger also contests the views of one of the major theorists of the phenomenology of our experience of the arts, Roman Ingarden, author of *The Cognition of the Literary Work of Art* and other studies of literature, film and music.

If one wanted to make a thorough comparison of, say, film, drama and the novel, one would also have to consider the spatial phenomenology of our experiences of works in these different media. For example, one might argue that drama in the theatre is experienced as spatially closer to us than film in the cinema — as *here* rather than *there*. If this is so, it might be explained fairly straightforwardly in terms of the differential crossability of the space between audience and stage, audience and screen. What we do in the cinema cannot affect what happens on screen; but our applause, laughter, signs of boredom, etc. can influence what happens on stage. Likewise, stage actors may forget their lines; screen actors never do. The stage actor is consequently closer to us psychologically: the boundary between imaginary and real world is not always sustained, as when an actor corpses or dries.

The subjective contrast between things *here* and things *there* is complemented by the temporal subjective contrast between what is experienced as happening *now*, and what experienced as happening *then* (or as to happen in the future). In *Camera Lucida* Roland Barthes suggests that photographs have a *here-then* character in experience. We experience photographs as spatially close, because they are the real traces of real events. But we also experience them as temporally distant, because they are the traces of events which are irretrievably and necessarily past. Thus the nostalgic character of photographs (q.v. 'Photography').

Such speculations could and have been developed at length. Within the framework provide by the concepts of space and time it is possible to conduct an extensive comparative study of the nature of the arts and of our experience of them. One can begin to see what is meant by saying that a work has an 'immediacy' or that it is boring or tedious. One can also raise interesting questions about the frame of mind in which we should approach different works. Roland Barthes used to say that 'readerly' texts needed to be read fast, 'writerly' ones (like the *nouveau roman*) slowly. In *Painting as an Art* Richard Wollheim indicates (p. 8) that he is only going to write about paintings which he has looked at for at least two hours. There is certainly scope in that statement for a discussion of how we set about experiencing Lessing's paradigm of spatial art.

Structuralism
(q.v. 'Semiology/Semiotics', 'Post-Structuralism', 'Tradition')

'Every novel has a beginning, a middle and an end. But not necessarily in that order.' Thus wrote Somerset Maugham, an unlikely structuralist, but in this sentiment entirely at one with structuralist theorists of narrative, including the first one, Aristotle, to whose *Poetics* Somerset Maugham is alluding (see Aristotle, *On the Art of Poetry*, Ch. 7).

Any structuralist account of narrative will distinguish between the subject-matter, events or history narrated and their narration, fabulation or discursive rendering. But if structuralism could tell us no more than Somerset Maugham told, it would be nothing to become excited about. In fact, structuralists have been able to tell us quite a lot more. For example, in the *Morphology of the Folktale* (1928), Vladimir Propp set out to show for a corpus of 150 Russian folk tales that all the stories could be generically classified in terms of thirty-one narrative functions distributed among seven dramatis personae. Each story is comprised of a subset of the thirty-one functions occurring, remarkably enough, in an invariant order. This interesting classificatory achievement becomes fascinating as soon as it is realized that Propp's empirically derived classification appears to fit an indefinite number of stories, oral, written, enacted or filmed and from diverse cultures.

Little Red Riding Hood, for example, begins in a way which, some ordering problems aside, you will have no difficulty in assigning to the first eight of Propp's functions, as they follow on from the delineation of what Propp calls the 'initial situation':

1 One of the members of a family absents themselves from home.
2 An interdiction is addressed to the hero.
3 The interdiction is violated.
4 The villain makes an attempt at reconnaissance.
5 The villain receives information about the victim.
6 The villain attempts to deceive the victim in order to take possession of the victim or their belongings.

7 The victim submits to deception and thereby unwittingly helps the villain.

8 The villain causes harm or injury to a member of the family.

Propp's attempt to specify a narrative structure underlying diverse surface content has suggested teaching strategies for creative writing which extend to the story techniques usually confined to poetry. Thus, instead of giving a story *title*, teachers can offer Propp's functions as a story *structure*, rather as they might give the structure of a haiku or a sonnet as the form in which a poem is to be written.

However, Propp's account is not without its problems, and it suggests some immediate questions. One problem concerns vagueness in the specification of functions, so that it is often or always a matter of interpretation whether something in a story is to count as, say, the violation of an interdiction. Not all cases are as clearcut as Little Red Riding Hood straying from the path when she has been told not to. One question arising is why there should be precisely thirty-one functions and seven dramatis personae. For an orally narrated tale, it is reasonable to suggest that hearers can hold in their heads only about seven characters (see G.A. Miller, 'The Magic Number Seven, Plus or Minus Two'), but thirty-one has no obvious explanation, and other structuralists, like A.J. Greimas, have sought to rationalize it to a more magical number.

Among contemporary structuralists, the most famous, Claude Lévi-Strauss, has always believed that underlying structures — whether in kinship systems, myths, rituals or objects such as masks — are evidence for the way the mind works. He assumes, like Chomsky, that the human mind always and everywhere works in the same ways. For Lévi-Strauss, following in the footsteps of another linguist, Roman Jakobson, the leading idea is that the human mind operates in terms of binary oppositions and that such oppositions structure all the phenomena of human culture. Myths, for example, provide an imaginary resolution of the contradictions into which our binary ways of thinking lead us. So the Oedipus myth is a meditation on the conflict between a society's belief that human beings spring from the earth (autochthony) and the evident fact that they are born of the union of man and woman, a meditation which makes sense of this opposition by putting it into parallel with the opposition between overvaluing blood relations (Oedipus's incest) and undervaluing them (Oedipus's patricide). (See Lévi-Strauss's essay, 'The Structural Study of Myth', for a full exposition.)

Binary oppositions are at work in plastic art too. In one of his most accessible books, *The Way of the Masks*, Lévi-Strauss seeks to show for the masks of the Indian tribes of the north-west coast of North America that those masks which are plastically similar in different tribes are linked to myths with opposite meanings, whereas masks which are opposite are associated with similar myths. So the Kwakiutl mask of Dzonokwa and the Cowichan Swaihwe mask are plastically opposites: one is black, the other white; one has sunken, the other protuberant eyes; one has no tongue, the other a noticeably large one; etc. But they are linked to similar myths: both Dzonokwa and Swaihwe are the source of riches.

These thumb-nail sketches from Lévi-Strauss show the characteristic structuralist concern with relational (diacritical) rather than inherent or intrinsic meanings. Neither Propp nor Lévi-Strauss tries to locate the meaning, significance or essence of a tale, myth or mask by reflecting, phenomenologically or psychoanalytically, on its own particular and peculiar properties. Rather, they work at meaning by locating each story or artifact in a set (what Lévi-Strauss calls a 'transformation set') such that each individual element stands in differential, contrastive or oppositional relation to every other.

There is a standard structuralist source and account of how and why this should be so which derives from the work of the linguists Saussure, Trubetzkoy and Jakobson. According to them, it is in the nature of languages as conventional systems of arbitrary signs that they can only generate meanings or values diacritically and not intrinsically. Thus the value of the phoneme /p/ in English is defined by the other phonemes of English and not by any intrinsic properties of /p/. Likewise, it is claimed for semantic units that the value of (say) *Sheep* is established in relation to *Lamb, Ewe, Ram, Mutton*, etc. and not intrinsically. Any textbook of structuralism, such as Terence Hawkes' *Structuralism and Semiotics*, emphasizes such points as defining what structuralism is all about.

This whole approach is fraught with problems. Phonemes are very different from semantic units, which have a reference as well as a sense, such that it seems untrue to say that they have no substantive meaning of their own. A less mysterious account of diacritical and differential meaning might be given by saying that the diacritical and differential on the plane of structure (what Saussure calls 'synchrony') is the product of real dialogue on the plane of history (what Saussure calls 'diachrony'). Let me elaborate.

Structuralism is, by definition, an ahistorical, synchronic approach to the study of the products of cultural endeavour, considered independently of their authors, consumers and circumstances of production. As such, it has been the target of reproaches by Marxists and others. Famously, Sartre and Lévi-Strauss argued over the very question of structure versus history: see Sartre's *Critique of Dialectical Reason* and the last chapter of Lévi-Strauss' *The Savage Mind*. But structure and history are mutually necessary, not mutually exclusive. It is because stories, myths, masks or novels develop historically, each creator working in a context established by predecessors, contemporaries, models and rivals with whose work his or her own is intertextual or dialogic (to use the language of Julia Kristeva and Mikhail Bakhtin: q.v. 'Tradition') that the results are sets of works internally related by differences and distinctions. In an important sense the audience always encounters such differences ahistorically, and for that reason the structuralist approach is validated. When, for example, I read a novel 'for pleasure', I do in large part read it without regard to its history and in such a way that the text is placed, though not quite in the way T.S. Eliot thought, in a simultaneous order of other texts, so that after my reading I might want to compare *Things Fall*

Apart with *The Mayor of Casterbridge* or *Empire of the Sun* with *What Maisie Knew*. Any particular comparison may be inept or far-fetched, but no logical howler is made in making it.

But to bring in the reader, the audience, in this way is a most unstructuralist thing to do. The scientific quest of structuralists from Propp through to Gerard Genette (in *Narrative Discourse*) is for structures considered independently of writers and readers alike, structures which are at work whether we know it or not. This strongly realist element in structuralism is one of its aspects from which, in works like Roland Barthes' *S/Z*, post-structuralism (q.v.) is a reaction.

Some Key Figures for Structuralism

Ferdinand de Saussure (1857–1913) Swiss linguist and inspiration for modern structuralism through his posthumous *Course in General Linguistics*, which sought to complement historical, diachronic linguistics with a cross-sectional static or synchronic linguistics. For an introduction see Jonathan Culler's *Saussure*.

Victor Shklovsky (1893–1984) Prolific Russian writer and leading figure in the Russian formalist movement 1913–1930, originating the idea — later appropriated by Brecht — that art works by creating estrangement. He described *Tristram Shandy* as the most typical novel in world literature. For an introduction see Tony Bennett, *Formalism and Marxism*.

Roman Jakobson (1896–1982) Another prolific Russian who eventually reached the USA during the Second World War, where Lévi-Strauss encountered him. He wrote and lectured in many languages. See his *Six Lectures on Sound and Meaning* and the famous essay, 'Linguistics and Poetics'.

Vladimir Propp (1897–1970) Russian folklorist, known almost entirely for his *Morphology of the Folktale*, but author of other works, some now translated as *Theory and History of Folklore*.

Claude Lévi-Strauss (1910–) Anthropologist, for many years professor at the Collège de France and the key figure in establishing structuralism in France. For an introduction see Edmund Leach, *Lévi-Strauss*.

Roland Barthes (1915–1980) French writer and critic influenced by Sartre and Brecht as well as Saussure. From his early Marxist-structuralist *Mythologies* he progressed through post-structuralism (*S/Z*) to autobiography (*Camera Lucida*). He was never an academic critic, much more the marginal, tubercular intellectual. For an introduction see Jonathan Culler, *Barthes* or Susan Sontag's *A Barthes Reader*.

Style

We speak of style in relation to a period, a school or movement in the arts, and we also use the term to pick out features or characteristics of works of art across periods, schools or movements. These are matters of what might be called *general style*. We also speak of the style of an individual artist: *individual style*. This distinction corresponds roughly to that which Roland Barthes makes for literature between writing (*écriture*) and style (*style*) in *Writing Degree Zero* (1953).

But does every individual artist have a style? Must they have one in order to count as an artist? Can an artist have more than one style? In *Painting as an Art* (1987) Richard Wolheim argues that for a painter to count as an artist, they must have an individual style (p. 26). The same could be argued for a writer or a film-maker and so on. It may not be easy to specify what the style is which makes an artist of a painter, but it is something definite, something real: says Wollheim, 'Individual style is in the artist who has it, and though, in the present state of knowledge, it must be a matter of speculation precisely how it is stored in the mind, style has psychological reality' (p. 26): to have a style is like knowing a language (p. 27). But in the case of style, 'we should be extremely reluctant, without evidence of massive psychological disturbance, to multiply styles by departing from the maxim, one artist, one style' (p. 35). The trouble with Wollheim's approach is that it tries both to deploy the concept of style normatively — to distinguish artists from (mere) painters — and to use the concept descriptively, as locating a psychological fact. There is a tension between these two uses, and it might be better to distinguish them.

Thus, on the one hand, we could think of individual style as like the individual idiolect — the idiosyncratic version of a language — which each individual speaks. Individuals may or may not be aware of particular features of their style, as likewise of their idiolect, though making progress in an art form almost certainly involves bringing more and more of the features of one's style under self-conscious reflexive control, so that they can either be intentionally deployed or actively modified. Equally, no one can have reflexive awareness of all aspects of their style or idiolect — at any rate, at any one time. This is a primary source of what is often called the surplus of

167

meaning, and is perhaps the insight which is expressed in La Roche-foucauld's famous maxim, *'Le style, c'est l'homme même'* (His style is the man himself) (q.v. 'Unconscious'). On the other hand, we use 'style' to pick out those features of an individual's work which we think deserve explicit eva-luation as 'good' or 'bad': as when we say, 'It is painted in a lurid style (or a delicate style, and so on)'.

Whereas a child apprenticed to its mother tongue will normally acquire just one idiolect of that tongue (though that idiolect will include different registers: that is, different forms appropriate for use on different occasions), it is not so clear that an artist apprenticed to painting or drawing or film-making or 'creative writing' will have learning experiences of a single or consistent system, even with a rigidly prescriptive education. Hence it is not impossible that an individual's style should develop as fragmented or incon-sistent or multiple. Part of the developmental achievement of the 'serious' artist is their success in moving out of what is, in effect, a confusion of styles into a consistent stylistic stance, which they make their own. This idea is basically that which Wollheim discusses as the distinction and movement in an individual artist's work from the pre-stylistic to the stylistic (p. 29) and yields whatever truth there is in the notion that for a painter to count as an artist, they must have a style (of their own). A muddle of styles is not enough. It is this developmental aspect of style which accounts for the fact that style is generally (perhaps necessarily) identified at least in part retrospec-tively, not just by the audience but also by the artist.

But just as there are virtuoso mimics, who can imitate many idiolects (this is what a Mike Yarwood does), there seems no reason why there should not be artistic mimics. Obvious candidates are forgers and pastichers of various kinds. But there seems to be no reason why a 'serious' artist should not also be a virtuoso mimic, that is, capable of handling more than one style — and not just in its superficial features. So an artist could display more than one style without 'massive psychological disturbance'; any writer of parodies has to be able to do this. Some composers (e.g. Mozart) have clearly been capable of displaying more than one style. And despite Wollheim's scepticism (p. 35), Picasso may have been a painter of such stylistic virtuosity: see John Berger, *Success and Failure of Picasso*.

In other words one should distinguish between the person who does not know enough to put together a consistent artistic act (of their own), and is consequently a mere copyist, or a pasticher, or simply muddled; and the person who knows so much that they can offer us a genuine and valuable case of artistic multiple personality. It is perhaps a merely contingent limita-tion of human ability that in most cases the maxim 'one artist, one style' holds good, sufficiently so for author studies to make sense, as it does in the *auteur* approach to the study of film.

For the teacher, the question of style is connected to questions about the role of emulation and imitation in arts education. This is discussed in Rod Taylor's and Gavin Bantock's contributions to *The Symbolic Order*, edited by Peter Abbs.

Sublime

Though semantically paired with the beautiful, the sublime has nothing like its currency. The use of the term may even strike some people as affected: to call a work 'sublime' is rather like calling it 'divine'. But if a critic uses 'sublime' to characterize a work which induces amazement, wonder or awe in virtue of its ambition, scope or a passion which seems to drive it, then this use is not far off that to be found in one of the major works of classical criticism, *On the Sublime*, historically attributed to Longinus but now generally reckoned to date from the first century AD, before Longinus' time.

On the Sublime deals with forms of expression which have the power to 'entrance' us, to 'transport us with wonder', as opposed to merely persuading or pleasing us. Sublime passages in literature (and, we add, in the other arts) exert an 'irresistible' force. Couched as rhetorical advice, 'a well-timed stroke of sublimity scatters everything before it like a thunderbolt, and in a flash reveals the power of the speaker' (all citations from *On the Sublime*, Ch. 1).

This power arises not from mere mastery of technique: not all technically competent artist are capable of sublimity. Rather, it can only be achieved by those artists who are able to form 'grand conceptions' and are possessed by 'powerful and inspired emotion' (*pathos*) — qualities which Longinus regards as 'very largely innate' (Ch. 8). Combined with technical competence, powerful thought and emotion produce the 'true sublime', works which 'uplift our souls', fill us with 'proud exaltation and a sense of vaunting joy, just as though we had ourselves produced what we had heard.'

Now there is clearly some slippage here between the idea of the genius of the sublime artist, as a superhuman figure, and the genius of a particular kind of work. The same slippage occurs in our contemporary cultures insofar as they transfer a suspicion of a certain kind of artist — the genius, the superman — onto certain kinds of work — the vast, the unrestrained and so on. Contemporary cultures prefer their art works, in general, to be modest and unassuming. And, in general, they are, so that there is little opportunity for critics to use the word 'sublime' even if they were willing.

But sublime works are produced, even in unexpected places. The conception which informs Werner Herzog's *Fitzcarraldo* is certainly grand — a man getting a steam boat hauled over a mountain in order to finance opera in the Amazon — and the filming is as passionate as the hero. Insofar as the film produces amazement, wonder or awe it is properly characterized as sublime. Again, the all-male Satyricon Theatre of Moscow performs a cabaret version of Jean Genet's *The Maids* with song, dance and mime which in virtue of the intensity of physically expressed passion conveyed undoubtedly renders the performance sublime — though we would probably simply say 'astonishing'. Perhaps one should start thinking of some contemporary fiction as sublime — Marquez's *One Hundred Years of Solitude*, for example.

On the Sublime was translated into French in 1674, and exerted a considerable influence in eighteenth century aesthetics, where beauty and sublimity are often paired. In this context the sublime often has a rather different meaning from what it has in Longinus, and this different meaning has also entered into our way of thinking. For example, in *A Philosophical Enquiry into the Origin of Our Ideas of the Sublime and Beautiful* (1757) Edmund Burke generates a conception of the sublime in connection with our encounter with nature as well as art. The sublime now becomes that which causes astonishment, 'that state of the soul in which all its motions are suspended, with some degree of horror' (p. 95). In lesser degrees the sublime produces admiration, reverence and respect (p. 96). In greater degrees the sublime is that which produces terror, 'terror is in all cases whatsoever, either more openly or latently the ruling principle of the sublime' (p. 97). So Burke's question then becomes, what terrifies us? Subjectively, it is the fear of pain. Objectively, we are terrified by vastness (the ocean), by obscurity (which hides the full extent of a danger from us), by what is powerful, and by what is infinite. (Says Burke, 'Infinity has a tendency to fill the mind with that sort of delightful horror, which is the most genuine effect, and truest test of the sublime' (p. 129); and recall Pascal's 'I am terrified by the emptiness of these infinite spaces', *Pensées*.) In relation to art Burke lists as sources of sublimity, magnitude (e.g. of a building), unfinishedness (as in preparatory sketches), difficulty (as when we imagine the immense force necessary to build Stonehenge), magnificence (especially when to some extent in a rich disarray) and colour (the sublime excludes white, green, yellow, blue, pale red, violet and the spotted and requires 'sad and fuscous colours, as black, or brown, or deep purple, and the like' — p. 149).

Burke's constant recourse to nature to characterize aesthetic experience is standard in eighteenth century and later writing; it is also found, for example, in Kant's *Critique of Judgement* (1790), where it is used — as it is by Burke — to get at the beautiful as well as the sublime. Of course, natural beauty is a concept of major importance to romantic thought. Here it is only to be observed that the relation of nature to the aesthetic is one which divides contemporary aestheticians: for some, the beautiful and sublime in nature are paradigmatic for understanding the aesthetic value of art; for others, this approach — which treats it as a contingent fact that we also get aesthetic pleasure from art as well as nature — is totally misguided.

My own inclination is to side with the eighteenth century, especially in relation to how we think of the sublime. In addition, though the sublime is in one aspect characterized through its power to effect loss of control over ourselves — we are thunderstruck by the sublime — in another aspect the characterization of the sublime is in terms of the mind at work: we are, says Burke, amazed, awe-inspired, astonished by the sublime. This does not sound so very different from the (sense of) wonder in which all serious scientific response to the world is (also) rooted. Educationally, we might be well-advised to think more in terms of ensuring that children encounter the sublime than that they are initiated into the beautiful.

The concept of the sublime, as articulated by Burke, contains a lurking paradox. It is that we are drawn to things which cause us pain — indeed, terror, says Burke. Yet our whole psychology is built on the notion that we seek pleasure and shun pain. This paradox can be dissolved by saying that we find pleasure in the encounter with imagined or fictional pain, or that the aesthetically painful is prophylactic of real pain, or that the 'pain' of the sublime is metaphorical — that there is a pleasure in the sublime which we characterize as painful. The paradox is rather more obstinate than these summary resolutions suggest, and further aspects of it are implicitly under consideration in the sections 'Holocaust', 'Mimesis and Katharsis', and 'Play'.

Symbol, Symbolism

The word 'symbol' and to a lesser extent its cognates — symbolism, symbolic — have a dual life. On the one hand, the word leads a boring existence as a synonym of 'sign' so that '*A* is a symbol of *B*' means no more than '*A* is a sign of *B*'. Studying for your driving test, nothing hangs on whether you think you are mugging up road signs or road symbols. But 'symbol' also leads an exciting, mysterious life. Artists search for symbols as knights errant might search for the Holy Grail, thinking of them as things which will capture, evoke or resonate with the depths of human experience. Critics search for the keys which will unlock the secrets of the symbols artists have intuitively found. See, for example, Ernst Cassirer's three-volume *Philosophy of Symbolic Forms* for an exhaustive study. I discuss the boring sense of 'symbol' elsewhere (q.v. 'Icon, Index, Symbol'). Here I consider the interesting sense.

One key issue is this: Are there natural symbols? That is, are there symbols which have a meaning or evoke a response independently of the context within which they are produced and encountered? Are there symbols with a natural history but no cultural history? (q.v. 'Archetype').

Dream symbols have often been considered candidates for the status of natural symbols with a fixed meaning, which can be spelt out in a dictionary. So if one dreams of one's teeth falling out, one is really dreaming about sexual intercourse: the former symbolizes the latter. Nor is there any reason to suppose that the symbolism can be explained — it is just a fact that the one thing symbolizes the other. In the example given it is quite clear that there is nothing culturally specific about one's teeth falling out (it happens to all children) or about sexual intercourse. (In these kinds of discussion there is always a tribe to be invoked, but in the case of sexual intercourse there isn't!)

The moment one tries to show a meaningful connection between the symbol and the thing symbolized, so that it is intelligible why the former should symbolize the latter, the symbol loses not only its mystery but also its naturalness: it begins to look more like a cultural phenomenon, even though it may be one which is very widespread. For example, if in a dream a house is said to symbolize a woman, then this might be intelligible in terms of the very widespread cultural connection between women and hearth and home, and so on. The symbol ceases to be mysterious.

In *The Interpretation of Dreams* (1900) Freud argues against the 'dream book' approach to dream symbolism and in favour of a view of dream symbols as determined in their use and meaning by particular associations individual to the dreamer or local to his or her culture. The meaning of a dream cannot be read off with the aid of a dream book but must be (re-) constructed with the aid of the dreamer's associations to the dream symbols. To take a simple example: I dream of chasing a Painted Lady butterfly. Unsurprisingly, this 'symbol' stands for a painted lady and the painted lady in question is the one I have just taken to the opera, to *Madam Butterfly*. There is not a hint of natural symbolism here — and apparently not much need for interpretation either. What, however, should not simply be taken for granted is the Freudian (and general) presupposition that when I dream about a Painted Lady butterfly I am *really* dreaming about something else, a painted lady. The interesting question is why no one seriously supposes that I was really just dreaming about a Painted Lady butterfly! Pleading that I am an amateur lepidopterist and saw a Painted Lady (*Vanessa cardui*) only last week is to no avail in this culture. Some would be tempted to say that ours is simply a symbol-crazy culture which does not realize that 'all keys to symbolism are part of symbolism itself' (Dan Sperber, *Rethinking Symbolism*, p. 50). There are cultures which are rather different. Roland Barthes in his book, *The Empire of Signs*, says as much of Japan: there, if someone paints a picture of a cucumber and two aubergines, that's exactly what it is a picture of. (I leave the reader to work out the symbol-crazy interpretation.)

The example takes us from dreams to art. Just as there have been theories of the natural or fixed dream symbol, so in all the arts we find artists and critics who have been completely committed to theories of the natural or fixed symbol. These theories are of rather different kinds, and of varying plausibility. It is worth trying to unpick them, though all I do here is sketch some of the varieties of theory which have been espoused.

Composers have believed in sound symbolism and painters in colour symbolism: in tones and colours which are believed to be connected to certain ideas or emotions, independently of intention or context (see, for example, Kandinsky's *Concerning the Spiritual in Art*). The problem with such a belief is that it may embrace phenomena which have nothing to do with symbolism. If the colour red or deep bass notes excite a certain psychophysiological response, it does not seem right to say that they are functioning as *symbols* in doing this. The artist who uses them is (merely?) orchestrating (manipulating?) a certain causally explicable response. What is missing is the dimension of meaning (q.v. 'Meaning'). In a slogan: no meaning, no symbol.

More interesting and sophisticated are the theories of poetic symbolism, found in Kant, the English romantics and elsewhere, for example in Jung. Very baldly, the leading idea here is not just that the poet's job is to express a general idea in a particular symbol, but that there is no other way of expressing certain general ideas other than through the particular. The particular work of art is our attempt to express the inexpressible idea, for

173

example the idea of God. We cannot give a literal translation or paraphrase of 'the meaning of the symbol' which we use. If we could, we would not have to use the symbol; as Aniela Jaffé summarizes Jung's position, he has pointed out that 'a true symbol appears only when there is a need to express what thought cannot think or what is only divined or felt' (Jung, *Man and His Symbols*, p. 281).

The creative artist's distinctive ability is the ability to find symbols for the inexpressible, and these are both meaningful (unlike the bass notes or red) yet not interpretable by reference back to what they are symbols of (unlike, say, the Painted Lady). They are evocative of something which can never be (fully) stated, though we may be driven always to try to state what is evoked: driven to render the ineffable effable. But in being so driven we are always in danger of committing what has been called the heresy of paraphrase. For a discussion of this concept of symbolism see Mary Warnock, *Imagination* (1976), Part 3. For a quite different account of the drive to verbal paraphrase, specifically in connection with painting, see Michael Stephan, *A Transformational Theory of Aesthetics* (1990).

Taste

What is taste? There are three possibilities.

1 Taste is a faculty of the mind, innate and *equal* in virtually everyone, which is capable of education, and by means of which we distinguish (or are struck by) the difference between the beautiful and the ugly, the tasteful and the tasteless.
2 Taste is a faculty of the mind, innate and very much *unequal*, which is capable of education, etc.
3 Taste is a set of socially inculcated dispositions or culturally transmitted abilities to respond to and distinguish objects, events, etc. as beautiful or ugly, tasteful or tasteless. What counts as beautiful is itself socially and culturally constructed as part of the construction of taste, and may vary without any evident restriction. Taste is always differentially distributed: some people get it, some don't. It thus can act as a social discriminator or distinguisher, and is used by individuals to define and distinguish themselves socially.

The third possibility sounds less like a short definition and more like a précis of a full-blown theory. The précis will probably be immediately intelligible because it indicates a common way of thinking about taste. Most (?) people like to think they have taste (good taste); many think that it is solely in virtue of their socialization (or enculturation or education) that they find tasteful whatever they do find tasteful.

So it is true that I find Laura Ashley home furnishings generally tasteful (they please my sense of taste), that I find Texas Homecare wallpapers, etc. generally tasteless, and that I find even more pleasing than Laura Ashley furnishings what is on offer from Sanderson or Osborne and Little. But, equally, I cannot fail to be struck by the facts that (a) I am offended by what is cheap and pleased by what is dear and (b) that the distribution of Texas, Laura Ashley and Sanderson wallpapers on the walls of people's homes corresponds quite closely to the social class or occupational distribution of their occupants: Texas (working-class to lower-middle), Laura Ashley (middle-middle), Sanderson (upper-middle). People who are aware of (a) and

(b) and embarrassed by these truths may end up painting their walls white! — though this, of course, has its own socially signifying value.

What is true of wallpapers is at least as true of music: what music people value, what they listen to on the radio or purchase as recordings, corresponds very closely to their social position. Choice in music (musical taste) has such strong socially signifying value as an indicator of social group membership or allegiance that music education in secondary schools has often enough simply foundered on the rock of such extramusical social signification. It has ended up thinking either that its task is to bring good music (= classical music) to the masses, who have then opposed this unasked for charity, or that its task is merely to confirm the choices which pupils have already made, often enough resulting in the embarrassing spectacle of Sir playing last year's pop music on the upright piano. (For discussion of this predicament in music education see Lucy Green, *Music on Deaf Ears*.)

A story of the social construction of taste, and its unequal distribution — largely related to years of formal education — could be told at great length and has been, for example, by Pierre Bourdieu in *Distinction* (1984). But what is missed in such stories is any serious consideration of the possibility that what is unequally distributed may nonetheless by built on, and perhaps even correspond to, real pre-social propensities to respond. For consider: mathematical knowledge is very unequally distributed, and higher mathematics is the preserve, the monopoly, of professional mathematicians. But that does not in itself lead anyone to think that there is nothing to higher mathematics (or physics, or chemistry), that it is no more than a social construction which one can take or leave as one pleases.

To this it may be replied that the difference between (higher) mathematics and (good) taste is that the former is the same everywhere in the world, whereas the latter is attached to very different objects in different cultures: every culture has its own good taste. This reply is too quick, and is certainly not decisive. It is true that objects of (good) taste vary from culture to culture. So classical Indian, Chinese or Japanese paintings are painted according to different conventions from those employed in European painting. Likewise, the ceramics of these civilizations look different from those made in Europe. But — and this is an important point — it is not true that to European good taste — to educated, upper-middle-class, etc. taste — these paintings or pots are found positively ugly. Rather, the reverse: they are found beautiful, and they are admired and sought after. (Conversely, European classical music found a ready reception in China and Japan.) In addition, the artifacts of non-literate cultures have often been appreciated in Europe — and not merely by collectors — as objects of beauty. For example, traditional African sculpture was valued by and influenced some of this century's most important European painters.

Lack of familiarity with the artistic conventions of another culture may render access to an understanding and appreciation of its art difficult in various ways. But this has not prevented such art being found or seen as beautiful, as pleasing to (the sense of) taste. So why not say there is an innate sense (or basis to the sense) of taste, whether equally or unequally distributed we do not yet know? Why not go on to look for evidence of what is (innately) pleasing to taste?

Three problems remain to be surmounted, or at least recognized. The first is less worrying. The last-ditch social construction of taste theorist may dismiss the cross-cultural argument suggested above by saying that it is merely a further mark of social distinction to be able to say that one finds beautiful the art of another culture. A true connoisseur is precisely one who can show such flexibility of response. About this one can only say that it looks as if an infinite regress of argument is about to begin, with no possibility of escape or decisive confrontation of views.

The second problem is more difficult. It is the problem created by people with bad or even appalling taste. If there is an innate basis to the sense of taste, even if it is unequally distributed, even if some people have no taste at all, that is surely not compatible with the fact that some people find positively pleasing that which others find positively ugly, and that systematically so. (If someone literally had no taste, then their choices would, as it were, be random, so they ought to hit upon the tasteful at least as often as upon the tasteless.)

I visit someone's house and, looking at the new, carefully chosen and expensive carpets, wallpapers, pictures on the wall, knick-knacks, etc. am overwhelmed by a sense of their ugliness and tastelessness — how can I possibly think that the sense of taste is innate? Is it not much more plausible to suppose that my response is one in which I have been trained (by my family, my school) or in which I have trained myself (in pursuit of my social aspirations, etc.)? The sense of taste, as innate, must surely be a very poor thing if it cannot withstand such aberrations as I am pointing to. There are, after all, whole factories engaged in the mass production of tasteless objects, some of them very expensive. (Think of High Street jewellery.) Perhaps the sense of taste is a very poor thing. Perhaps it does require careful nurture if it is to develop. Perhaps it is easily perverted. These are possible responses to the second problem. They are not possible responses to the third problem.

The third problem is this. Young children have a positive preference for things which adults, who take these things seriously, though they keep their mouths shut, find excruciatingly tasteless. Young children love things which are gaudy, gross, sentimental, formless (have you ever *read* a story in a *My Little Pony* comic?) and so on. There is precious little evidence of a sensibility to things of beauty. This last sentence is, I hope, provocative and may lead the reader to continue the debate. The debate is, in effect, continued elsewhere in this book, in sections where references to classical philosophical discussions of these issues are to be found. (q.v. 'Beauty' 'Judgment').

Tears and Laughter

'Tears and laughter are, aesthetically, frauds', says Ortega y Gasset in *The Dehumanisation of Art*. Why should anyone think like that, or think (like Thomas Mann) that film is not art because it makes you cry. Well, don't tears and laughter belong to *real* situations which call for an emotional response, not to the unreal situations of art? Isn't it an index of a common disability that people find it easier to cry over a fictional tragedy than over a real one? Is there a terrible indulgence in tears shed in the theatre or the cinema, especially when they do not flow over an earthquake or a famine?

Aren't tears and laughter responses which can be too readily manipulated? Don't we often feel resentment when a film or play elicits tears or laughter we should like to withhold: tears over the denouement of a sexually stereotyped romance, laughter at a racist joke? And if tears and laughter were in place as aesthetic responses, wouldn't sexual arousal, or excitation to some act of violence, be in place too?

Isn't the job of the audience, the reader, to engage in imagination with a world shown, represented or expressed in a work of art, not to seek emotional gratification from it, or to allow emotional responses to be elicited? But how could there be imaginative involvement without emotional response? We can be terrified by the thought that in this dark place something is about to reach out and attack us. Why not terrified by the thought that in the dark place represented on the screen something is about to reach out and attack the hero with whom we are identifying? But should we identify? The question invites the reaction: identifying with a character is a natural response, and so consequently are the possibilities of emotional response which follow. Children as young as one or two can cry over the fate of a character in a story being read to them, feel sad when something sad is narrated (q.v. 'Mimesis and Katharsis').

Of course, our natural reactions can be exploited and often are by the authors of sentimental romances, the makers of pornographic films, the producers of doubtful sitcoms which make us laugh despite ourselves. So what? The problem of emotional exploitation is not solved by proposing a division between, say, entertainment and art (this is Collingwood's distinction in *The Principles of Art*), such that entertainment is designed to (and does) elicit emotional responses, whereas art is not so designed, and is abused by us if we seek emotional gratification.

The truth in what Ortega y Gasset is saying might be this: in a proper relationship to art there is always something of the reflective, if not always of the contemplative (in the everyday sense of that term). There *are* serene paintings upon which we may gaze contemplatively. But even caught up in the unfolding of a terrible tragedy, or swept along in the tumult of a symphonic finale, we are still exercising judgment and with it the possibility of reflection: still conceptualizing the experience into the experience which makes it an aesthetic one — an experience with a shape and a movement. But like any experience, it has the potential to evoke an emotional response, and often does so.

There is one further point about emotional reactions to art: the emotion is most commonly elicited through the construction of a narrative or temporal context in which it finds an appropriate place. It is not the *fact* of death, a murder, a bereavement which makes us weep; it is its insertion into a narrative which has prepared us for it and for such a response. Likewise, it is not a musical passage in isolation which arouses us, but its presence at a particular point for which we have been prepared. There are few if any opening lines or opening bars which move us to tears. Perhaps it is because the reports of disasters and tragedies which comprise so much of our daily radio and TV news have no narrative context, but rather appear as bald, isolated incidents, that we are so often untouched by them. For a useful discussion, see Malcolm Budd, *Music and the Emotions*.

Text and Context
(q.v. 'Interpretation', 'Meaning', 'Intention and Convention')

It is sound practical advice when disputing the meaning or the interpretation of a poem, play, painting, etc. to 'stick to what's in front of you', which is the text, canvas, etc. Otherwise, the text, canvas, etc. becomes merely a stimulus to more or less idiosyncratic, more or less interesting associations, meditations, reflections. What the speaker says then tells us things about the speaker, not about what the speaker is supposedly speaking of.

Yet 'sticking to the text' is easier said than done. For the text only reveals itself to us under a complex of contextual assumptions brought to it, consciously or quite unconsciously. For instance, knowing the Roman alphabet, you have no difficulty in seeing 'I Vitelli Dei Romani Sono Belli' as text. But *what* text it is depends on whether it is read as Italian or Latin, for it can be either: in Italian it means 'The Romans' cattle are beautiful'; in Latin, 'Go, O Vitellius, to the war-cry of the Roman Gods.' The right language context for this text is not written on its face, and has to be supplied from the context of its occurrence, or assumptions about that context, even if the context or the assumptions are obvious and do not have to be thought about. On an obviously Roman monument the words are Latin; in the middle of a text being read in Italian they are Italian: the *context* is then the context for this text.

I make a joke at your expense, but you don't hear it as a joke, and look cross, so I say, 'It's a joke', and you smile. In other words I provide you with a context for what I said (my text), in this case the context of my intentions and/or the genre to which I saw my words as belonging. I interpret my words to you, helping you make sense of their force and meaning. It is not much different when, reading Swift or Jane Austen, we assume on the basis of what we know or have been told about these authors that there will be lots of irony. Now, of irony we know that 'its presence or absence changes nothing in the text except its fundamental meaning' (E.D. Hirsch, *The Aims of Interpretation*, p. 23). So 'sticking to the text' in some po-faced fashion is going to mislead us when it comes to making sense of Swift's text or Austen's text.

To cut a long story short, we make sense of texts potentially using all and always using something of what we have in the way of contextual knowledge, and there is no other way of proceeding. Generally, we do not even have to think about the contexts we assume in making sense of something. It is only when those contexts fail us that we have to think about what we are doing. So you ask me, 'Where would you expect to find a legless tortoise?' and I am stumped for an answer: I can't think in what sort of place you would find such an unfortunate creature — until you say, 'Exactly where you left it' — which tells me that the answer was obvious all along, except to someone looking in the wrong place. Criticism often does the job of showing us the right place to look for the sense of a text, a canvas, but when it does that successfully, we can all too easily feel that it is merely stating the obvious, forgetting that things have only fallen into place for us because the critic was clever enough to show us where to look.

As an undergraduate student of philosophy, I read, like all such students, Descartes' *Discourse on Method*. Later I read a remark of Hugh Kenner's that the *Discourse* is written as an autobiography. I re-read, and, yes, of course, it is written as an autobiography. It's obvious. But I hadn't noticed before Kenner pointed it out to me, nor does any student of philosophy notice. That's because we are looking for the arguments, not the form in which they are presented.

But is there a right context for reading a text, looking at a painting? So far I have only suggested that either we hit on the right context automatically or unconsciously, or that when we get a context wrong or are baffled we can (easily) be shown the way to the right context: 'It's a joke', 'It's ironic', 'It's an autobiography.' But in the case of a complex work of art is there always or necessarily one right context, albeit comprised of various subparts? For example, Marxist critics will generally want to insist that there is always a right context, and that it has as one dominant or determinant subpart the class-related ideological complex which the individual work will (necessarily) express, even if unbeknown to its author (see, for example, Lucien Goldmann's study of Racine and Pascal, *The Hidden God,* or Nicos Hadjinicolau's *Art History and Class Struggle*; q.v. 'Marxist Critical Theory'). The Marxist critic is no different in terms of making a claim about a right context than, say, the Jungian critic, for whom archetypes are everywhere, even if unbeknown to their authors (q.v. 'Archetype'). It is just that Marxists and Jungians make different, incompatible claims about what the right context is.

One might say that Marxist or Jungian contextualizations are in order to the extent that they are illuminating, that is, relevant to our interests in understanding (see Habermas's essay, 'Knowledge and Human Interests'). The trouble is then that it seems they will be relevant to our interests in understanding to the extent that we are already Marxists or Jungians. In other words the question of whether there is one right context is not separable from the question of whether there is one right (true) theory of the world.

Tradition

Who could possibly be against tradition? Well, most important twentieth century artists have at some point thought themselves to be against it. But they have been against different things, and they have not always in practice been against what they said they were against.

Artists have said they have been against tradition when they have been against academicism: the lifeless repetition of motions and motifs no longer rooted in art but the requirements of the classroom for order, predictability and assessability. For the academicism of a turn of the century German art school, see George Grosz, *A Small Yes and a Big No*. Presumably, only academics are in favour of academicism, though they wouldn't call it that.

More significantly, artists have proclaimed themselves against tradition, meaning the art of the past. But the key difference is between those who have learnt from the past, and need to move beyond it to find new ways of expressing new things — as Karl Kraus finds a new way of expressing horror of that new thing, world war, in *The Last Days of Mankind* — and those who having failed to learn from the past are doomed either to repeat it or to produce work which, in retrospect, is merely the evidence of a protest movement, as with much of Dada and futurism.

There will often be ambivalence on the part of the creative artist towards the artistic past, especially the recent past. On the one hand, there is the desire to be truly creative, to produce something new and not merely a novelty within well-worn and well-understood forms (q.v. 'Creativity'). On the other, there is the pressing need for genius to learn from genius. The tension produces perfectly researchable *anxieties of influence* — to take the title of a well-known book by Harold Bloom. Some artists can happily enter into and work through an encounter with the art of their predecessors, acknowledging that they are learning and what they are learning from them. Others are anxious lest influence spoil their own individual talent, and have to deny and repress such influence. Most artists will move more or less uneasily between these two relationships to what has already been created.

In T.S. Eliot's famous 1919 essay, 'Tradition and the Individual Talent', acknowledgment of the indispensability of tradition is linked to a (classical) stress on the value of achieving impersonality in art — this against a (romantic) stress on self-expression (q.v. 'Classicism and Romanticism'). The poet is someone who excels in having a feeling for words, not one who readily finds words for a feeling. Indeed, for Eliot, the poet need make no distinction between emotions he has experienced and emotions he hasn't in fashioning feelings in words. And fashioning feeling in words requires not that one looks inside oneself, examining the phenomenology of subjective experience, but rather that outside oneself one is able to locate an 'objective correlative' for an emotion. As Eliot puts it in the other essay of 1919, that on *Hamlet*, 'The only way of expressing emotion in the form of art is by finding an "objective correlative", in other words, a set of objects, a situation, a chain of events which shall be the formula of that *particular* emotion; such that when the external facts, which must terminate in sensory experience, are given, the emotion is immediately evoked' (p. 48).

Eliot sets out not only an account of how he thinks the artist ought to engage with tradition (the Dead Poets' Society) but also how a tradition is constituted in a culture and for an audience. The leading idea here is that a living tradition is one in which the present (new art) can alter the meaning, the perception of the monuments of the past:

> The existing monuments form an ideal order among themselves, which is modified by the introduction of the new (the really new) work of art among them. The existing order is complete before the new work arrives; for order to persist after the supervention of novelty, the *whole* existing order must be, if ever so slightly, altered; and so the relations, proportions, values of each work of art toward the whole are readjusted; and this is conformity between the old and the new. Whoever has approved this idea of order ... will not find it preposterous that the past should be altered by the present as much as the present is directed by the past. And the poet who is aware of this will be aware of great difficulties and responsibilities. ('Tradition and the Individual Talent', pp. 38–9)

This idea of Eliot's, that in a living tradition past and present form a simultaneous order, is comparable to the structuralist idea that a living language exists for its speakers in a single synchronous state even though it is the product of historically reconstructible (diachronic) processes and practices (q.v. 'Structuralism'). In both cases a living tradition is distinguished from a dead one — in the latter case there is no simultaneous order, no synchrony, for any living person, merely historical (archival, philological) records.

In this perspective a large part of active arts education must be concerned with keeping alive the past, and that implies deciding *what* to keep alive and *how*. For example, no one believes that *Beowulf* can be kept alive in Anglo-Saxon; it has to be translated if it is to have any chance of staying in a simultaneous order (and even then it may be beyond recall). But what of Chaucer and Shakespeare? No sooner do we name these names than familiar disputes recall themselves. The friend of Shakespeare who wants Shakespeare to stay in a living and widely accessible arts tradition will be happy to take on new rewritings and adaptations of the original. The friend of Shakespeare who thinks that what matters is not any old living tradition but a particular simultaneous order in which it is the *language* of Shakespeare which matters, will resist, seeing in *West Side Story* or a comic-strip *Othello* nothing which serves to sustain the tradition as he (usually he) would wish to define it. One might add that those whose concern is with Christian theology and morality will be happy to see the Bible endlessly retranslated and modernized; those who care for a church more than for Christianity, and for the Bible as part of ritual or literature rather than as revealed truth, will insist on the King James' Bible, the Book of Common Prayer, etc.

The controversies here align to a large extent with the division between the friends of the people (populists) and the friends of the established order — queen and country, church and state, culture and tradition — that is, those who are called elitists. It is very hard to buck this division and opposition. In the end every teacher has to take a view on whether, say, Shakespeare is important and, if he is, what is essential in him. The only point of serious agreement between populists and elitists appears to be a shared commitment to the idea of a living arts tradition. No one is interested in preserving Shakespeare merely as history, as an archeological curiosity not so very different from the Rose Theatre.

There have been those who have said they would dispense with any and all traditions in the interests of self-expression, paralleling in the world of arts education the position of artists who have rejected tradition (for some, though not indisputably, the common, central characteristic of modernism — q.v.). But as Peter Abbs shows in *Living Powers* and *A Is for Aesthetic*, the attempt to evade tradition is misguided because ultimately incoherent: without tradition (an inherited language and culture) there is very little, if any, self, and consequently little or nothing to be expressed (q.v. 'Self-Expression', 'I').

Unconscious/The Unconscious

Doing something, there are many other things of which I am unconscious, in the sense unaware of, but which may be relevant to what I am doing. I may be unaware that you are also writing a book on aesthetics at the same time as me. In this case what I am unaware of might be called *external* to what I am doing. I may be unaware that the sentence I am writing contains a spelling mistake, a grammatical error, an alliteration, a mixed metaphor. In this case what I am unaware of is *internal* to what I am doing.

It would seem that because our minds are finite, we cannot be aware of everything relevant to what we are doing, even everything internal to it, since there is an infinite number of things which can be truly said of what we are doing, and we cannot be aware of all of them. Nor need these features of which we are unaware be unpatterned aspects. For example, a writer may have a style of which he or she is unaware, even though that style is patterned and could be (for example) defined and used to identify an author's work, as it is in computer-based analysis of texts (q.v. 'Style').

What the writer (or painter or composer) is unaware of may be noticed by others and — especially if it is patterned — may be assigned a meaning and a value by them. For example, an unconscious style may be seen as expressive of a writer's personality or of a vision of the world. In this way it is clear that texts (paintings, musical compositions) can elicit responses based on features not intended by the creator, yet indubitably present. These features constitute what some would call a surplus of meaning — meaning additional to that intended. As E.D. Hirsch puts it, 'An author almost always means more than he is aware of meaning, since he cannot explicitly pay attention to all the aspects of his meaning' (*Validity* in *Interpretation*, p. 48). (I would delete the 'almost' and substitute 'must'.) In contrast, a work can only contain, say, an allusion if the creator intended the allusion,

The very general claim that works have aspects or features, even patterned ones, of which their authors were unaware and hence were not using as vehicles of (intended) meaning, may be supplemented by a more specific claim that works contain aspects, patterned or unpatterned, symptomatic or expressive of their author's unconscious. More specifically still, one might claim that to these aspects the author will be blind, unless after the event, when they are pointed out. In other words it is in the nature of the unconscious to find ways of expressing itself in which it will not be recognized as expressing itself by the person whose unconscious it is (see Sigmund Freud, *The Psychopathology of Everyday Life*).

The idea that there is unconscious as well as conscious mental agency is still controversial: Sartre, for example, sought to reanalyze alleged instances of the unconscious at work as instances of bad faith, in which we seek to deceive ourselves about what we are saying or doing (see Sartre's *Being and Nothingness*). Even those who accept the general idea of an unconscious disagree about what it contains and hence about what to look for as expressive of it: there is a Freudian account of the unconscious, but also a Jungian one, and others besides.

Psychoanalytic accounts of art and artists, and criticism of individual works attempt much more than to show the unconscious at play in individual works or in named artists, but that is one of the central things such accounts do provide. In doing this, the psychoanalytic critic or theorist proceeds suspiciously, like a detective, looking for clues to interpret as symptoms of the unconscious at work. In addition, the psychoanalytic critic or theorist may seek to explain all or part of the appeal of a work to an audience, especially its overtly emotional appeal, in terms of the unconscious of the audience and to which the work gains access, even (and even especially) unbeknown to that audience. Thus, to give an almost banal example, an open or disguised Oedipal drama stirs up an Oedipal response, though we may be *unaware* that our response is an Oedipal one. (For varieties of psychoanalytic criticism see Elizabeth Wright, *Psychoanalytic Criticism*).

By all accounts the unconscious ought to have no difficulty in finding ways to express itself in an artist's work, since by all accounts the unconscious has at its disposal precisely those ways of expression which we take as characteristic of art. The unconscious is not boringly literal but richly symbolic. Like the artist, it uses signs metaphorically and metonymically (q.v. 'Figurative and Literal'). Take, for example, Freud's account of the construction of dreams in *The Interpretation of Dreams* (1900). For Freud, dreams express unconscious, repressed wishes (the unconscious here being thought of quite generally as the depository of what was once open but is now repressed). To circumvent the anxieties which overt expression of these wishes would cause, dream work produces dreams in which the wishes are expressed in a form which disguises them from the dreamer. Two key devices used by the dream work are condensation and displacement. Condensation is like metaphor: a chain of thoughts or cluster of desires are crystallized into and attach to a non-literal image; the attachment is motivated, but not transparent to conscious understanding. Displacement is like metonymy: rather than express a thought or desire directly, we represent it through some other thought, desire or image which has a motivated connection to it, either as part of it standing for the whole (this is the sense 'metonymy' has in rhetoric) or by some associative link.

The images or symbols produced by the work of displacement and condensation are not, in general, fixed and drawn from a pre-existing repertoire. They are idiosyncratic and novel or creative. This is why, in Freudian psychoanalysis, dreams cannot be interpreted by means of a dream book (or dictionary of symbols), but require the cooperation of the dreamer in providing associations to the explicit content of the dream, so that the processes of condensation and displacement can be worked back to the original motivating wishes. In contrast, in Jungian psychoanalysis, a much greater place for fixed symbolism has been granted (q.v. 'Symbol, Symbolism'), the fixed symbols thought of as archetypes, images given a priori, independently of and prior to experience (q.v. 'Archetype').

Visual Arts in Education

The visual arts in education comprise a complex and varied range of 2-D, textiles and 3-D activities, closely connected in that all involve the reordering and transformation of materials — from the highly resistant to the most malleable — under the impulse of visual and tactile experiences and sensations. They are, therefore, primarily concerned with aesthetic values as they manifest themselves through the two sense of sight and touch. Wood, metal, stone, perspex and plastics; clays, earth and pigments; fleece, fibres and pulp in various states provide artist and craftsperson with their essential raw materials. Though use of the hands plays an important part in the shaping and forming of these materials, a wide variety of tools and equipment is also employed. Some of these reflect recent technological advances, but others have hardly changed through centuries of usage. Artists and craftspeople have a highly developed design sense and can clearly visualize in the mind's eye and further clarify their intentions in various graphic forms. Nevertheless, concepts are also formed and modified, as well as realized, through the actual manipulation of the materials themselves. Through this creative act of working materials many likewise testify to profound feelings of identification and kinship with other practitioners, ranging across time, place and cultures, who have worked in related ways. Practical activity itself can therefore provide access to the symbolic system of the aesthetic field (q.v.) in the broadest possible sense, for many visual arts processes are universal, being practised across the world.

The visual arts have many obvious connections with the other major art forms, sharing their profoundly expressive qualities by likewise addressing issues to do with birth, life, death and the whole human dilemma, in the most potent ways. They are also practical and functional for many of their forms are determined by basic everyday human needs; architect, potter, weaver and designers help satisfy our need for shelter, clothing, furniture, containers and utensils and for aesthetically pleasing domestic, leisure and work places and environments. The visual arts occupy a crucially important place in the school curriculum, relating naturally to all the other major art forms but having a further important role to fulfill because of the vital ways in which they can inform and give meaning to the more functional activities which take place within the field of design and technology. Every branch of the visual arts has its history and contemporary practitioners. This means that the critical studies approaches pioneered within the subject can help pupils to understand the degree to which the visual arts have direct bearing on every aspect of their lives — through the design of cars and the house they live in, the cup they drink from and the clothes they wear, as well as through their study and practice of the fine arts such as painting and sculpture.

Critical studies are now widely recognized as comprising an essential element in any balanced visual arts education; young people should have opportunity to know about, understand and enjoy the visual arts as practised by others, as well as having opportunities to practise their own art-making. For many years art teaching was so weighted towards making that this often led to an emphasis on technique in isolation, with pupils copying from, or relying unduly on, second-hand source material, so great was the pressure to produce acceptable end-products by whatever means. Where art history and appreciation were taught, this was usually to older, more able students, but even then invariably treated almost as a separate subject divorced from studio practice. Recent critical studies developments have highlighted how beneficially these two major strands can be brought into tandem, and how, when this happens, it can be relevant to the needs of young people of all ages, intelligence and aptitude, with the experience in each area enriching learning in the other.

Many schools have been led to a reconsideration of the resources necessary for this type of work and are rectifying the years of neglect with regard to building up a range of art books, slides and video, and reproductions — unfavourable though the present climate is. Until quite recently it was also customary to see only the school pupils' work displayed, but there are teachers currently engaged in devising ingenious ways of introducing a variety of original works into their schools — in addition to loan collection examples — as well as more fully utilizing the potential of the pupils' work as a teaching resource. There was equally a time when it was unfavourable to embark on gallery visits, but this trend has also been largely reversed, in spite of government legislation militating against planning out-of-school visits.

Some schools have even successfully created gallery spaces of their own, providing the whole school population with ongoing access to the work of others. These developments have placed the visual arts in an ideal position to address all four phases of making, presenting, responding and evaluating, which define the aesthetic field, and are particularly in accord with the notion of the field as denoting 'the dynamic interactive element both in art-making and in and between works of art' (Abbs).

Recent consideration has also been given to how artists and craftspeople might most effectively operate in schools. There is now a better understanding of the crucial role they can fulfil in making the nature of artistic concepts and their realization comprehensible to young people in vital ways, and also how pupils too might work in related ways. Through these twin approaches, pupil insights can deepen, horizons broaden and their own practice gain in impetus, often taking unexpected new directions at a far remove from the norms of 'school art'. It is now far more common for residencies to be supported by attractive and informative displays of the artist's work, past and ongoing, set up and used in ways which clarify both the artist's motivations and working procedures. Where these are further substantiated by examples of other artists' works which have influenced the development of the resident artist, or which he or she simply admires, these displays can open up the whole symbolic system of the aesthetic field not just as it appertains to that artist, but also to the pupils through their related activity. Artists' interests are diverse, so this support material will frequently range across place, time and cultures, with examples coming potently alive through the link with the 'living artist'. Black and women artists working within these schemes can open up new horizons and bring important race and gender issues to the fore, challenging some of the prevailing notions of society in the process.

The content, forms, process, mood model also provides an invaluable analytical tool which opens up many points of access to the aesthetic field. It enables pupils to engage with art works in greater depth by posing questions in relation to what they are about, how they have been arranged and ordered, how they have been made and what with, and what kind of mood or atmosphere they encapsulate and convey. The four areas provide rich fields for negotiation between teacher and pupil, with each having potential to develop specific aspects of art vocabulary. Pupils can effectively relate aspects of the works of others to which they are particularly responsive to their own practice, and the model provides them with clear criteria for the evaluation of their own work and to make sense of the ideas and opinions of others with regard to the visual arts. Students experienced in the use of the model comment particularly on how it enables them to engage in depth with art objects about which they have no prior knowledge. Traditionally, art history and appreciation courses were impaired by undue attention to external factual data, but the four areas provide means whereby the pupil can explore the intrinsic qualities of works. In any course, particular areas will inevitably come into prominence at different times, but throughout any balanced course all four should be held in equilibrium, with the issues raised by each fully explored. These can then provide criteria for the meaningful exploration of the broader contexts which give rise to art and within which art exists; the social, cultural, historical and technological, for example.

Though current legislation appears to be as disadvantageous to the visual arts as to the other major art forms, it is interesting that the important developments in the subject over the last decade or so are complemented by a consistent increase in the numbers opting to study it to 16+ examination levels. Around half the school population now choose to study GCSE art and design. Providing the National Curriculum can allow the necessary scope for young people to exercise their preferences to some degree, the visual arts in education will continue to flourish.

For further reading see R. Taylor, *Educating for Art*; D. Thistlewood, (Ed.), *Critical Studies in Art and Design Education*; R. and D. Taylor, *Approaching Art and Design*; R. Taylor, *The Visual Arts in Education*.

RT

Willing Suspension of Disbelief
(q.v. 'Imagination')

I go to the theatre; I take my seat. I know it's only a play I'm going to see. But as the lights dim, I forget the real world, and willingly prepare to enter the imaginary world of the play, to believe in that world enough to laugh and cry, and to hang on the fate of its characters.

For children it seems to be easier. They don't need the lights to dim, the props of the stage, just a teacher who says, 'Let's pretend', and who then leads them into make-believe, as Dorothy Heathcote's 'teacher in role'. Indeed one might doubt whether children start from a disbelief which has to be suspended. It is rather as if they start from a belief which is only unwillingly or with difficulty given up. We take young children to the theatre, and they are all too really distressed. So we smile and cajole, 'It's only a play', 'They are only pretending.' It doesn't always work. Sometimes we have to take the children out of the theatre back into the 'real' world, a less threatening place. Adult reactions to horror films are no different. And here is Roland Barthes putting words into the reader's mouth, '"I know these are only words, but all the same" ... (I am moved as though these words were uttering a reality)' (*The Pleasure of the Text*, p. 47).

One might conclude: there is at least a level at which our minds do not discriminate between the real and the imaginary, between the original and its representation; or, alternatively, that feeling (emotional) response is to situations as conceived, and imagination is always involved in the conception. It is only in *action* that we discriminate the real and the imaginary, not in *reaction*. As far as reaction is concerned, there is always belief and it is never suspended — or, if it appears to be, we have to do with a pathological condition of imaginative weakness, a condition of anaesthesia, or else of emotional weakness.

If you can sit through certain films, certain plays, and not bat an emotional eyelid, that is not evidence of clear-headedness ('But it's only a film!'), nor evidence of a refusal ('I am unwilling to suspend my disbelief'). It is evidence of imaginative disability, if not of simple hard-heartedness (emotional disability). But how do you tell imaginative weakness and hard-heartedness apart? One response is to say that they are not so separate as here suggested. To be able to engage imaginatively is *not* separate from the capacity for sympathetic involvement with others. The person of feeling is a person of feeling for others. L.C. Knights puts it this way, 'The feelings that literature arouses are sympathies with something or other' ('Literature and the Education of Feeling', in P. Abbs (Ed.), *The Symbolic Order*) This is an interesting response, not least because it connects the idea of aesthetic education with that of moral education: to develop imagination is to develop sympathy, to foster sympathy is to nurture imagination. The central concern in both cases is with seeing and taking another person's point of view. It is no accident that all the theorists of drama in education have argued what is in effect either a moral or political case for it: the educative power of drama is to make people *better* than they would otherwise be, since the capacity to respond to (say) imagined distress is not separate from the capacity to respond to real distress. It is a parallel thought that leads Sartre, famously, to say, 'Nobody can suppose for a moment that it is possible to write a good novel in praise of anti-semitism' (*What Is Literature?*, p. 46). That is, no one. capable of the imaginative effort to write a good novel would be devoid of the human sympathy to see that anti-semitism is detestable.

But the drama-in-education story cannot be the whole story of the relationship between imagination and sympathy. There are clear cases where imagination is not the same thing as sympathy. In music, for example, the capacity to take pleasure in the music is at least in some measure dependent on the capacity to animate the music with a feeling-tone: to hear the music as happy or sad, and so on through an increasingly sophisticated vocabulary (see Peter Kivy, *The Corded Shell*). But this capacity to animate does not in any obvious way involve ability to identify sympathetically with others. One has to be capable of feelings to take pleasure in music, but there seems no bar to those feelings being self-centred. My own self-centred capacity for happiness or sadness is enough for me to take pleasure in the gaiety or melancholy of music.

In the visual arts the capacity for response is arguably most connected not to one's capacity for human sympathy (after all, there are landscapes and still-lifes to be accounted for), nor to one's ability to animate pictures with a feeling-tone, but rather to one's capacity to respond to what is depicted *as if* it were a real object (in other words not to be afflicted by disbelief). This is the position defended by Michael Stephan in *A Transformational Theory of Aesthetics*, where he argues that the 'level' at which we do not disbelieve in paintings is, in fact, the right hemisphere of the brain which handles the non-discursive pictorially presented information content of figurative paintings, and saves us from even the possibility of disbelief.

Further Reading

Though the bibliography lists all works cited in the text, the following works (not all listed there) have proved of special interest over the years to students on the University of Sussex's MA in Language, Arts and Education, from which much of this book arises. They may prove helpful for users of this book, specifically in the areas of aesthetics, criticism and critical theory.

BARTHES, R. (1975) *S/Z*, London: Jonathan Cape.
BENJAMIN, W. (1973) *Understanding Brecht*, London: New Left Books.
EAGLETON, T. (1983) *Literary Theory*, Oxford: Basil Blackwell.
FULLER, P. (1980) *Art and Psychoanalysis*, London: Writers and Readers.
MOI, T. (1985) *Sexual/Textual Politics*, London: Methuen.
PROPP, V. (originally 1928) *Morphology of the Folk Tale*, University of Texas Press.
SCRUTON, R. (1979) *The Aesthetics of Architecture*, London: Methuen.
SCRUTON, R. (1983) *The Aesthetic Understanding*, London: Methuen.
SHEPPARD, A. (1987) *Aesthetics*, Oxford, Oxford University Press.
SONTAG, S. (1979) *On Photography*, Harmondsworth: Penguin Books.
WOLLHEIM, R. (1987) *Painting as an Art*, London: Thames and Hudson.

Bibliography

Note: All works cited in the text are listed here. In the case of 'classics', the date of first publication is given, but the publisher reference is always to a contemporary edition.

ABBS, P. (1982) *English within the Arts*, London: Hodder and Stoughton.

ABBS, P. (1987) *A Is for Aesthetic*, Lewes: Falmer Press.

ABBS, P. (Ed.) (1987) *Living Powers: The Arts in Education*, Lewes: Falmer Press.

ABBS, P. (Ed.) (1989) *The Symbolic Order*, Lewes: Falmer Press.

ABOUD, F. (1988) *Children and Prejudice*, Oxford: Basil Blackwell.

ABRAMS, M.H. (1953) *The Mirror and the Lamp*, Oxford University Press.

ADSHEAD, J. (1981) *The Study of Dance*, London: Dance Books.

ALLEN, J. (1979) *Drama in Schools*, London: Heinemann.

ALQUIÉ, F. (1965) *The Philosophy of Surrealism*, University of Michigan Press.

ALTHUSSER, L. (1970) *Lenin and Philosophy and Other Essays*, London: New Left Books.

ANSCOMBE, G.E.M. (1957) *Intention*, Oxford: Basil Blackwell.

ARISTOTLE *On the Art of Poetry*, in *Classical Literary Criticism*, ed. T.S. DORSCH (1965), Harmondsworth: Penguin Books.

ARORA, R. and DUNCAN, C. (1986) *Multicultural Education: Towards Good Practice*, London: Routledge.

ARTS COUNCIL OF GREAT BRITAIN (1988) *The Arts and Cultural Diversity*, London.

ARTS IN SCHOOLS PROJECT (1990) *The Arts 5–16 Project Pack*, Edinburgh: Oliver and Boyd.

AUTY, G. (1977) *The Art of Deception*, London: Libertarian Books.

BAKHTIN, M. (1968) *Rabelais and His World*, MIT Press.

BAKHTIN, M. (1981) *The Dialogic Imagination*, University of Texas Press.

BAKHTIN, M. (1984) *Problems of Dostoyevsky's Poetics*, University of Minnesota Press.

BANFIELD, A. (1982) *Unspeakable Sentences*, London: Routledge and Kegan Paul.

BANKS, J.A. (1981) *Multi-Ethnic Educaton: Theory and Practice*, Boston: Allyn and Bacon.

BARKER, F., *et al.* (1977) *Literature, Society and the Sociology of Literature*, Essex University.

BARKER, F., *et al.* (1978) *1848: The Sociology of Literature*, Essex University.

BARTHES, R. (1953) *Writing Degree Zero*, London: Jonathan Cape.

BARTHES, R. (1957) *Mythologies*, London: Jonathan Cape.

BARTHES, R. (1961) 'The Photographic Message', in R. BARTHES, *Image, Music, Text* (1970).

BARTHES, R. (1964) *Elements of Semiology*, London: Jonathan Cape.

BARTHES, R. (1964) 'Rhetoric of the Image', in R. BARTHES, *Image, Music, Text* (1970).

BARTHES, R. (1968) 'The Death of the Author', in R. BARTHES, *Image, Music, Text* (1970).

BARTHES, R. (1970) *Image, Music, Text*, London: Fontana.

BARTHES, R. (1975) *S/Z*, London: Jonathan Cape.

BARTHES, R. (1976) *The Pleasure of the Text*, London: Jonathan Cape.

BARTHES, R. (1982) *Camera Lucida*, London: Jonathan Cape.

BARTHES, R. (1983) *The Empire of Signs*, London: Jonathan Cape.

BATESON, G. (1973) *Steps to an Ecology of Mind*, London: Paladin.

BELL, C. (1913) *Art*, London: Chatto and Windus.

BENJAMIN, W. (1970) *Illuminations*, London: Fontana.

BENJAMIN, W. (1973) *Understanding Brecht*, London: New Left Books.

BENNETT, T. (1979) *Formalism and Marxism*, London: Methuen.

BENNINGTON, G. (1987) *Lyotard: Writing the Event*, Manchester University Press.

BERGER, J. (1965) *Success and Failure of Picasso*, Harmondsworth: Penguin Books.

BERGER, J. (1972) *Ways of Seeing*, Harmondsworth: Penguin Books.

BERGER, J. and MOHR, J. (1982) *Another Way of Telling*, London: Writers and Readers.

BERGONZI, B. (Ed.) (1986) *Innovations: Essays on Art and Ideas*, London: Macmillan.

BERNAL, M. (1987) *Black Athena*, London: Free Association Books.

BEST, D. (1991) *The Rationality of Feeling*, London: Falmer Press.

BLACKING, J. (1973) *How Musical Is Man?*, Seattle: Washington University Press.

BLOCH, E., *et al.* (1977) *Aesthetics and Politics*, London: New Left Books.

BOURDIEU, P. (1984) *Distinction*, London: Routledge and Kegan Paul.

BOWIE, M. (1991) *Lacan*, London: Fontana.

BRECHT, B. (1964) *Brecht on Theatre: The Development of an Aesthetic*, London: Methuen.

BRECHT, B. (1965) *The Messingkauf Dialogues*, London: Methuen.

BRECHT, B. (1977) *The Measures Taken and Other Lehrstücke*, London: Methuen.

BRECHT, B. (1980) *The Life of Galileo*, London: Methuen.

BRITTON, J. (1963) *The Arts in Education*, London: University of London Institute of Education.

BUDD, M. (1985) *Music and the Emotions*, London: Routledge.

BÜRGER, P. (1984) *Theory of the Avant-Garde*, Manchester University Press.

BURKE, E. (1757) *A Philosophical Enquiry into the Origin of Our Ideas of the Sublime and Beautiful*, Oxford: Basil Blackwell.

CARBY, H. (n.d.) *Multicultural Fictions*, Race Series SP No. 58, Centre for Contemporary Cultural Studies, University of Birmingham.

CARDINAL, R. (1985) *Expressionism*, London: Paladin.

CARTER, A. (1983) 'Alison's Giggle', in E. PHILLIPS (Ed.), *The Left and the Erotic*, London: Lawrence and Wishart.

CASSIRER, E. (1955) *The Philosophy of Symbolic Forms*, Yale University Press.

CHADWICK, W. (1990) *Women, Art and Society*, London: Thames and Hudson.

CHOMSKY, N. (1956) *Syntactic Structures*, The Hague: Mouton.

CLEMENT, C. (1989) *Opera, or, the Undoing of Women*, London: Virago.

COLLINGWOOD, R.G. (1938) *The Principles of Art*, Oxford University Press.

COOKE, R. (1987) *Velimir Khlebnikov*, Cambridge University Press.

CRAFT, M. (Ed.) (1984) *Education and Cultural Pluralism*, Lewes: Falmer Press.

CROCE, B. (1953) *Aesthetic: As Science of Expression and General Linguistic*, London: Peter Owen.

CROOK, J.M. (1987) *The Dilemma of Style*, London: John Murray.

CULLER, J. (1976) *Saussure*, London: Fontana.

CULLER, J. (1983) *Barthes*, London: Fontana.

CURRIE, G. (1988) *An Ontology of Art*, Basingstoke: Macmillan.

D'AGOSTINO, F. (1986) *Chomsky's System of Ideas*, Oxford: Clarendon Press.

DERRIDA, J. (1982) *Margins of Philosophy*, Brighton: Harvester Press.

DES (198) *The Arts 5–16: A Curriculum Framework*, London: HMSO.

DES (1985) *Music from 5 to 16*, London: HMSO.

DICKIE, G. (1974) *Art and the Aesthetic: An Institutional Analysis*, Cornell University Press.

DONOGHUE, D. (1983) *The Arts without Mystery*, London: BBC Publications.

DUNLOP, V.P. (1980) *Dance Education*, London: Macdonald and Evans.

EAGLETON, T. (1981) *Walter Benjamin or Towards a Revolutionary Criticism*, London: New Left Books.

EAGLETON, T. (1990) *The Ideology of the Aesthetic*, Oxford: Basil Blackwell.

ECO, U. (1977) *A Theory of Semiotics*, London: Macmillan.

EICHENBAUM. B. (1926) 'The Theory of the "Formal Method",' in L.T. LEMON and M.J. REIS (1965), *Russian Formalist Criticism*, University of Nebraska Press.

ELIOT, T.S. (1917) 'Tradition and the Individual Talent', *in Selected Essays*, London: Faber and Faber.

ERLICH, V. (1981) *Russian Formalism*, Yale University Press.

ESSLIN, M. (1987) *The Field of Drama*, London: Methuen.

FANCHER, G. and MYERS, G. (1981) *Philosophical Essays on Dance*, New York: Dance Horizons.

FELDMAN, H., *et al.* (1978) 'Beyond Herodotus: The Creation of Language by

Linguistically Deprived Deaf Children', in A. Lock (Ed.), *Action, Gesture and Symbol: The Emergence of Language*, London: Academic Press.

Ferrari, G. (1989) 'Plato and Poetry', in G.A. Kennedy (Ed.), *The Cambridge History of Literary Criticism, Vol. 1: Classical Criticism*, Cambridge University Press.

Fischer, E. (1963) *The Necessity of Art*, Harmondsworth: Penguin Books.

Fish, S. (1980) *Is There a Text in This Class?*, Harvard University Press.

Foucault, M. (1983) *This Is Not A Pipe*, University of California Press.

Freud, S. (1900) *The Interpretation of Dreams*, Harmondsworth: Penguin Books.

Freud, S. (1904) *The Psychopathology of Everyday Life*, Harmondsworth: Penguin Books.

Freund, E. (1987) *The Return of the Reader: Reader-Response Criticism*, London: Methuen.

Fuller, P. (1986) *Images of God*, London: Chatto and Windus.

Gardner, H. (1984) *Frames of Mind: The Theory of Multiple Intelligence*, London: Heinemann.

Gasset, O.Y. (1972) *Velazquez, Goya and the Dehumanization of Art*, London: Studio Vista.

Genette, G. (1980) *Narrative Discourse*, Oxford: Basil Blackwell.

Gill, L. (1990) *The Arts: Do We Need Them?*, London: Watts.

Goldmann, L. (1964) *The Hidden God*, London: Routledge and Kegan Paul.

Gombrich, E. (1961) *Art and Illusion: A Study in the Psychology of Pictorial Representation*, London: Phaidon.

Gombrich, E. (1963) 'Meditations on a Hobby Horse', in *Meditations on a Hobby Horse*, London: Phaidon.

Goodman, N. (1968) *Languages of Art*, Indianapolis: Hackett.

Goodman, N. (1972) *Problems and Projects*, Indianapolis: Bobbs–Merrill.

Gosse, E. (1983) *Father and Son*, P. Abbs (Ed.) Harmondsworth: Penguin Books.

Green, L. (1988) *Music on Deaf Ears*, Manchester University Press.

Greer, G. (1979) *The Obstacle Race: The Fortunes of Women Painters and Their Work*, London: Secker and Warburg.

Griffin, S. (1981) *Pornography and Silence*, London: The Women's Press.

Grosz, G. (1982) *A Small Yes and a Big No*, London: Alison and Busby.

Gulbenkian Report (1982) *The Arts in Schools*, London: Calouste Gulbenkian Foundation.

Habermas, J. (1972) 'Knowledge and Human Interests', in J. Habermas, *Knowledge and Human Interests*, London: Heinemann.

Hadjinicolau, N. (1978) *Art History and Class Struggle*, London: Pluto Press.

Halliwell, S. (1987) *The Poetics of Aristotle*, London: Duckworth.

Hamburger, K. (1973) *The Logic of Literature*, Indiana University Press.

Hawkes, T. (1977) *Structuralism and Semiotics*, London: Methuen.

Haynes, A. (1987) 'The Dynamic Image: Changing Perspectives in Dance Education', in P. Abbs (Ed.), *Living Powers*, Lewes: Falmer Press.

Hirsch, E.D. (1967) *Validity in Interpretation*, Yale University Press.

HIRSCH, E.D. (1976) *The Aims of Interpretation*, University of Chicago Press.

HOCHBERG, J. and BROOKS, V. (1962) 'Pictorial Recognition as an Unlearned Ability', *American Journal of Psychology*, pp. 624–28.

HOLQUIST, M. (1990) *Dialogism*, London: Methuen.

HOLUB, R. (1984) *Reception Theory*, London: Methuen.

HORNBROOK, D. (1989) *Education and Dramatic Art*, Oxford: Basil Blackwell.

HORNBROOK, D. (1991) *Education in Drama: Casting the Dramatic Curriculum*, London: Falmer Press.

HUGHES, R. (1980) *The Shock of the New*, London: BBC Publications.

HUIZINGA, J. (1949) *Homo Ludens*, London: Routledge and Kegan Paul.

HUME, D. (1739) *A Treatise of Human Nature*, Oxford: Clarendon Press.

HUME, D. (1777) *Dialogues Concerning Natural Religion*, Harmondsworth: Penguin Books.

INGARDEN, R. (1973) *The Literary Work of Art*, Northwestern University Press.

INGARDEN, R. (1973) *The Cognition of the Literary Work of Art*, Northwestern University Press.

JAKOBSON, R. (1956) 'Two Types of Language and Two Types of Aphasic Disturbance', in R. JAKOBSON and M. HALLE, *Fundamentals of Language*, The Hague: Mouton.

JAKOBSON, R. (1960) 'Closing Statement: Linguistics and Poetics', in T. SEBEOK, (Ed.), *Style in Language*, MIT Press.

JAKOBSON, R. (1978) *Six Lectures on Sound and Meaning*, Brighton: Harvester Press.

JAMES, A. and JEFFCOATE, R. (Eds) (1981) *The School in the Multicultural Society*, London: Harper and Row.

JENCKS, C. (1987) *What Is Post-Modernism?*, London: Academy Editions.

JOSIPOVICI, G. (1977) *The Lessons of Modernism*, London: Macmillan.

JUNG, C.G. (1963) *Memories, Dreams, Reflections*, London: Fontana.

JUNG, C.G. (1964) *Man and His Symbols*, London: Aldus.

JUNG, C.G. (1966) *The Spirit in Man, Art and Literature*, London: Routledge and Kegan Paul.

JUNG, C.G. (1980) *The Archetypes and the Collective Unconscious*, London: Routledge and Kegan Paul.

KANDINSKY, W. (1912) *Concerning the Spiritual in Art*, New York: George Wittenborn.

KANT, I. (1790) *The Critique of Judgement*, trans J.C. Meredith, Oxford: Clarendon Press.

KAPPELER, S. (1986) *The Pornography of Representation*, Cambridge: Polity Press.

KITSES, J. (1966) *Film and General Studies*, London: British Film Institute.

KIVY, P. (1980) *The Corded Shell*, Princeton University Press.

KIVY, P. (1985) *Sound and Semblance*, Princeton University Press.

KLOEPFER, D.K. (1989) *The Unspeakable Mother: Forbidden Discourse in Jean Rhys and H.D.*, Cornell University Press.

KRAUS, K. (1974) *The Last Days of Mankind*, New York: Frederick Ungar.

KRISTEVA, J. (1974) *The Revolution in Poetic Language*, Columbia University Press.

KRISTEVA, J. (1980) *Desire in Language*, Oxford: Basil Blackwell.

KUHN, T.S. (1970) *The Structure of Scientific Revolutions*, 2nd ed., University of Chicago Press.

LABOV, W. (1977) 'Rules for Ritual Insults', in *Language in the Inner City*, Oxford: Basil Blackwell.

LACAN, J. (1977) 'The Mirror Phase as Formative of the Function of the I', in *Ecrits*, London: Tavistock.

LANGER, S. (1942) *Philosophy in a New Key*, Harvard University Press.

LANGER, S. (1953) *Feeling and Form*, London: Routledge and Kegan Paul.

LEACH, E. (1970) *Lévi-Strauss*, London: Fontana.

LEAVIS, F.R. (1948) *The Great Tradition*, London: Chatto and Windus.

LEAVIS, F.R. and THOMPSON, D. (1933) *Culture and Environment*, London: Chatto and Windus.

LERDAHL, F. and JACKENDOFF, R. (1983) *A Generative Theory of Tonal Music*, MIT Press.

LESSING, G.E. (1766) *Laocoön* (most accessibly in *German Aesthetic and Literary Criticism: Winckelmann, Lessing, Hamann, Herder, Schiller, Goethe*, ed. H. NISBET, Cambridge Universtiy Press, 1985).

LÉVI-STRAUSS, C. (1966) *The Savage Mind*, London: Weidenfeld and Nicolson.

LÉVI-STRAUSS, C. (1972) 'The Structural Study of Myth', in *Structural Anthropology*, Harmondsworth: Penguin Books.

LÉVI-STRAUSS, C. (1982) *The Way of the Masks*, Seattle: University of Washington Press.

LEWIS, D. (1969) *Convention*, Princeton University Press.

LONGINUS *On the Sublime*, in Aristotle, Horace, Longinus, *Classical Literary Criticism*, (Ed.) T.S. DORSCH (1965), Harmondsworth: Penguin Books.

LUKACS, G. (1950) *Studies in European Realism*, London: Merlin Press.

LYNTON, N. (1980) *The Story of Modern Art*, Oxford: Phaidon.

LYONS, J. (1977) *Chomsky*, London: Fontana.

LYONS, J. (1977) *Semantics*, Cambridge University Press.

LYOTARD, J.F. (1984) *The Post-Modern Condition*, Manchester University Press.

MACHEREY, P. (1978) *A Theory of Literary Production*, London: Routledge and Kegan Paul.

MacINTYRE, A. (1981) *After Virtue*, London: Duckworth.

MARCUSE, H. (1978) *The Aesthetic Dimension*, London: Allen Lane.

MARX, K. (1859) *A Contribution to the Critique of Political Economy*, London: Lawrence and Wishart.

MARX, K. (1970) *Economic and Philosophic Manuscripts of 1844*, London: Lawrence and Wishart.

MAYNE, J. (1985) 'Feminist Film Theory and Criticism', *Signs*, 11, 1.

MERQUIOR, J. (1985) *Foucault*, London: Fontana.

METZ, C. (1974) *Language and Cinema*, The Hague: Mouton.

MILLETT, K. (1971) *Sexual Politics*, London: Rupert Hart-Davis.

MOI, T. (1985) *Sexual/Textual Politics*, London: Methuen.

MOI, T. (Ed.) (1986) *A Kristeva Reader*, Oxford: Basil Blackwell.

MOTHERSILL, M. (1984) *Beauty Restored*, Oxford University Press.

MULVEY, L. (1975) 'Visual Pleasure and Narrative Cinema', in Mulvey (1989).

MULVEY, L. (1989) *Visual and Other Pleasures*, Basingstoke: Macmillan.

MURRAY, P. (Ed.) (1989) *Genius: The History of an Idea*, Oxford: Basil Blackwell.

NEWTON-DE-MOLINA, D. (1976) *On Literary Intention*, Edinburgh University Press.

NORRIS, C. (1982) *Deconstruction: Theory and Practice*, London: Methuen.

NORRIS, C. (1988) *Paul de Man*, London: Routledge and Kegan Paul.

NORRIS, C. (1984) *Derrida*, London: Fontana.

NÖTH, W. (1990) *Handbook of Semiotics*, Indiana University Press.

ORTONY, A. (Ed.) (1979) *Metaphor and Thought*, Cambridge University Press.

OWESI, K. (1986) *The Struggle for Black Arts in Britain*, London: Commedia.

OWESI, K. (Ed.) (1988) *Storms of the Heart*, London: Camden Press.

PARKER, R. and POLLOCK, G. (1981) *Old Mistresses: Women, Art and Ideology*, London: Routledge and Kegan Paul.

PARMELIN, H. (1977) *Art Anti-Art*, London: Marion Boyars.

PASCAL, R. (1977) *The Dual Voice*, Manchester University Press.

PATEMAN, T. (1983) 'How Is Understanding an Advertisement Possible?', in H. DAVIES and P. WALTON (Eds), *Language, Image, Media*, Oxford: Basil Blackwell.

PATEMAN, T. (1986) 'Transparent and Translucent Icons', *British Journal of Aesthetics*, vol. 26, n. 4, pp. 380–82.

PAYNTER, J. (1982) *Music in the Secondary School Curriculum*, London: Schools Council.

POPPER, K. (1957) *The Poverty of Historicism*, London: Routledge and Kegan Paul.

PRATT, M. (1977) *Toward a Speech Act Theory of Literary Discourse*, Indiana University Press.

PROPP, V. (1928) *Morphology of the Folktale*, University of Texas Press.

PROPP, V. (1984) *Theory and History of Folklore*, Manchester University Press.

REID, L.A. (1961) *Ways of Knowledge and Experience*, London: George Allen and Unwin.

REID, L.A. (1986) *Ways of Understanding and Experience*, London: Heinemann.

RENOIR, J. (1974) *My Life and My Films*, London: Collins.

RICHARDS, I.A. (1924) *Principles of Literary Criticism*, London: Routledge and Kegan Paul.

ROBERTSON, S. (1963) *Rosegarden and Labyrinth*, Lewes: Gryphon Press.

ROSS, M. (1975) *Arts and the Adolescent*, London: Schools Council.

ROSS, M. (1989) *The Claims of Feeling*, Lewes: Falmer Press.

SARTRE, J-P. (1950) *What is Literature?* London: Methuen.

SARTRE, J-P. (1957) *Being and Nothingness*, London: Methuen.

SARTRE, J-P. (1976) *Critique of Dialectical Reason*, London: New Left Books.

SAUSSURE, F. DE (1916) *A Course in General Linguistics*, trans R. Harris, London: Duckworth.

SAVILE, A. (1982) *The Test of Time*, Oxford: Clarendon Press.

SCHILLER, F. (1793) *On the Aesthetic Education of Man in a Series of Letters*, Oxford University Press.

SCRUTON, R. (1974) *Art and Imagination*, London: Routledge and Kegan Paul.

SCRUTON, R. (1981) 'The Impossibility of Semiotics', in *The Politics of Culture*, Manchester: Carcanet Press.

SCRUTON, R. (1983) *The Aesthetic Understanding*, London: Methuen.

SCRUTON, R. (1986) *Sexual Desire*, London: Weidenfeld and Nicolson.

SEARLE, J. (1979) 'Literal Meaning', in *Expression and Meaning*, Cambridge University Press.

SEARLE, J. (1983) *Intentionality*, Cambridge University Press.

SELFE, L. (1977) *Nadia*, London: Academic Press.

SHKLOVSKY, V. (1917) 'Art as Technique', in L.T. LEMON and M. REIS, (1965), *Russian Formalist Criticism*, University of Nebraska Press.

SHKLOVSKY, V. (1984) *A Sentimental Journey: Memoirs 1917–1922*, Cornell University Press.

SHOWALTER, E. (1977) *A Literature of Their Own: British Women Novelists from Brontë to Lessing*, Princeton University Press.

SIMPSON, K. (1975) *Some Great Music Educators*, Borough Green: Novello.

SLOBODA, J. (1985) *The Musical Mind*, Oxford University Press.

SMALL, C. (1987) *Music of the Common Tongue*, London: John Calder.

SONTAG, S. (1982) *A Barthes Reader*, London: Jonathan Cape.

SPERBER, D. (1975) *Rethinking Symbolism*, Cambridge University Press.

SPERBER, D. and WILSON, D. (1986) *Relevance*, Oxford: Basil Blackwell.

STALLYBRASS, P. and WHITE, A. (1986) *The Politics and Poetics of Transgression*, London: Methuen.

STEEDMAN, C. (1986) *Landscape for a Good Woman*, London: Virago.

STEINER, G. (1989) *Real Presences*, London: Faber and Faber.

STEPHAN, M. (1990) *A Transformational Theory of Aesthetics*, London: Routledge.

STEVENS, A. (1982) *Archetype: A Natural History of the Self*, London: Routledge and Kegan Paul.

STORR, A. (1988) *The School of Genuis*, London: André Deutsch.

SULTER, M. (Ed.) (1990) *Passion Discourses on Black Women's Creativity*, New York: Urban Fox Press.

SWANWICK, K. (1988) *Music, Mind and Education*, London: Routledge.

TAYLOR, R. (1986) *Educating for Art*, London: Longman.

TAYLOR, R. (1991) *The Visual Arts in Education*, London: Falmer Press.

TAYLOR, R. and ANDREWS, G. (1991) *The Arts in the Primary School*, London: Falmer Press.

TAYLOR, R. and TAYLOR, D. (1990) *Approaching Art and Design*, London: Longman.

THISTLEWOOD, D. (Ed.) (1989) *Critical Studies in Art and Design Education*, London: Longman.

TORMEY, A. (1971) *The Concept of Expression*, Princeton University Press.
TREVARTHAN, C. (1979) 'Communication and Cooperation in Early Infancy: A Description of Primary Intersubjectivity', in M. BULLOWA (Ed.), *Before Speech*, Cambridge University Press.
TROTSKY, L. (1925) *Literature and Revolution*, University of Michigan Press.
VENTURI, R. (1966) *Complexity and Contradiction in Architecture*, New York: Museum of Modern Art.
VOLOSINOV, V. (1973) *Marxism and the Philosophy of Language*, New York: Seminar Press.
WALTON, K. (1970) 'Categories of Art', *Philosophical Review*, 79, pp. 334–67.
WARBURTON, N. (1988) 'Seeing through Seeing through Photographs', *Ratio*, pp. 64–74.
WARNOCK, M. (1976) *Imagination*, London: Faber and Faber.
WEBB, E. (1991) *Literature and Education: Encounter and Experience*, London: Falmer Press.
WHORF, B.L. (1956) *Language, Thought and Reality*, MIT Press.
WILDE, O. (1891) '*The Decay of Lying*', in O. WILDE, *The Artist as Critic*, ed. R. ELLMANN, London: George Allen.
WILDEN, A. (1968) *The Language of the Self*, Baltimore: Johns Hopkins University Press.
WILLIAMS, R. (1977) *Marxism and Literature*, Oxford University Press.
WILLIAMSON, J. (1978) *Decoding Advertisements*, London: Marion Boyars.
WIMSATT, W. (1954) *The Verbal Icon*, Kentucky University Press.
WINNICOTT, D.W. (1971) *Playing and Reality*, Harmondsworth: Penguin Books.
WITKIN, R. (1974) *The Intelligence of Feeling*, London: Heinemann.
WOLFF, J. (1981) *The Social Production of Art*, London: Macmillan.
WOLLHEIM, R. (1979) 'The Cabinet of Dr Lacan', *New York Review of Books*, 25 January, 1979.
WOLLHEIM, R. (1984) *The Thread of Life*, Cambridge University Press.
WOLLHEIM, R. (1987) *Painting as an Art*, London: Thames and Hudson.
WRIGHT, E. (1984) *Psychoanalytic Criticism*, London: Methuen.
ZIFF, P. (1981) 'About the Appreciation of Dance', in G. FANCHER and G. MYERS, *Philosophical Essays on Dance*, New York: Dance Horizons.

Index

Names of individuals are generally not indexed when in the text they are only mentioned, e.g. in bibliographical information. Titles of art works mentioned are, however, generally indexed as they may serve a mnemonic function for some readers. Main chapter heads are not indexed.